History of Tibet and Great Tibet

Hashmatullah Khan

Translator
Zain-ul-Aabedin Aabedi

Foreword by
Salman Haider

ATLANTIC
PUBLISHERS & DISTRIBUTORS (P) LTD

Published by
ATLANTIC
PUBLISHERS & DISTRIBUTORS (P) LTD
7/22, Ansari Road, Darya Ganj, New Delhi-110002
Phones : +91-11-40775252, 23273880, 23275880, 23280451
Fax : +91-11-23285873
Web : www.atlanticbooks.com
E-mail : orders@atlanticbooks.com

Branch Office
5, Nallathambi Street, Wallajah Road, Chennai-600002
Phones : +91-44-64611085, 32413319
E-mail : chennai@atlanticbooks.com

Printed in India at Nice Printing Press, A-33/3A, Site-IV,
Industrial Area, Sahibabad, Ghaziabad, U.P.

Foreword

Salman Haidar
Ambassador; President, IPCS;
Former Indian Foreign Secretary;
Former Indian Ambassador to UK, China and Bhutan;
Former permanent representative of India to the UN
in New York
Email: shaidar@airtelmail.in

When Hashmatullah Khan was born somewhere near Lucknow in 1860, the aftershocks of the Great Rebellion of 1857 were still being felt. The Muslims of Oudh, regarded as the chief instigators, became the prime victims of British wrath. It was an unsettled time and the future was uncertain, especially for North India's Muslims. In the circumstances, Hashmatullah's family must have faced hardships but yet was able to provide him with an education at a maktab, where he was grounded in the traditional learning of the time. When he finished, he had to find some way of earning a living. There was not much to be had around Lucknow, so the young man had to try his fortune elsewhere. His first stop was the princely state of Nahan where he found employment for a few years. Hashmatullah then moved further North and in 1894 found work in the office of the British Agent in Gilgit. A year later he was sent to Chitral in the aftermath of a sharp little colonial war, and there he got to know the locals as well as a number of other neighbouring people like the Kafirs, Kyrgyz, Yarqandis, Badakhshanis and others. Finally, in 1898 he obtained an appointment in the State of Jammu and Kashmir where he was to remain for the rest of his working life. During his service he was transferred from place to place, including Gilgit, Muzaffarabad, Rajouri, Kargil, Ladakh, eventually to retire in 1928 as Wazir-e-Wazarat of Baramula. From these wanderings he learnt a number of languages of the region, becoming proficient in as many as seven, all told, including English, which he must have largely taught himself. He also got to know the local people, familiarized himself with their history and customs, and gathered many documents in various languages which he later put to use in the book he was to write.

Hashmatullah Khan was my paternal grandfather, already long retired before I was born, but still a vigorous and active old man. He was a somewhat forbidding personality, a strong and forthright individual, a serious, weighty man. He was of Afghan stock, Yusufzai Pathan, and his people must have come to India from their barren homeland in search of opportunity. His Pathan ancestry was Hashmatullah's great source of pride: he often told me that he was 'pure Pathan', as was grandmother. He wore the Afghan turban with the Western-style suits that were his invariable dress and was emotionally drawn to his country of remote origin. After his retirement, Hashmatullah went to Kabul on a deeply satisfying pilgrimage of sorts, driven there on an unpaved road through the Khyber Pass by my father.

My grandfather did not talk a great deal about his days of service, though he did mention a couple of things that had obviously pleased him. He was proud of having constructed the first ever public works project in Ladakh, an irrigation channel. I looked for it on an early visit to Leh but drew a blank. Only much later, to my delight, did I find that the channel did indeed exist but in Kargil, where it still survives, having been expanded but still following Hashmatullah's alignment. And, after more than three-quarters of a century, Hashmatullah's name as the originator of the project was not yet forgotten. The other piece of work he recalled with some pride was a garden he had laid out in Baramula, named in the fashion of the time as 'Hashmat Bagh'. On the only occasion that I have visited Baramula I asked about it, thinking it might have survived though most likely by now to have been renamed. But I could not find it.

Tarikh-i-Jammu

Hashmatullah Khan's major legacy is the extensive history he compiled of the State of Jammu and the many appurtenant regions conquered by the Dogras. *Tarikh-i-Jammu*, or "History of Jammu", is its short title. An account of Jammu and the achievements of Maharaja Gulab Singh was the principal subject but the project kept expanding to include accounts of Kishtwar, Inner Tibet (Lhasa), Greater Tibet (Ladakh), Outer Tibet (Baltistan), Purig (Kargil and Zanskar), Gilgit (Dardistan), Muzaffarabad, and other parts of the Maharaja's vast domain. It is a painstaking and meticulous record, compiled largely from documents in many languages collected by Hashmatullah, which throw light on the history, geography, politics, religion, social customs, etc. of the many regions where he served. His personal experience is a valuable part of the narrative. The wealth of information he acquired through his individual effort in the isolated locations where he served gives unique value to what he wrote. He lists kings and dynasties of half forgotten states that had never figured in anyone's records and might well have passed into oblivion without the benefit of his labour.

Tarikh-i-Jammu was published in 1939 in Lucknow and was welcomed as a serious, solidly constructed narrative, written with command and authority. Seventy years after it came out, it remains a singular treasure house of information about the border areas and the dynastic achievements of the Dogra rulers of Jammu. Being written in Urdu, the book has unfortunately not received in India the attention it merits. It is known only to a few scholars and is impossible to procure. A pirated edition came out a few years ago in Muzaffarabad, which is perhaps just as well for it made the volume more widely available. The only real remedy to ensure the continued availability of the book is to have it translated into English. This is something I have been trying for years to persuade my friends in Jammu University to undertake—what better place for a major work dedicated to the glory of the Jammu Durbar. But my efforts have been unavailing, and *Tarikh-i-Jammu* still awaits translation.

It is thus all the more welcome that Mr. Zainul Abedin should have mounted an effort to translate a part of the book into English, the portion that relates to Ladakh. Hashmatullah spent the best part of his service in Ladakh and his most intimate professional association is with that territory. His book contains an extensive section on Ladakh which needs to be made more widely available to both scholars and to general readers, especially in the present time when Ladakh claims ever increasing interest at home and abroad. I trust that this effort will stimulate others to carry on the work begun here. *Tarikh-i-Jammu* merits much more attention than it has received and its availability in English will be a real contribution to Jammu and Kashmir studies.

While welcoming the book, we should also acclaim the author. In recognition of his many-sided contribution to the state, it would be an elegant and appropriate gesture for the Government of J&K to name after Wazir Hashmatullah Khan the irrigation channel in Kargil that he built. It is my hope that the publication of this volume will encourage that demand.

Salman Haider

History of Tibet (Lhasa) and Great Tibet (Ladakh), 3rd Part

Actually this part of history has 4 sub parts. The first part deals with the History of Tibet (Lhasa); the 2nd to 5th part deals with "The History of the Ladakh Dynasties"; and 6th to 10th part deals with "The Invasion and Conquest of Ladakh and Baltistan and Invasion of Lahsa" by Wazir Zorawar Singh, "The Ladakh Expedition" by Diwan Nihal Chand and Wazir Ratnu, and the "Baltistan Expedition" by Wazir Lakhpat. The 11th to 14th part deals with the miscellaneous topics.

"The History of Lhasa" is a translation of a Tibetan history. My friend Shash Kushok of Rizong Gonpa provided me with the valuable information and I have added some information from the history books of English. "The History of Ladakh" is based on the Tibetan history and I have added much more, because of my personal efforts and research for many years and with the help of the history books of the foreign authors and have tried to reveal the events clearly as per my capacity.

I am highly thankful to my friend, Nono Tsetan Paljor and Shash Kushok of Rizong Gonpa, who provided me with valuable information and helped me to translate the Tibetan history, and stayed with me for a whole winter season and worked till midnight each day, and because of their personal knowledge and sincere efforts I was able to clear the doubts and translate the events and have added the information. It is a fact that without their noble efforts I could not have accomplished the translation of the Tibetan book.

The historical events about the Dogra's expedition and conquests have been taken from the *Gulab Nama* and I have incorporated my own observations and findings during the

Hashmatullah Khan Luckhnavi

research. Moreover I was benefited by the available written records and historical documents.

As far as the local researches are concerned, a respectable person of Pashkum, Mirza Mohammad Khan, and Molvi Mohammad Hussain of District Jehlum helped me and provided me with their valuable information and guidance for which I am highly thankful to both of them.

My friends Pandit Nand Ram and Pandit Damodar Koul helped me to accomplish the statistical and miscellaneous topics. I am also thankful to them.

"The Tibetan History of Lhasa and Ladakh", as has been mentioned above, is having very ancient base. The rest of the events have been written from the undermentioned works. I am grateful to the authors of these books.

1. *Tarihke Rashide* (Persian) by Mirza Haider Gorkan
2. *Tarikhe Firishta* (Persian) by Abul Qasim
3. *Gulab Nama* (Persian) by Diwan Kirpa Ram
4. *Mukammal Tarikhe Kashmir* by Mohammad Din Foq
5. *Tarikhe Hindustan* (Urdu) by Zakaullah
6. *Tarikhe Aazimi* (Persian)
7. *Tarikhe Hassan* (Persian) by Hassan Shah
8. *Travel Notes of Padri Dezidery* (English) by Fillipo de Fillipi
9. *Jammu and Kashmir* (English) by Duro
10. *The History of Western Tibet* by A.H. Franke
11. *Tibetan Tarikh of Gonpa Hemis*
12. *Tibetan Tarikh of Gonpa Lamayuru*
13. *Encyclopedia Britanica.*

As far as the research of Ladakh and Baltistan is concerned, I have traveled to all the parts of the area so many times and tried to find out the facts from the folk songs, folklore, traditions and historical monuments. Since I have utilized all the available local facts and sources, it is the beginning and there might be some loopholes, which I could not rectify at the movement and will be done in the future.

I have followed the "Tibetan History of Lhasa" to fix the period of the Kingdom of Lhasa and the same method has been utilized to fix the period of the Kingdom of Ladakh. Later, when the history of Ladakh was linked with the foreign countries, the period was established as per the historical documents and orders issued in the name of Ladakhi Kings, by the Rajas of other countries. This part has been bifurcated into fifteen chapters. The first chapter is related to Tibet, from where the Lachhen dynasty of Ladakh starts. In the beginning, it was not my intention to write the history of this country but some events of this country are inter-related with Lhasa, and that is why I have narrated a brief history of Lhasa to make clear the facts. Probably, this will be fruitful and interesting.

The second chapter starts with the history of the Lachhen Kingdom of great Tibet, i.e. Ladakh. The invasion of Sultan Sayeed Khan, ruler of Kashgar started during the last period of this dynasty. At that time the Lachhen Kingdom was divided into two parts. The capital of the first kingdom was Shay as usual and the second independent kingdom was established at Tingmogang. "The History of Ladakh" was linked with other countries after this invasion.

The third chapter deals with the detailed history of the invasion of Sultan Sayeed Khan of Ladakh, Baltistan and Kashmir. His General for Ladakh expedition, Mirza Haider Gorkan, has recorded these events in his valuable book *Tarikhe-Rashidi*. Though the history of Kashmir has no direct link with Ladakh, yet Mirza Haider's invasion of Kashmir started after his invasion of Ladakh and it is not out of place to mention the 500 year old history of a civilized neighbouring country, so I have included it in this chapter.

The fourth chapter deals with the dynasty, whose kings conquered the Kingdom of Shay and established their own new Government of Ladakh and was called Namgyal (The victorious).

The fifth chapter is in continuation to the fourth chapter, regarding the history of Namgyal Dynasty. Since it was very long, it starts in the fourth chapter and is concluded in the fifth.

The sixth chapter deals with Wazir Zorawar Singh's expeditions to Ladakh, and is the most important part of this book. The first expedition is mentioned in the sixth chapter, when the power and position of Raja Tundup Namgyal was restored when he promised to be loyal and pay the tribute. Thus, Wazir went back towards Jammu. Later, because of the instigation of the King of Ladakh, the Raja of Purig revolted against the Dogras. Hence Wazir had to return from Zanskar. This has been mentioned as the second expedition, when King Tundup Namgyal was dethroned and Morup Stanzin was appointed as the Raja of Ladakh. The Raja of Purig was also dismissed.

The seventh chapter deals with the third expedition of Wazir Zorawar Singh Kalohria, when he conquered Baltistan and Ladakh. Raja Morup Stanzin was dismissed and Ladakh was completely annexed with the Government of Jammu. In Baltistan, Mohammad Shah was appointed as Raja of Askardo.

The eighth chapter deals with the Tibet expedition of Wazir Zorawar Singh Kalohria, when he conquered a vast area of Tibet up to Purang, where the Dogra Army was ruined by the Tibetans, and Zorawar Singh Kalohria was killed at Purang.

The ninth chapter deals with the Tibetan invasion to Ladakh and the revolt of the Rajas of Purig and Baltistan, and describes the fourth expedition of Diwan Hari Chand and Wazir Ratnu. In this expedition, the brave General conquered the region of Sod and Chiktan and defeated the Tibetan Army. A treaty was signed between the Dogras and the Tibetans. Tibetan officers were transported to Jammu as hostages and the arrangement of Ladakh was made in an efficient manner.

The tenth chapter describes the fifth Dogra expedition of Wazir Lakhpat, when he suppressed the revolt of Baltistan and made good arrangements for Baltistan and Purig.

The eleventh chapter deals with the trade, commerce, handicrafts, agriculture production and minerals of Ladakh.

The twelfth chapter is about the able administrators, who played a vital role for the development of Ladakh.

In the thirteenth chapter, comparative studies have been made between the old regime and the new administration. In this connection, I could not have a written document as a proof. My research is based only on the verbal statements of Gyalpo Sonam Namgyal and his old courtiers. In the fourteenth chapter, I have described the customs and traditions of the Buddhists.

In the fifteenth chapter, discussions have been made on the miscellaneous topics, like the Buddhist festivals, the arrangement of the Gonpas, the rights and duties of the Lamas, the Bodhi calendar and the census of Ladakh. The census statements of the two border provinces are very interesting, underlining that in spite of the polyandry system, the birth rate of male and female are almost equal and they have not been affected by the local traditions.

The last chapter will reveal how this far flung and backward area has progressed culturally, socially and economically, under the peaceful and sympathetic attitude of the Government of Jammu and Kashmir since there was no peace and prosperity during the reign of the old regimes. Some friends provided me with photographs relating to this portion, which I have placed on the proper places. I got the photograph of Mr. Johnson from his daughter Miss Aida Johnson, for which, I am grateful to her.

Hashmatullah Khan

Preface

It gives me immense pleasure to translate the 3rd part of the book entitled *History of Tibet and History of Great Tibet* authored by Wazir Hashmatullah Khan Lukhnavi (1936), from Urdu to English. I thought this would expand the reach of this magnificient and beautiful piece of writing and also because many of my good friends, who are not well versed with Urdu, have been requesting me to translate the same into English. I have used very simple language for easy understanding by the readers. Though I have tried my best to keep the content in its original form using very subtle language while translating, there may still be shortcomings and readers are most welcome to bring them to my notice so as to incorporate the same in future editions.

The author was the Wazir-e-Wazarat of Ladakh for a long time under the Dogra regime and had the opportunity to travel to almost all the villages of Leh, Kargil and Baltistan. During his journeys in various parts of the region he passionately observed the cultural, social, religious, economic and historical monuments. He also did a thorough research with the help of the religious and village heads, influential people of the area, and through available documents, manuscripts, folklore, songs and monuments.

It is hoped that the English version of the book will be useful for the researchers, historians and students and especially those trevellers and tourists who want to get an in-depth knowledge of various facets of the history, culture and tradition of this region. My thanks are due to Mr Salman Haider, the grandson of the author and the then Foreign Secretary to Government of India, for writing an excellent Foreword for the book.

Zain-ul-Aabedin Aabedi

Preface

Pedigree Table of Kings of Tibet (Lhasa)

1. Nyathi Chanpo	About 380/ 355 BC
2. Mothi Chanpo	About 330
3. Tangthi Chanpo	About 305
4. Sothi Chanpo	About 280 (Seven Thi kings)
5. Mirthi Chanpo	About 255 BC
6. Dakthi Chanpo	About 230
7. Sabthi Chanpo	About 205
8. Tigom Chanpo, Lonpo Longnam	About 180
9. Shathi, Nyathi	Chathi or Poti Kongyal 155 BC.
10. Aey Sholik	About 130BC
11. Tay Sholik	About 105
12. Thi Sholik	About 88 (Six lik kings)
13. Guru Lik	About 55
14. Dongji Lik	About 30
15. Eshu Lik	About 05
16. Zanam Zain Ldey	About 20 AD
17. Ldeythol Namjong Chan	About 45
18. Saysnol Nam Ldey	About 70
19. Saysnol Pol Ldey	About 95 (Eight Ldey kings)
20. Ldey Snolnam	
21. Ldey Snolpo	About 120
22. Ldey Gyalpo	About 145
23. Ldey Tan Chan	About 170
24. Tory Long Chan	About 190
25. Thi Chan Tam	About 245
26. Thida Pong Chan	About 270
27. Thitok Jai Chan	About 295
28. Latho Thori Nain Chan	About 373
29. Thi Nain Zong Chan	About 437
30. Dong Nain Ldeve	About 501
31. Mozlong Konpata	About 565
32. Namri Shongchan Gyalpo	About 629

33. Shongchan Zangbo About 642
34. Kongri Kongchan About 675
35. Mangshong Manngchan About 700
36. Doshong Mangjay About 725
37. Thi Ldey Sokstan About 750
38. Jangsa Lah on (Ist wife) assisinated
38. Thishong Ldey Chan IInd wife About 820
39. Motik Chanpo Morup Chanpo Monay Chanpo About 880
40. Lang Tarma Ralpa Chan Lundup Lharjey Sangma About 898
41. Yumstan (Ist wife) Otshong (IInd wife).
    Kingdom east Tibet Kingdom west Tibet
42. Ldey Spal Khorsan (king of west Tibet)
43. Skit Ldey Nimagon (Purang) Thi Tashi Sagspa Pal
    1. Spalgi Gon Raja Ladakh About 990 AD 1. Paldey
    2. Tashi Gon Raja Purang 2. Hodey
    3. Ldey Sud Gon Raja Kugay 3. Keeday

Contents

1

History of Tibet (Lhasa)

The Researchers and Scholars of the Lhasa are of the opinion, that once in the past, the whole Lhasa was under the sea. Gradually, the water began to flow downwards and dry land appeared and with the passage of time, the region of Lhasa, emerged under the sea. Gradually, the mountains were covered with snow and ice. The river and streams began to flow. After a long time the snow melted and green grass and forest began to grow on the hills and plains. Consequently, various kinds of animals began to live in the forest. The God and Goddess desired that the human beings should be created now on this universe. As a result, the God Chanraziks appeared in the shape of a male ape and Goddess Dolma took the shape of a terror female ape. Because of the sexual contact of these two animals, six children were born. The three of them possessed noble nature like their father and the rest three were terror like the mother. The number of the off springs increased very fast and gradually took the mental and physical shape of the human beings. They began to live in different groups. This view confirms the Darwin's evolution theory of geology.

During this period a child was born in the palace of an Indian King, whose name has been mentioned "Maggyapa" in the Tibetan books. Whose father was alive, during the fourth generation of Lord Buddha. His great grand father Sargyal was contemporary to Lord Buddha, if we divide each generation with thirty years. Then the child might have born 150 years after the birth of Lord Buddha and it should be about 400 year

BC. He was a boy of very strange feature. His eyebrow was upwards, eyelid were blue like lucky stone, having teeth at the time of birth. The fingers were long and strange. His father was afraid to see the child of strange feature so he kept him in a box and was thrown in the river. A man found the box, the child was alive. He took the child to his home and was brought up under his care. Later, he came to know that his father has expelled him from the home because of the strange feature. He became very sad and left the house of the man, who brought up him. He was wandering in the forest and hills. At last he reached on a hill of Lhasa called "Lahri Thonpo", where from he saw the beautiful valley of Yarlung. He came down from the hill and reached in the village of Chanthang Zgotse. There were twelfth shepherds, they inquired, where from you came? There was communication gap. The boy could not understand their language. So he raised his finger towards the hill. The shepherds thought that the boy is pointing towards the sky. Certainly, he must have come from the country of the God and Goddess. They discussed that there is no king in our country. Hence we should take this God to there to make the king. Thus, four men took him on their shoulders up to the town of Yarlung. Because they took him on their shoulders. So he was called "Nyathichanpo" (shoulders king). He founded the kingdom and constructed the palace "Yumbu Lazgang", which is still in tact.

The researchers are of the opinion, that Nyathichanpo was the fifth son of the King Parasnajit of Kosala. His eyes were defective. He run away from Kosala and reached in this country on the north of Himalaya which is today known as Tibet. Here the chiefs of twelfth tribes of middle and southern Tibet accepted him as their king. He started living in the Yarlung area, which is in the south of present Tibet. However it is true, that the culture, tradition and the Government of Tibet was founded by a prince of India. Nyathi Chanpo married with a Tibetan lady Nam Mog Mog and Mothi Chanpo was born and the race continued as follows:

1. Nyathi Chanpo
2. Mothi Chanpo

3. Tangthi Chanpo
4. Sothi Chanpo
5. Mirthi Chanpo
6. Dakthi Chanpo
7. Sabthi Chanpo

These are the genealogical tree of the seven Thi kings. Nothing is known about their style of administration. However it is believed, that they never die, but after completing their worldly duties, they use to fly towards the sky. Later Tigom Chanpo became the king. Lungnam was his minister. Tigom Chanpo had three sons:

1. Shathi
2. Nyathi
3. Chathi or Poti Konggyal

There was a quarrel between the King Ti Gom and his Minister Lungnam. Thus, Lonpo Lungnam assassinated the king. All his three sons ran away to Kongbo and Lonpo Lungnam ruled over Tibet. In the mean time, a child was born to the widow of Tigom, due to adulteration with the God, Yarla Shampo, whose name was Rola Skeys. During his adulthood, he took the revenge with the Lonpo and got him killed. Now Chathi came back and ascended the throne and appointed his step brother Rola Skeys as his Minister. It is said, that because of the bloodshed and killings, their journey to heaven ceased. And the burial system of the dead body started. The surname of Chathi was Poti Konggyal. The Bon religion flourished in Tibet during his reign. As per the history of Tibet, this was the ancient religion of this country. He got constructed the palace of Changbar Staktse. During this period, the Minister Lonpo Rola Skeys and Lapok Gokar jointly did developmental works. They got constructed the kohls, and started the agricultural work. Silver, bronze and iron were extracted from the raw minerals and bridges were constructed over the streams and rivers. These two Rajas are called Pargay Stangnas, and the last one is considered the father of the Tibetan culture and civilization.

Chathi's son Aey Sholik ruled over Tibet during 130 BC, his son Tay sholik 105 BC, his son Thi Sholik 80 BC, his son Guru Lik 55 BC, his son Dongji Lik 30 BC, and his son Eiy Sholik 5 BC. These are called six Lik kings and nothing is known about their way of administration and events.

The son of Aey Sholik was Zanam Zain Ldey 20 AD.

Ldeythol Namchong chan	45 AD
Saysnol Nam Ldey	70 AD
Saysnol Poldey	95 AD
Ldeysnol Nam	120 AD
Ldeysnol Po	145 AD
Ldey Gyalpo	170 AD
Ldey Tangchan	195 AD

The chain of above mentioned eight kings are called Ldey Kingdom. Nothing has been mentioned in the Tibetan history about them. There after the series continues as follows:

Torylong Chan	220 AD
Thichan Nam	245 AD
Thidapong Chan	270 AD
Thitok Jai Chan	295 AD

Latho Thori Nain Chan, birth 245 AD and death 373 AD. Buddhism flourished in Tibet, during the reign of this king. It is believed, that the following religious books were brought down from the heaven, during the reign of this king.

1. Pangkong Chhaggyapa
2. Dozday Zamatokgi Sningpo Egay Tukpa

A golden Stupa and Chanta Maney Kos Phur (i.e. a model to mould the Stupa or Chhortain) were also brought down. A mysterious voice was heard. This said, "the benefit of these things will appear, during the fifth generation. Nobody was able to understand the meaning of these things, at that time, but considering them very sacred, lighted the lamp, offered flowers and kept them under proper care". The Raja lived a life long of 140 years.

According to the Tibetan history and calculation, the king was born in the year 254 AD. He was a man of 80 years, when the religious books of Buddhism reached in Lhasa. It was happened in 333 AD. Thereafter, he ruled over Tibet for 40 years. Accordingly he died in 373 AD. When we compare the year recorded in the Tibetan books with the English date it indicates that Lord Buddha was born in the year 557 BC and died in 477 BC. The calculations of the year mentioned in this chapter have been made accordingly.

His son was Thining Zongchan (437 AD). His son was Mozlong Konpata or Stagri Nyangzak (565 AD). He was a blind. A foreign doctor cured him and he was able to see the animals grazing on the hills, and called "Stagri Nyangzak" which means watcher of animals on the hills.

His son was Namri Shongchan Gyalpo (629 AD). During his period, Medical education and mathematics was brought from China. And these educations were implemented verbally in Lhasa. The king got constructed a magnificent palace in Lhasa. It is believed that the mud used in the construction of the palace was prepared with the milk of brown color cow and yak. It was called Raskes Bumzoks palace. The king started to find out the salt from the lake of Daksum Lding. Prior to that there was no tradition of using salt.

His son was Shongchan Zangpo (650 AD). This king was born 1508 years after the death of Lord Buddha. It is also believed that the king was born 296 years after the Buddhists religious books were brought in Lhasa. Probably he was born in 629 AD and ascended the thorn in 642 AD. He got constructed a magnificent palace on the Potala hill and began to live in it. This palace is still in good condition and Dalai Lama use to live in it. The king gave some gold and ornaments to Sambota, the son of his Minister Aano and deputed him to India to learn the alphabets. He learned reading and writing of Sanskrit language from Tamzay Pandit Lichan and learned Sanskrit language from Pandit Laragpo Singay and went through the following three books; *Pani Bayakaran*, *Kalapa* and *Jantrapa*. Later he came back to Lhasa and with the help of Sanskrit alphabet, invented a separate alphabet for the language of Lhasa. At that time there were two letters in use in India. The first is called "Lansa" in Tibetan books. According to the specimen of Lansa, he invented the Uchain letters, the religious books are being maintained in this very language. Till now these alphabets are also being used for printing purposes. The second type of letters is called "varto". Sambota invented the "Tha-ik" alphabets according to it. The business letters and other correspondence are being made in these alphabets. Basically both the alphabets are one. Only the difference is what the two Roman alphabets are having.

The scholars of the foreign countries were invited to Lhasa. They are, Komara Deva from India, Shilamanzo from Nepal, Tanato, Ganota and Tamzay Lechan from Kashmir and Hashang Mahadeva from China. With their help and cooperation Sambota and Dharma Kosha translated 21 books from Chinese and Sanskrit languages into Tibetan language. Eight books were written by Sambota himself. The king also learned the Tibetan alphabets and maintained the rules and regulations for the country.

The king deputed his men to Nepal and married with Planza Thichon, the daughter of Raja of Nepal and brought various kinds of goods and statues to Lhasa. Later another representative was sent to the court of King of China along with presents and got married with his daughter. The Chinese Princes also brought so many articles and statues to Lhasa. The king who was 25 years old at that time got constructed Rasa Gonpa over a lake so as to keep the statues in it. Because of the interaction with the foreign countries, so many art and craft were flourished in Lhasa. For instance, to make wine with the rice, to make curd with the milk, to extract butter from the curd, to make the Lassi, to run the water floor mill, to weave the clothes and to prepare the beautiful ornaments, etc.

During the period of this king Buddhism reached in Lhasa, along with the alphabets. His two queens, one the Princes of Nepal was the daughter of Raja Joti Verma and the second was the Princes of China. They helped the king for the propagation of Buddhism and pressurized the people to accept this religion. He was a very ambitious king. He founded the city of Lahaldan in 639 AD. It is known as Lhasa now. He conquered the neighbouring small states and extended the kingdom. He developed the diplomatic relations with the big neighbouring states and exchanged the presents.

This king was very popular as a conqueror. In the north he conquered the Kiyang tribe. In the west, he extended the kingdom up to Ladakh. In the south he ruled over Nepal and after crossing Himalaya reached in India. It is not clear, how far he reached within the territory of India, but has mentioned in the history, that Nepal and the country of Brahmans revolted against the Government of Tibet. The third generation of Shongchan Zanpo, who was suppressing the revolt, was killed in this battle. It has not been mentioned in the history of India, about Tibet's rule over India, however the Chinese history reveals that during the 10th century the Tibetan rule was up to the sea, and the name of Bay of Bengal was Tibetan Ocean. The researchers have found recently some proof about the race and language regarding the Tibetans rule over Bengal.

However, the history of India is mum about it.

He could not have any issue with the above mentioned two queens. Hence, he married with three more queens. It is said that one of them was from the Country of Royong, another one was from Monyul. In Tibet those people are called Monpa, who resides between the territory of Tibet and India (presently the inhabitants of district Tawang in Arunachal Pradesh are called Monpa). Nothing has been mentioned about the tribe of the third queen. Out of these three queens, two were childless and the third gave birth to Kongri Kong Chan, who ascended the thorn at the age of thirteen in the year 675 AD. His son was Mangsong Mangchan, who ruled over Tibet up to 700 AD. His father died during his childhood. Therefore his grandfather Shongchan Zangpo took the reign of the government again. After his death his grand son Mangsong ascended the thorn. He conquered the Tatars of Lokhon in the vicinity of Kokonor in 663 AD. Later he invaded China and defeated them. But the Chinese took the full revenge and they invaded Tibet and reached up to Lhasa. Here they burnt the royal palace Pombo Lahkhang. Lonpo Gar, who was the General of the Tibetan Army, was killed in the battle.

His son was Doshong Mangjay, who ruled over Tibet till 725 AD. His surname was Lungnam Tholgi Gyalpo. His seven ministers were very brilliant and wise.

His son was Thi Ldey Sogsan. His second name was Miza Aqsum. He ruled over Lhasa till 750 AD. Art and literature flourished during this period. Two Indian scholars, Sangais Snangwa and Sangais Jhiwa came for the pilgrimage of Kailash Parbhat. The king wanted to invite them to translate some religious books but they denied. However, they taught the five books to the king's representatives and they got translated the books in Tibetan language. These books are still prevalent in Lhasa and are considered very important religious books. He made good efforts for the propagation of Buddhism. The king brought the medicine books from China and got translated them into Tibetan language and introduced the medical education in the country.

The king invited some of the religious persons from Lee City of China, and a religious group was formed in Lhasa. Gradually this group became very stronger and endangered the kingdom.

His son was Jangsa Lhaon. The prince was very brilliant and handsome. His engagement was made in China. She was Kaimshang the daughter of Joy Sang the King of China. She was on her way to Lhasa when Jangsa Lhaon was killed by Lonpo Nyathi Zang. Since the Lonpo wanted to marry his daughter with the prince, but the prince rejected the offer and preferred for the Chinese princess. When the bridegroom reached Lhasa, Miza Aqsum the father of Late Jangsa married her and made her the queen. She gave birth to Thishong Ldey about 731 AD. Some of the male and female attendants accompanied the Chinese queen from her country. One of the maid servant claimed that Thishong was actually born to her but everybody knew that the queen was pregnant. Therefore the people rejected the claim of the maid servant. Finally, to settle the dispute, it was decided that when the child began to walk on his feet a public meeting was convened. The king offered a cup of wine to the child with the direction, to take the cup of wine to his mother. It was decided that both the women are the claimant of being the mother of the prince, therefore whoever the child offer the cup of wine she will be consider the mother of the child. The child straightly went to the queen and gave the cup and it was decided in presence of the public that really he is the son of the queen, the right lineage prince and heir of the thorn and crown. The king's decision is really praiseworthy.

Thishong's father Miza Aqsum died when he was a child. Hence Lonpo Majing spread the rumour against the late Miza Aqsum in public that the death of young son is because of his conversion to Buddhism and its propagation. He motivated the people to fight against the ill-omened religion. Therefore the statues which were brought from Nepal and China to Lhasa were thrown away on the hills and the big statues were buried in the ground.

When Thishong was grown up, a man called Sangshi found three books between the boulders and handed it over to Thishong. He realized that these books were of his forefathers and had been destroyed because of religious enmity by his enemies. Hence he decided to fight with the enemies, and keep the religion alive so that his ancestor becomes immortal. In spite of the efforts of the enemies of the religion, there were so many supporters and followers of Buddhism, hence Thishong, with the consultation of these people deputed a person Basal Nang secretly to India in order to convene an Indian scholar and pious man to Lhasa. He invited Khanpo Bodhi Sato from India. His surname was Shanta Rakeeta. Basal Nang kept the scholar in Mangyul and he himself went to Lhasa to report the king. The king consulted his ministers and supporters, who were the followers of Buddhism. If the scholar is convened in Lhasa, what should be done to Lonpo Majing who is very powerful and opponent of Buddhist religion? Everyone suggested that the astrologers should be asked to announce that Lhasa would be struck by a natural calamity and the only way to avoid this and to save the country, the Prime Minister should be imprisoned for a period of three months. According to the decision, when the astrologers issued the decree in the court, a thorough discussion was held and it was unanimously decided that Lonpo Majing and Lonpo Gozgan should face the prison for the sake of the country. Lonpo Gozgan was briefed earlier, whenever Lonpo Majing will be put in the prison, you should run away from that place. Accordingly, the two ministers were brought in front of the prison. In this country the prisons were like a cave, it was very wide in the bottom and their passages were narrow. The prisoners were being put in the prison through its passage and a big slab of stone was kept on the passage. When Majing was brought down in the prison Gozgan ran away as planned earlier. A big slab of stone was put on the passage and was covered with earth and was left to die. When they overcame and overpowered the enemy of the religion, they decided to work for the welfare of the religion with full bloom. Basal Nang was deputed again to Mangyul to bring the Indian scholar Khanpo Bodi Sato to Lhasa. Within few days Khanpo reached Lhasa. He propagated Buddhism with full swing and got repaired the sacred sites damaged by Majing and Buddhism began to flourish once again.

But suddenly famine hit the country after a few days and there was an epidemic resulting in the loss of a large number of animal and human beings. Though the roots of the new religion began to strengthen in the hearts and mind of the people, but the people linked the calamity with the Government of Buddhist religion and began to abuse and accuse the religious heads. The people were thinking to eradicate the religion, but Khanpo was wise enough to befool the people. He made the people understand that the famine and natural calamity was not because of the Buddhist religion but was because of the quarrel of their Gods with the evil sprits of their a country. Khanpo suggested that, if they invite the Indian scholar, Guru Padma Jungnes to Tibet, he could eliminate these evil sprits from the soil of Tibet. Accordingly, Sonam Dorjay and Dojoms were deputed to India. Guru Padma was already informed about the events but Guru made it appear that he came to know about this through revelation. Hence, before arrival of Sonam Dorjay in India, Guru Padama left for Lhasa. They met at Mangyul which is in between Lhasa and Nepal. From that very place he began to eliminate the evil sprits of Lhasa and thus, reached there. Guru Padma Jungnes reached Lhasa in 750 AD, when Thishong Ldey was 19 years old. In the mean time Khanpo Bodhi Sato went back to Nepal. When Guru Padma reached Lhasa, Bodhi Sato was called back from Nepal. Both the scholars advised the king to construct a Gonpa by the style of Indian temple Otanta Puri and should be called Sum-Yas. The length of the Gonpa was an archer's arrow shooting distance. Khanpo enrolled seven men in this Gonpa and imparted religious education to them. The Gonpa was constructed when king was 21 years old. Khanpo died after completing this task and Padma was alone he went to another country in the south-west direction. During the reign of this king Buddhism was flourished in Tibet. The statues damaged by the enemies of this religion were repaired and the religion was consolidated in every respect. The king died in his old age. King Shongchan had three sons:

1. Monaychanpo, 2. Mourupchanpo and 3. Motikchanpo whose surname was Satnalik Jingyon.

Monaychanpo ascended the thorn in 821 AD and died after ruling over Tibet for one year and seven months. He wanted to eradicate the poverty in the country so as to remove the differences between the rich and the poor. He compelled the rich to distribute their wealth among the poor and destitute people so that the poor can also live a better life. He continued the process thrice but failed. Rich people who were made poor by distributing their wealth among the poor became rich again over a period of time as they did hard work and made efforts. The poor who got the wealth again became poorer due to their idleness and useless expenses. On observing this astonishing situation, the religious heads blamed this on their deeds in the past life and with time these noble efforts ended.

After the death of Monaychanpo, Motikchanpo ascended the thorn because his elder brother Mourupchanpo was assassinated by Lonpo Jingnatam. He did remarkable job for the welfare of the Gonpas and got translated the religion and other important books into Tibetan language. He got constructed a new Gonpa called Karchhong. He had five sons:

1. Sangma, 2. Laharjay, 3. Lundup, 4. Tarma, and 5. Ralpachan.

Lundup died in his childhood. Laharjay died at the age of fifteen. Sangma became a Lama. Hence Ralpachan ruled over Tibet till 901 AD. The text of the Buddhist religion books that were translated during the period of his ancestors into Tibetan language was qualitatively poor. He made the intention to correct them. Therefore he invited Khanpo Zina Mita, Soranta Bodhi and Dana Shila from India. Under the able guidance of the Indian scholars the Tibetan translators Kawa and Chogro, etc., revived and made the corrections. By doing so he became very popular in Tibet. He also got constructed a magnificent Gonpa at Ushangdo. His relation was not good with the Government of China. There was a battle between the two and Ralpachan conquered a portion of the Chinese area and annexed with Lhasa. Finally the battle ended after an agreement was signed. The border was demarcated and a big slab of stone was placed at the border by inscribing the agreements of both Lhasa and China and promised by the two governments to strictly keep the sanctity of the border. This agreement was completed and signed at Changnan in 821 AD. The next year a copy of the agreement was placed in the palace of the King of China and another copy inscribed on a slab of stone was fixed in the palace of the King of Lhasa, which still exist. During the period of this king the regards, respect and powers of the Lamas improved. They were provided the highest seat in the court and were granted the rewards. The ministers and other dignitaries observed that the king is more interested in religion they feared that one day the government will be in the hands of Lamas, so they got issued a "Fatwa" by the astrologers that "If king's brother Lama Sangma is not expelled from the country, Lhasa would have to face a great calamity". Consequently, Sangma was expelled towards India. The worldly people were not satisfied with this act. One day his minister Lonpo Azyas Tagna killed the king and his brother Tarma Utumchan was made the king and Azyas Tagna was made the minister.

King Tarma and his minister Lonpo Azyas Tagna disliked the Buddhism and was looking for a suitable chance to damage the religion. Unfortunately an epidemic disease was spread in the country and many people died. The standing corps got destroyed because of the hail storm. The minister inquired the causes of the calamity from the people. The people replied that they know nothing. Tarma said that evil sprits have entered the country along with the statues brought from China and these statues have created all these problems for us. It is better to destroy them. Thus, they destroyed the statues mercilessly. The small statues were thrown away in the river. The big statues which could not be moved were buried in the ground. The religious books were burnt and some were thrown in the river. The rest were thrown down the hills. The Indian Pandits and the Tibetan translators were assassinated and some ran away towards India. The Lamas were compelled to do the agricultural work. Those who refused to do so were asked to be hunters. The doors of the three big Gonpas, Rasa, Ramosay and Samyas were completely closed and locked. Boards were placed on the doors saying that these are the Bars of the Lamas. He was not content with these actions as he ordered to destroy the Rasa Gonpa completely.

During this period, a scholar Lama Lalung Palgi Dorje was observing meditation. When he heard about these unfortunate events, he discontinued his meditation and came out of his hut with the intention to eliminate the enemy of the religion from the soil. A white horse was colored black and a special dress was prepared with the outer layer of the dress being black and inner as white. This dress had very wide sleeves so as to hide the bow and arrow. He reached before the king riding on the horse. At that time, Tarma was reading the agreement of the Government of China inscribed on a slab of stone and fixed on the wall of the palace. Lama Palgi Dorje bowed before the king as per the tradition of the country. In the mean time, he swiftly shot the arrow which struck on the chest of the king. He fell down and died. Palgi Dorje left the bow and arrow there and changed the dress by reversing the inner layer to outer side and ran away on the horseback. He crossed the river and as a result the color of the horse got washed away and it became white. King's army followed him but he could not be recognized because of the change of his dress and the color of the horse.

Tarma was born about in 870 AD. At the age of twenty-eight he ascended the thorn. He ruled over Tibet for one year six months and fifteen days. According to this calculation he was died in 899 AD. At the time of Tarma's assassination, the second queen was pregnant. After knowing this the first queen also covered a piece of cloth around her belly and pretended to be pregnant. When the second queen gave birth to a male child, she too managed to bring a child from outside and tried to indicate that she also had a male child who was having teeth at that time as observed by the second queen. She argued that if was really her child then she should properly take care of the child. The second queen was looking after her child carefully and used to keep the lamp lit the entire night by the bedside of the baby. Therefore he was called "Otshang", i.e. light. The name of the child of the first queen was "Yumstan".

When the two princes became young they recovered the statues buried in the ground by Tarma and installed in the Gonpas and the Gonpas were repaired and renovated. There was a dispute for succession between the two therefore Otshang occupied the Yunro, the western Tibet and Yumstan occupied the eastern Tibet called Yazro in 935 AD. But even after the division of the kingdom the battle did not end and history of the Tibet became more complicated.

After Otshang his son Ldeyspal Khorsan became the king of western Tibet. He died after ruling over Tibet for thirteen years. He had two sons, Thi Tashi Sag Papal and Thi Skid Ldey Nimagon. The later went to Purang and established his own government at Purang. He had three sons, the elder son Spalgi Gon went to Mangyul and made himself the King of Ladakh. The second son Tashi Gon occupied Purang and the youngest son Ldeysud Gon became the King of Shang Shong (Kugay). The two sons of the later did extra ordinary job for the promotion of Buddhism. Among them the elder became a Lama. The younger son Khoray succeeded his father as king, whose offspring became king one after another for twenty generations. Tashi Sag

Papal also had three sons, Paldey, Hudey, and Keedey. The offsprings of the elder son ruled over Gong Tang, Logyalwa, Chipa, Lahtsay, Langlung and Sakor. There they became the separate ruler of the small kingdoms. The offsprings of Keeday also became the separate ruler of small kingdoms in the districts of Mo, Jung, Tang, Yaro Lag, and Rgyaltse. Huday had four sons; they were Pheydey, Thi Dey, Thichong and Gangpa. Among them the elder and the youngest two brothers became the ruler of San Dong. The second son occupied the Amdo and Dzongkha. The third son Ozu became the king of central Tibet and made Yarlung his capital which is in the south of Lhasa. His offsprings continuously ruled over central Tibet for eleven generations. Nothing has been mentioned in the history about Yumstan, the King of eastern Tibet, but the geographical name of the western Tibet mentioned above indicates that this family occupied the eastern parts also. The family lineage of this period is not available. During this period, when Khoray's offsprings ruled over Kugay and Thi Chong's family over Uou, one more government was established in Tibet. Finally, it dominated both the kingdoms. Khoray's son Lahdey succeeded him. Lahdey had three sons, who ruled over Tibet after him. The youngest son invited from India the famous Buddhist scholar Atishah in Tibet from the temple of Vikram Shila. He began to live in the largest Gonpa of Naris, called Thoding. He not only published the religious books and imparted religious education but also introduced the counting system of the Tibetan calander by sixty years in 1026 AD. This system was in practice in the Indian Province of Shambala (I could not recognize, the Shambala in India). Ati Shah was the first Lama who because of his knowledge and power dominated all the Government of Tibet. Many more scholar Lamas were holding good power. The Okay Kingdom had a great regards and respect to these scholars. For instance the seventh king of this dynasty had patronized the scholar Sakya Pandita. Because in 1246-48 AD, on the request of Koyok, the successor of Ogdai, the Pandita came into the court of the king and up keep the honour and glory. Five years later Kablai Khan conquered the eastern Tibet and after ascending the thorn of China, the Mongol King invited Phagspa Loyi Gyalsan, the nephew of the Pandita in his court. He remained with the king continuously for twelve years. On the request of the king he invented an alphabet for the Mongol language on the style of Tibetan letters. But it was not popular in the public and after fifty eight years it disappeared without becoming popular among the common masses. In recognition to his services, Kablai Khan granted the power to Phagspa, to rule over the provinces of Tibet, i.e. the province of Kham, Amdo and thirteen districts of Ursang. From that very period, the Sakyapa Lama became the King of Tibet. Thus twenty-one Lamas ruled over Tibet one after another for 70 years from 1210 to 1340 AD. Since Gonpa Sakya was their residence and headquarter, due to this relation they were called "Sakyapa". They used to appoint a deputy among them to run the day to day administration.

When the Government of Sakyapa became weak, the other Gonpas like Degung, Phagdup and Vishal began to improve their power. Ultimately, they dominated the successors of the Phagspa and subdued them. During this unfortunate period, Changchub Gyalsan alias Phagmodo appeared and conquered the Tibet and Kham. But he had to fight many years to consolidate its government. Finally, he succeeded in his mission and formed his own government, with the consent of the Peking, which continued during the period of his twelfth successors. When the Mongol Kingdom ended in China, the kings of the Mang dynasty extended and consolidated the Government of Tibet. Moreover, they recognized the Head Lamas of eight great Gonpas of Lhasa. Because of the sympathetic attitude of this dynasty, there was peace and prosperity in the country. Consequently, people inclined towards a luxurious life, and the government became weak. There was a civil war between the nobles and other dignitaries in the province of Ursang, during the reign of the second last king. This was the period, when the last king of the Mang dynasty was fighting against the tyranny of the Manchu tribe. Because of the disturbance in the country, a Mongol King of Khoshot dynasty got the opportunity to interfere in Tibet. In the Tibetan history his name was mentioned as Tnggarto King of Konor. The Mongols were having keen interest with the religion of the Lamas. Particularly, when Altan Khakan Tomaid and his cousin brother invited a great Lama of Tibet in his court. He was Lama Sonam Gyatso the third successor of Lama Gedun Drupa founder of the Tashnal Honpo Gonpa. This Gonpa was completed in 1447 AD. Thereafter the founder of this Gonpa, Lama Gedun Drupa was appointed as the Head Lama of Gonpa Galdan. Gonpa Galdan is just near to Lhasa and is considered one of the eminent Gonpa. He was the first great Lama of Tibet, who was conferred the title of "Dalai Lama".

The first successor of Lama Gedun Drupa, who was the ruler of Tibet from 1475 AD to 1541 AD got appointed a person to run the administration whose designation was "Depa". Lama Sonam Gyatso was conferred the title of "Dalai Lama" by the Mongol King in the year 1576 AD. During the period of third Dalai Lama, when he was a minor, the Mongol King Tnaggarto began to interfere in the affairs of administration, pretending to strengthen the religion in Tibet. At that time Lama Panchhen Lozang Choki Gyalson paid a huge amount to the invaders as penalty and they went back. Later, he sought the assistance from the King of Mancho dynasty of China, who was the ruler of China at that time. The Mongol displeased with this action and Goshri Khan the son and successor of King Tanggarto invaded Tibet and dismissed all the Rajas of the small provinces of Tibet, including king of Sang. He subdued the entire Tibet and the 5th Dalai Lama was made the ruler of Tibet in 1645 AD. Later in 1653 AD, the Chinese Government also gave the consent to the Government of the Dalai Lama and he was invited at Peking in the court of King of China.

In 1706 AD, the Mongol Khoshot and in 1717 AD, Mongol Songar raised questions about the succession of Dalai Lama and interfered in Tibetan affairs. But in 1720 AD, the Chinese Army invaded Tibet and completely conquered it and set the rules and regulations for the government, which is still in practice. It was China who kept away Tibet from the interference of the foreign countries so as to form an independent country in the middle to protect from the invasion of the Europeans. In 1872-73 AD, the British Government in India tried to start the trade relation with Tibet. Later it was renewed in 1884 AD. In 1886 AD, they decided to depute a trade delegation to Lhasa. In the beginning, the Government of China issued a passport to the delegation but later objected the entry. Hence they changed the idea. The Tibetans considered it the weakness of the British Government and invaded Sikkim. Therefore, in 1888 AD, an expedition was sent to Sikkim under the command of General Graham to evacuate the Tibetans from Sikkim. In 1890 AD, an agreement was signed and later in 1893 AD, a trade regulation was drafted. On the ground that the agreement was done with the Kingdom of China, Tibetan Monks started feeling that they were left out of this agreement, therefore they not only refused to stick by the agreement but also took certain steps which further widened the gap between them.

A Lama by birth, he was a Mongolian but politically he was a citizen of Russia. His Russian name was Varjew. He entered Lhasa in 1880 AD. Later when he went back to Russia, he invited the attention of the Russian Government towards Lhasa. He presented himself in Lhasa, as a non Government representative of the Government of Russia. He maintained a good relation and approach with the Dalai Lama, and briefed him about the dangerous motto of British rulers against Tibet. He motivated him to make the security arrangement through the Government of Russia. He gave assurance and possibility to convert Czar and Russian people into Buddhism. Dalai Lama agreed the proposal and was ready to go to Saint Petersburg but the council of ministers objected. Thus, he deputed his representative in the court of Czar. He was a great officer. He was able to attend the court of Czar. He returned back with a proposal of a draft of the agreement. According to it, a Russian prince has to appoint in the court of Lhasa, so as to develop the relations between the two countries. But the council of ministers and the Chinese officers posted in Lhasa, both objected the proposal. Dalai Lama under the influence of Varjew tried to create problems, by provoking the British Government. He was sure of Russian support and the Russian arms and ammunition reached in Tibet. There was uncertainty regarding the drafted agreement, that Russia will patronize the Tibetan Government. Though, Russia denied. The Tibetans interfered in Sikkim, a British dominion and did ungraceful activities there. Lord Curzon, the Viceroy of India decided to take strict action against Tibet. Initially the British Government agreed to depute Col. Young Husband to Khamba Jung with a small number of security force, so as to draft the agreement. Khamba Jung is just on the north border of Sikkim. The expedition reached in Sikkim on 7th of July 1903 and stayed there till 11th of December. There was no representative from Tibet and the agreement proved useless. Finally, on 3rd December the British Government allowed to capture the valley of Champi, and arrangements were made to invade Gyantse of Tibet. It was also discussed, how to overcome the problems of transportations. Col. Young Husband proceeded with this expedition. General Ronald MacDonald was the commander of the Army. On 12th December 1903, after crossing the pass of Jilab, the British Army entered in Tibet, wherefrom it reached at Tona, where a section of army stayed till the winter season is over. On 31st of March 1904, they marched further. At Guru the Tibetans attacked but they were defeated. The march continued, and had to face minor opposition on the way. On 12th April, the expedition reached at Gyantse and captured it. A fierce battle took place, and a portion of British Army was defeated. Finally the expeditionist entered the capital Lhasa on 3rd August. Dalai Lama ran away, along with Varjiu. The officers of the Government of China did efforts to come on a conclusion, but because of the attitude of the Lamas and absence of Dalai Lama, it could not be matured.

Finally, the agreement was signed on 7th September. The main conditions are as follows:

1. The Tibetans has deviated the border of Sikkim, it should be avoided in future.
2. For the purpose of British trade, trade centre should be established at Gyantse, Gartog and Yatong.

3. Tibet will have to pay 5 lakh ponds as war penalty. Later it was reduced to one third.
4. No foreign country should have any sort of concession in respect of earthly, trade, commerce, etc., with the Government of Tibet. Partial modification were made later, and the Government of China confirmed it through a declaration dated; 27th April, 1906.

According to the agreement of 1907, with the Government of Britain and Russia, the following conditions were laid down for Tibet:

1. Tibet will be an autonomous region, consolidation of its area under the patronage of Government of China.
2. No officer from British Government or Government of Russia will be appointed as their representatives in Tibet.
3. The above mentioned two countries will not do any effort to get concessions regarding railway and mine, etc. in Tibet. In the appendix it was decided, that without the consent of the Government of Russia and British, no educational team should be allowed to enter Tibet for three years. In January, 1908, the last installment of the penalty was paid to the British Government, and the valley of Champi was restored to Tibet. Now the government of China convened the Dalai Lama at Peking and issued royal order that the reign of the Government should take in his own hand. Dalai Lama continued the services of the officers, who were appointed temporarily during the British expedition, and those who supported the expedition among the Tibetans were pardoned. But in 1909, Chinese Army was deputed to suppress the rebellion Lamas, at the border of Zamichan, and the Lamas were treated very harshly. When the Dalai Lama did the effort, to issue order to abstain from strict actions, the Chinese officers appointed in Tibet refused to accept it and called the Chinese Army in the city. Dalai Lama fled away from Tibet to India and stayed at Darjeeling.

This happened in 1910. The Chinese Army followed him up to the border. He was dethroned, as per the royal order. When the British Government felt that the Chinese Government wanted to establish an effective rule over Tibet. They invited the attention of the Government of Peking towards the agreement, especially, the autonomous status of the surrounding states like Nepal, Bhutan and Skim should be considered. Dalai Lama tried to seek the support of British Government in Pecking. But Britishers stated that he doesn't have any authority as a person and the British Government recognize only the real Government of Tibet. However, Dalai Lama, rule over Tibet continued and still exists.

GEOGRAPHY OF TIBET

Here it is necessary to mention the geography of Tibet. This country is situated in the central Asia. In the north there are the mountain ranges of Koinlon which separates it from the eastern Turkistan. China is in the east. The Himalayan ranges are in the south, which bifurcate this country from the British India, Bhutan and Nepal, etc., and in the west there are Ladakh and the State of Jammu and Kashmir. It is the highest plateau in the world and is about 1600 feet high from the sea level. The half of the northern part of this country is barren because of extreme cold. There are many ranges of mountains and many lakes are in the valleys. Most of these are salty. There are many hot springs in Tibet. In the south of Tngla hills the atmosphere is normal; hence this part of the country is populated. The sources of the great rivers and the valleys are situated in this part. For instance the Brahamputra, Indus, Sutlej, and Ghagra follows towards India, and Maikang, Salvey, Kowangho, and Yangzi Kyang follows towards China. In the north of Brahamputra, there are a great range of mountains; its peaks are almost equal to the peaks of the south Himalayan mountains. Among them the three Chan, Tangla and Hlonpo Gangri are very popular. Gold are in abundance in Tibet, it is found on the bank of rivers in the sand, and also obtained by digging the earth and washing the sand. According to the researchers there are many portions in the north and east of Tibet, where gold is available, and which has not been touched even now. The gilding work is being done at some places, where as some gold are being sent to China. Iron and azure are also available there, but mercury is found in a small number. Salt and borax are obtained from the lakes. Change of climate is frequent in this country, but most of season in the year remains cold and dry. The climate of this country is being affected by the winds of south-west and usually dust storms are there. It rains heavily at some places, but few places are completely dry. Some parts of the country are very cold during the winter and very warm during the summer. Sheep and cattles are their pet animal and they also kept goats, pig and hen. Horse, mule and donkey are used in large numbers. Many species of wild animals are there, i.e. Yak, deer, stag, gizala, antelope, leopard, beer, and wolf, etc. A rare type of pigeons and many species of "Kabaks" are also found there. Tibet is also the country of Kashmiri fowls. Trade is being done with China, Turkistan, Mongolia, Ladakh, India, and Indian Islands. The imported goods are; silk, carpets, tea, horses, and sheep, and the exported goods are wool, woolen goods, salt, blanket, lamb's skin, medicines, borax, lucky stone, gold, silver, and Chinese tea.

The population of the region is Mongol race and their language is called Tibetan, which is similar to the Brahmi language. The pronunciation differs from place to place. Their religion is Lamaism Buddhist, which is prevalent in Ladakh. Brief description has been made in the Ladakhi portion of history. The polyandry system of marriage is prevalent here, that means all the brothers share one wife. It is an old tradition, and not known much about it. Tibet is consisting of five provinces; they are:

> 1. Amdo, 2. Khams, 3. Wada, where Lhasa city is situated, 4. Sang and 5. Naris. The latter is the western province, whose border touches with Ladakh, Nepal, and British India. Dalai Lama is the highest authority, whose capital is in Lhasa. There is a National Council in Lhasa to assist Dalai Lama, called "Songdo". All the

important matters are decided by this council. The maintenance of relations with the foreign countries rest with this council. The system of government is very flexible. The length and breadth of this country is about 463200 square miles and the population consists of only twenty lakh people. Some awareness is seen in the administration, after the British expedition to Tibet in 1904. The British Government did the arrangement of post and telegraph up to Gyantse. Beyond Gyantse, the Government of Tibet has made the arrangement of post and telegraph. It has been already mentioned above, that Spalgi Gon had three sons: The elder son conquered Ladakh and became the King and the founder of the Kingdom of Ladakh. It has been revealed in the 2nd chapter.

Genealogical Table of Lahchhen Kingdom of Ladakh

1.	Skit Ldey Nima Gon (Yathi Keeda) 975-990, AD. King of Kugay, Purang and Ladakh		
2.	Spalgi Gon (990-1020) King Ladakh, Zangskar and Spiti	Tashi Gon (Purang)	Ldey Sog Gon (Kugay)
3.	Chhosgon 1020-1050)	Dogon	
4.	Lahchhen Takspa Ldey	1050-1075 AD	
5.	Lahchhen Chang Chhub Semspa	1075-1100 AD	
6.	Lahchhen Gyalpo	1100-1125 AD	
7.	Lahchhen Otpala	1125-1150 AD	
8.	Lahchhen Naghlog	1150-1175 AD	
9.	Lahchhen Gaybum	1175-1200 AD	Lahchhen Gaibay
10.	Lahchhen Joldor	1200-1230 AD	
11.	Lahchhen Tashi Gon	1230-1265 AD	
12.	Lahchhen Chhospail	1265-1290 AD	
13.	Lahchhen Mourup Gon	1290-1340 AD	
14.	Gyalbu Rinchen (Malik Sadruddin Shah, King of Kashmir, Who died in Kashmir in the year 1327 AD		
15.	Lahchhen Sherab	1340-1430 AD	
16.	Lahchhen Thisog Ldey	1400-1430 AD	
17.	Lahchhen Malik Bum Ldey Raja Shey	1430-1470 AD	Lahchhen Takpa Bum Raja Tingmogang
18.	Lahchhen Lotus Chhogdan, Tongpa Ali Brother and Lapstan Sherab Brother	1470-1534 AD	
19.	Lahchhen Bara	1430-1455 AD	
20.	Lahchhen Bhagon	1475-1500 AD	
21.	Lahchhen Tashi Gon	1500-1532 AD	

Lahchhen Lahwang Gon brother of Lahchhen Tashi Gon was made blind and Imprisoned.

2

History of Great Tibet (Ladakh) Lahchhen Kingdom Ladakh

After the civil war among the offsprings of Lang Tarma, as mentioned earlier, the power slipped from the hands of his descendents. The son of Otshang, Ldey Spal Khorsan spent his life in a pitiable manner. His elder son Thi Sagspa Pal lived in a village. But his younger son Skit Ldey, according to some also known as Thi Keeda Nima Gon considered this a humiliation and could not bear this. He left for Naris i.e. western Tibet, along with 100 horse men. The country of Naris is four "Padao" (stopover) away from Mansarovar lake towards Lhasa. It is considered from Maryumla to border of Kashmir. Purang, Kugay, and Spiti, all are included in it. Since, he left the home in a helpless condition. He had to face shortage of food during the travel. So they ate the fish and the eggs of the fowls, which are found in large number on the bank of lakes. Thus hunting and eating, these valor people reached Rala that is between Tashigang and Gar and made Rala their capital, from where they began to attack the neighboring villages. When they besieged some villages they began to build a fort at Rala. This is known, as Kharmar or Red fort. The ruins of the fort are still there. There was an influential religious head at Purang called Lama Gashes Chan. He was well aware of the worldly affairs. He convened Nimagon at Purang, and well behaved with him. Under his guidance Nimagon conquered the whole Purang within few days, and build a fort at Tsesway, the capital of this region, called Nilza Zong. This fort still exists, but has converted into a Gonpa. Lama Gashes Chan got married Nimagon with Doza Khor Skoyong and he began to rule over Purang contentedly.

The second name of Naris was Maryul, divided in two parts; i.e. Stot Maryul and Sham Maryul (upper and lower) when we move from Nemo village towards Leh, the road pass through a nallah and reaches at a plateau. Here is a pass at the top of the plateau. It is called "Ladakh Kongkah" and is the border of both the Maryuls. Thus the upper side is called Stot Maryul and the lower Sham Maryul. During that period a good number of populations were there in Sham. Mostly they were "Brokpas". In ancient time, these people had migrated from Dardistan (Gilgit) and Karja. The history of Lama Yuru Gonpa reveals, the time when the Tibetan kings entered in Naris, there was a Brokpa Bagdur Skyap ruling over Sham. Bagdur seems to be a member of the Thata Khan's clan, whose rule was up to Khalsey. At that time, there was no population, in the Indus valley up to Changa-Martselang in Stot Maryul. During this period the populations in Stot Maryul were right from Gya village to Rong region, Sakti, Tanchey, Durgup and Shayok. Regarding the population, the history reveals that a group of people migrated from Monyul Karja and settled in Gya. Gradually they established their population at Rong, Sakti, Tanchey and Shayok. A person among them ruled over these people, whose capital was Gya. In his capital, he was well known as Gyapa Chow (Raja of Gya). The ruins of his fort in Gya are still there. A portion of the fort has been converted in to Gonpa, which is in good condition and the rest has fallen. The ruins of other forts of Gyapa Chow are found at different places of Rong, Tangtse and Sakti, and are known as "Monkhar". There were no strong government at Sham Maryul and Stot Maryul. So it was not a difficult job for Nima Gon to conquer it. Incidentally a natural reason occurred for the cause is as follows; during this period the nomads of Khotan reached up to Shayok and began to take the benefit of the pastures of the surrounding areas. They were the quarrelsome people. So due to fear Gyapa Chow constructed a fort at Shayok for security purposes, and kept a group of soldiers there. Consequently, the Khotani nomads and Ladakhi Mon's used to fight off and on with one another. Finally, an army was deputed to subdue the "Mons". This army ruined the Mons and reached up to Chiktan Purig and after looting and taking some prisoners with them, went back to their own country. While returning Khotan this army left some of the nomads to be inhabited at Yurgolog. Gyapacho displeased with this action. After few years when the Mons strengthened their position, they plundered the village of Yurgolog. When the Khotanis came to know about this destruction, they again deputed an army to subdue the Mons. Gyapacho became aware of this invasion but he was not in a position to fight the Khotani's army. Therefore he requested the ruler of Purang for help. Thus Nima Gon riding on the horse back along with his men reached for help and with the collaboration of the Mons, he defeated the Khotanis. In recognition to his services, Gyapacho offered the uncultivated land below Martselang to Nima Gon for cultivation. Initially he settled at Shay village and irrigated the lands there. Gradually the companions of Nima Gon settled in the Indus belt and he became a very influential person. Similarly the power and influence of Gyapacho diminished. As a result the descendents of Nima Gon overpowered him and his position became like that of a Kalon or a Governor of a province. Raftan Kalon Mulbe was from this clan. During my visit to Ladakh, the renowned persons among his offsprings were Heraman Zildar Tangtse, Jigsmat Nambardar Mulbe and Haider Khan Mafidar Tambis. In short he conquered all the regions of Naris, consolidated his position and established a regular government. He had three sons;

1. Spalgi Gon 2. Tashi Gon and 3. Ldeysog Gon. Nima Gon, during his old age distributed his country among his three sons as under:

> Spalgi Gon got the Stot Maryul and Sham i.e. from Rudok to the border of Kashmir, (Zojila) including Zangskar and Spiti. Tashi Gon got the Purang. Ldeysog Gon got the Kugay which is called Tsang Tsong.

SPALGI GON RAJA MARYUL, ZANGSKAR AND SPITI (about 990-1240 AD)

Spalgi Gon constructed a fort at Shay, and made it his capital in the Stot Maryul. No further achievement has mentioned about him. He had two sons; Dogon and Chhosgon.

Dogon died during the life time of his father. Nothing has been mentioned about him in the history. After the death of Spalgi Gon his son Chhosgon ascended the throne (about 1029-1050 AD).

Propagation of Buddhism by Lotsawa Rinchen Zangpo (about 1050 AD).

It is not out of place to mention here that, after the death of Ldeysog Gon his son Khoray ascended the throne, when Khoray's son Naka Raza became adult, he himself became a Lama and handed over the throne to Naka Raza. He made Lotsawa his disciple and was deputed to Kashmir and Hindustan to seek education. When he came back, after receiving education, he devoted himself for the cause of religion; His full name is Lotsawa Rinchen Zangpo. It has mentioned about him in the history of Lama Yuru Gonpa, that he got constructed 108 Gonpas and 108 Chhortens (stupa) between Zojila and Kailash Prabhat, and propagated Buddhism in this country. The following Gonpas constructed by him are still in good conditions.

Alchi, Sumda, Mangyu, Laido, Tholing (Kugay) Chiktan (Purig) and the ruins at Mulbe and Bazgo can be seen. The Gonpa of Tholing is one of the best architects of Lotsawa. I have not seen it personally. This Gonpa is among the first Buddhist architect in his country. Though the Lama yuru Gonpa is the oldest one but it is considered that prior to Buddhism it was the Gonpa of Bonchhos. When the inhabitants of Lamayuru converted to Buddhism, then they changed it into the Gonpa of their new faith.

LAHCHHEN TAKSPA LDEY (1050-1075 AD)

He was the son of Chhosgon.

LAHCHHEN CHANGCHUP SAIMSPA (1075-1100 AD)

He was the son of Lahchhen Takspa Ldey.

LAHCHHEN GYALPO (1100-1125 AD)

He was the son of Lahchhen Changchup Saimspa. He devoted himself towards the religious activities and constructed the 1st royal Gonpa at village Lukhil, which is presently called Likir. He enrolled Lamas in this Gonpa and started religious education through them. During the period about 100 to 500 Lamas used to stay at Mansarowar Lake and Kailash Parbhat.

They had to face the problems of food, etc, being far away from the local inhabitants. The king made the suitable arrangements and redressed the problems.

LAHCHHEN UTPALA (1125-1150 AD)

He was the son of Lahchhen Gyalpo. He collected a huge army of Ladakh and invaded Nyungti (Kullu) and defeated him. The king of Kullu bound himself by an oath, "so long as the glaciers of Kailash does not melt away, or the Mansarowar Lake dry up, to pay his tribute to the King of Ladakh, 'in particular Dzos and iron,' and shall be loyal to him." This treaty remained in force, as long as his offspring's ruled over Kullu. The king even conquered the province of Lowo of Tibet, which is in the east of Purang. Prior to that Purang was already annexed with the Kingdom of Ladakh. His empire was even greater than that of his ancestors.

LAHCHHEN NAGLOG, (1150-1175 AD)

He was the son of Lahchhen Utpala. This king built the palaces at Wanla and Khalsay. There was a bridge across the Indus River in front of Balu Khar, where the traders had to pay the taxes. When Naglog built the palace at Khalsay, he wanted to uplift this village; therefore he constructed a new bridge, near the village across the Indus at the very same place where the present bridge is situated and the custom office from Balu Khar was shifted to this place.

LAHCHHEN GAYBAY AND LAHCHHEN GAYBUM (1175-1120 AD)

Lahchhen Naglog had two sons; Lahchhen Gaybay and Lahchhen Gaybum.

LAHCHHEN JOLDOR (1220-1230 AD)

He was the son of Lahchhen Gaybum.

TASHI GON (1230-1265 AD)

He was the son of Lahchhen Joldor. He got copied some religious books with golden ink.

LAHCHHEN CHOSPAIL (1265-1290 AD)

He was the son of Lahchhen Tashi Gon; he set the social, political and religious rules for the country.

LAHCHHEN MOURUP GON (1290-1340 AD)

He was the son of Lahchhen Chospail. During the reign of this king the novices going to central Tibet for seeking religious education was first introduced. He also repaired the monasteries which had been built by his ancestors. He offered gold, silver, copper, coral beads and pearl, etc, through Lama Chhosgi Jai Jigstain Sumgi Gonpo, who was the first Head Lama of Degungpa sect, to the monasteries of Lhasa. He also got copied two sets of Kangur (a library of 108 volumes) considered to be the sacred books of Buddhism. His son was prince Rinchen, who ruled over Kashmir and converted to Islam. His Islamic name was Malik Sadruddin Rinchen Shah, who died in Kashmir.

PRINCE RINCHEN (MALIK SADRUDDIN KING OF KASHMIR) (1324-1327 AD)

He was the son of Lahchhen Mourup Gon. That is all that we learn about him from the Ladakhi chronicles, and no more is said of him. Since he is called Gyalbu or Prince, it indicates that he could not rule over Ladakh and left the country during his prince hood, and did such a wonderful job in wilderness, which perhaps would not have done in his own country. It is not out of place to mention here, a brief history of Kashmir that during the beginning of the 14th century Kashmir was ruled by Raja Sahadev. The people were free minded and never cared for religious principles. They could not differentiate between good and bad. It happens so before revolutions and social changes occur. In 1319 AD, a Muslim traveler Shah Meer migrated from Sawad Kuner and reached Kashmir. He became a member in the court of Raja Sahadev. In the mean time a Ladakhi Prince Rinchen, who was ill treated by his father reached Kashmir and became a very close confidante of Ram Chander, who was Commander in Chief. In 1323 AD, a Tatar King Zulkadar Khan invaded Kashmir with a huge army and helpless Sahadeva could not face it and fled to Kishtawar for shelter. Zulkadar plundered the valley of Kashmir and went back but because of extreme and inhospitable weather conditions, on the way Zulkadar Khan and his army perished. During this period Ram Chander was stationed in his fort at Gagangir. Rinchen and Shah Meer accompanied him. After the departure of Zulkadar Khan, when Ram Chander got assured he concentrated his energy towards restructuring of the administration. In the meantime another tribe invaded Kashmir and looted the people. Ram Chander deputed Rinchen and Shah Meer to counter the enemy. Rinchen fought courageously and due to his good strategy, he not only defeated the enemy but imprisoned and gave severe punishment to them and restored peace in the country. Due to this brilliant and well planned success he became very popular in the country. But very soon his hunger for power got over him and with the collaboration of Shah Meer he plotted against Ram Chander. Once when Ram Chander was staying at Inder Kot and Rinchen was at his estate in Laar region, He loaded weapons on the horses of the Ladakhi traders making appear as if they were transporting goods for trade and reached Srinagar along with his companions. After reaching there he distributed the arms to his loyalist who attacked Ram Chander during the night. At that time he was asleep and got killed. Rinchen immediately took over the reign and ruled over Kashmir. Later King Sahadev struggled to capture the Government but failed.

In 1324 AD, Rinchen sat on the throne of Kashmir, and married with Kota Rani, the daughter of Ram Chander. In this way he wanted to keep the relation with the former ruling family. But because of the biased nature of the Brahmans, he could not make a space for himself in their fraternity. Now he was in search of such a religion, in which he could find space for him easily. Because of the companion of Shah Meer he was already inclined towards Islam. In the mean time a religious scholar Bulbul Shah entered Kashmir; he got the opportunity to interact with him, and embraced Islam. His Islamic name was Malik Sadruddin. After the change of the government he brought religious revolution in Kashmir. But he could not have much time to observe this revolution, since he died in 1327 AD, after ruling over Kashmir for a short period of two and half years.

In Kashmir chronicles Rinchen's father's name has mentioned as Baghin. It indicates that Lahchhen Bhagan son of Lahchhen Bhara might be his father. But as per the Tibetan chronicles, Lachhen Bhara has no son with this name. Moreover the period of Rinchen does not match with Lachhen Bhara. Most probably, the last name must have misspelt as "Chen". (I am of the opinion that it is not Baghin or Chen but Lahchhen. Because the former and later kings have added this surname with their name and Rinchen too was a prince of this dynasty (Z. Aabedin). It indicates when Rinchen became young, his father as per the tradition engaged him in the affairs of administration, but due to political differences between the two, the son had to left the country and wandered. Prior to that he had a son. No difference has been shown in the heredity, except his name was mentioned as Prince (Gyalbu) in the Ladakhi chronicles. No doubt the founder of the new dynasty of Kashmir was prince Rinchen. Really it is a matter of proud for the Ladakhis.

LAHCHHEN SHERAP (1340-1400 AD)

Prince Rinchen's son was Lahchhen Sherap. He was enthroned in young age, after the death of his grandfather. He got constructed a fort over the Hangtse hill at village Saboo and founded a village in the surroundings called "Singay

Zgang". The name of the fort is "Saboo Changkhar" and the ruines of the fort is still there.

LAHCHHEN THISOG LDEY (1400-1430 AD)

He was the son of Lahchhen Sherap. He got constructed more than 100 "Chortens" in Leh town and two such "Chortens" in Saboo. (Chorten is a religious structure, like that of a dome, where the ashes of the death people are being kept. In Ladakh it is grinded, mixed with dust and mud is prepared. This is molded in blocks of different type of small statues and finally kept inside the "Chortens" in memory of the departed souls.

During this period the following different sects of Buddhism prevailed in Lhasa:

1. Sningma, 2. Kadampa, 3. Talspo Kargyut divided in four sub-sects viz., (i) Karmapa, (ii) Degungpa, (iii) Drukpa, (vi) Taglungpa, 4. Shangspa Kargyut 5. Saskyapa, 6. Tsechat, 7. Chotrigs, and 8. Chonagpa.

In Kham a man Lobzang Takpay Spal was born in village Tsonkha. He became a Lama. Received religious education in Lhasa, from the scholars of Kadampa, Kargyutpa and Saskyapa sects. And he became a great scholar. Later, he found discrepancies in the Buddhism prevailing in Lhasa. So he wanted to reform and revive the Buddhism. He drafted a new rules and way of life and introduced among the masses. He was having many students and a large number of people became his followers. He built a magnificent Gonpa, called "Galdan". Hence his followers are called "Gelukspa" after the name of the Gonpa. The visible difference regarding the dress was the cap. All the Lamas of other Gonpas used to wear red dress from top to bottom, but he asked his disciples to wear yellow cap. This tradition is still prevailing. This new religion is popular after the name of "Tsongkhapa", the birth place of the great saint.

Lahchhen Thisog Ldey had two sons; the elder Lahchhen Tak Bum Ldey and the younger, Lahchhen Takpa Bum. The two brothers were of very different character. The elder was of a good nature and merciful disposition, where as the younger was cruel and stone hearted. The elder was a strict follower of religion as against the young, who didn't care for the religion at all. The elder was very much concerned about the upliftment and empowerment of his community particularly the down-trodden and poor, but the young was so greedy and selfish that he could not bear the idea of having a brother king beside him. As per the tradition, after the death of his father, the elder son Tak Bum Ldey sat on the throne in (1430-1470, AD) but taking the opportunity his younger son captured the Sham region and established his own separate government.

King Tak Bum Ldey commenced his career with the erection of a number of religious buildings. First he erected the Chamba Marpo Gonpa "Red college" in Leh. He also built a triple temple, one surmounting the other, on the pattern of an ancient popular temple Tholing at Kugay. In the north-west of Leh town the Tivoo Serpo hill was considered ill-omened and unlucky. To eradicate this fatality and make the fatal power ineffective, he built a Gonpa over the hill. It looks like a Chorten from outside but it is a temple from inside, consisting of 108 temple shrines, called Tivoo Tashi Ottho. All the three temples still exist. The former two are in good conditions but the later has ruined.

Now he was planning to built a Gonpa on the crag resembling an elephant, in the lower part of Leh and keep Lamas there. In the mean time two representatives from the famous scholar Konkhain Tsongkhapa chhenpo Lobzang Takpay Spal, arrived in Leh. They were carrying a statue of Tsepakmat, about as long as a finger joint, which originated from the blood of his nose. He entrusted the same to the two ascetics and said, "Give it either to Takpa Bum or Tak Bum Ldey. When the representatives reached in Ladakh, the one Takpa Bum was in Nubra, they went there in his presence, but he did not deign to look at it, and ignored them completely, this attitude of Takpa Bum towards them made them feels ashamed and they went back to Ladakh without expressing purpose of the visit.

The day when they had to reach Ladakh, concisely or it was the blessing of Lama Tsongkhapa, that King Tak Bum

Ldey gave command. "At today's council, whoever attends, be it ascetic or a low-caste man, he should not be refused admittance." Now, when the two ascetics came into his presence, the king rose and greeted them. They presented the statue sent by Lama Tsongkhapa and the king was delighted and kept the statue with regards and respect. Tak Bum Ldey as per his previous intention got constructed a Gonpa, (Spituk monastery) to keep the sacred present over the hill resembling elephant.

It is considered that it came into existence because of miracles. A large number of his follower Lamas were enrolled in this Gonpa.

The Lahkhang constructed by Ol Ldey during the period of Lotsawa existed there. Tak Bum Ldey with the consultation of these two Lamas, who came as representatives of Tsongkhapa, converted this Lahkhang into Gonpa, and handed over to the Gelukspa sect. The name of one of the Lama seems to be Lahwang Lotus. The present Gonpa of Likir was built much earlier also gave under the care of the Gelukspa sect. During this very period a man of village Thiksay, called Lama Sherap Zangpo, went to Lhasa for higher studies. He got the education from Lama Tsongkhapa, and came back to Ladakh. He built a Lahkhang inside the Nalah Thiksay at Stagmo. (Lahkhang is that type of Gonpa, where statue is not kept). He also got constructed the Phugtal Gonpa at Zangskar. His nephew Lama Paldan Sherap got the religious education from him and he built the Thiksay Gonpa, but it is not known that under whose period it was completed.

TAKPA BUM KING SHAM REGION (1430-1455 AD)

Takpa Bum was busy in Nubra in connection with some official work but it has not been mentioned, what the work was. After staying few years in Nubra, he reached in Tia Tingmogang via Largyap. He captured the Sham region, built a very strong and magnificent fort at Tingmogang, and made it his capital. He got construct a fort at Bazgo, called Rafstan Kartsey, and ruled over Sham region. In this way the United Government of Ladakh was distributed in two separate autonomous governments. The one was the Stot Maryul, Shay as its capital and another was the Sham Maryul and Tingmogang was the capital. King Tak Bum Ldey could not compete with his brother and was contented with his small government at Shay.

LOTUS CHOGDAN KING STOT MARYUL (1470-1535 AD)

After the death of Tak Bum Ldey, his son Lotus Chhogdan sat on the throne of Shay. He conquered the Naris Korsum and extended his government towards east. He received the following articles as tribute from this region, armor 18, sword 18, dari 18, lucky stone 15, saddle 20, horses 150, yak female 40, yak male brown color 20, sheep and goat number less.

LAHCHHEN BARA KING TINGMOGANG (1455-1475 AD)

After the death of Takpa Bum his son Lahchhen Bara ascended the throne of Tingmogang.

LAHCHHEN BHAGON KING TINGMOGANG (1475-1500 AD)

After the death of Lahchhen Bara, his son Lachhen Bhagon ascended the throne. According to the Ladakhi chronicles, he was very greedy of power. There were many people of different tribes at Shay, the capital of Lotus Chhogdan. Lachhen Bhagon formed an alliance with these people and plotted against the King of Shay, and got killed King Lotus Chhogdan and his two younger brothers Tongpa Ali and Labstan Targais and conqured the whole Ladakh, thus he fulfilled the desires of his grand father Takpa Bum. But it seems to be not correct. It has just revealed to hide the factual events of the invasion of Sultan Sayeed Khan. The fact is, till the departure of the Mughals, there were two separate governments at Shay and Tingmogang, and the two were annexed by Tsewang Namgyal, after the return of Mirza Haider Gorgan, when he captured Shay. The details are as follows:

TASHI GON KING TINGMOGANG (1500-1530 AD)

Lahchhen Bhagon King of Tingmogang had two sons; Lahchhen Lahwang Gon and Lahchhen Tashi Gon. According to the tradition, Lahwang Gon was to be the successor but the bad example set by their fathers showed its influence on the sons. Tashi Gon's ambition strove after the crown. The brothers are characterized in the history as follows:

> Lahwang Gon had great bodily strength and was clever in any kind of sport; but Tashi Gon was very crafty and greedy. To attain his aim, Tashi plotted a plan and his elder brother's eyes were plucked out. Then he sent him to Lingshed, on the borders of Zangskar, along with his family members, for imprisonment. And himself became the King of Tingmogang, from (1500-1530 AD).

Nothing has been mentioned in Ladakhi chronicles about the events of King Lotus Chhogdan, but according to the foreigner authors he never interrupted with Lahchhen Bara and Lahchhen Bhagon, which later proved very harmful to him. But he tried to extend his government, beyond the border of Ladakh. The Raja of Sot Jadim Bag had captured the Ladakhi areas up to Lamayuru, and he fixed the border at Khalsay Bridge. This system of administration, according to the Sot chronicles continued for eleventh generations. But during the period of Doru Cho the son of Murid Khan, people were fed up with his cruelty. King Lotus Chhogdan invaded Sot and restored the areas captured by Raja Jadim Bag and the border of the Sot Government was shifted from Khalsay to Nalah Kanji. After Doru Cho his son Habib Cho became the Raja of Sot. At that time, Islam was flourishing in Baltistan and Purig. Raja Habib Cho with the collaboration of the Rajas of Khapolu, Shigar, and Skardo, invaded Ladakh and besieged the king, which took a long time. But the Baltis never moved. Finally the Raja of Ladakh had to make a compromise and paid a huge amount as tribute. The name of the Ladakhi Raja has not been mentioned with this event; most probably it might be the period of King Lotus Chhogdan.

Besides these two events the third one occurred during the period of King Lotus Chhogdan of Shay and King Lahchhen Tashi Gon of Tingmogang. When Sultan Sayeed Khan Ruler of Kashgar invaded Ladakh, under the command of Mirza Haider Gorgan and Sultan Sikandar Khan. The detail of the invasion will be narrated in the next chapter. According to the Ladakhi chronicles King Tashi Gon was a religious minded person. He convened Lama Chhosjay Ldanma from the Degung Gonpa of Lhasa, and according to his advice got constructed a magnificent Gonpa at Fiyang, called Tashi Chhoszong. He got enrolled Lamas for this Gonpa among the population of Fiyang. Going downwards from Leh at the spot where this Gonpa is seen for the first time, he placed a long prayer flag. Whosever whether thief or liar, in short anyone guilty of offence against the Government, if he escaped to this spot, should be rid of his crime. But it seems to be not correct because Fiyang was beyond the jurisdiction of Tingmogang. Probably, being a religious matter, Lotus Chhogdan might have permitted to construct the Gonpa. The fact is that just to hide the factual events of Mughal invasion to Ladakh; the Ladakhies has mutilated the history. The king made the usual offerings of prayer flags and gold water to the statues of the most famous Gonpas of Lhasa like, Degung, Saskya, Galdan, Rasa, and Samyas, etc. The Lamas were invited for feast and precious presents were offered to the Head Lamas of these Gonpas. He got copied the 108 volumes of Kangyur and Stangyur and other important religious books and erected many Chortains. But in spite of these offerings and prayers, he remained childless and during the lifetime of his elder brother, who was made blind and imprisoned at Lingshed, he was got killed without an issue, by Sultan Sayeed Khan. After his assassination his elder brother and children's were released from the prison. The blind, Lahchhen Lahwang Gon had three sons:

1. Tsewang, 2. Gonbo, and 3. Jamyang. Tashi Gon was succeded by his nephew Tsewang. After capturing Shay, he annexed both the Governments and founded the new dynasty, and called "Namgyal" or Victors. The details about him has revealed in the next chapter after the invasion of Mughals.

3

The Invasion of Mughals on Tibet

1. Preface, 2. Invasion of Mirza Haider to Bloor (Dardistan), 3. The Tibet expedition of Mirza Haider on behalf of Sultan Sayeed Khan, 4. The invasion of Sultan Sayeed Khan to Baltistan, 5. The invasion of Mirza Haider to Kashmir, 6. The return of Sultan Sayeed Khan from Ladakh and death, 7. The expedition of Mirza Haider to Ursang, 8. Mirza Haider reached in Ladakh in a deplorable condition, 9. Return of Mirza haider, 10. Conquer of Kashmir again by Mirza Haider from Lahore side. During the period when King Lotus Chhogdan was ruling over Stot Maryul from Shay, and King Tashi Gon was ruling over Sham Maryul from Tingmogang as its capital. The Mughals invaded Ladakh and Baltistan, and after looting and plundering these countries, the Mughals reached up to Kashmir on one side and up to Purang on the other side. About this important events, the Ladakhi chronicles has mentioned like this. That Tashi Namgyal fought the enemies with bravery. Defeated them and they run away. Many Yarkendi armies were killed. Tashi Namgyal celebrated the victory by constructing a Lahkhang on the Tsemo hill, its foundation were filled by the death bodies of the Yarkendies, and the statue of Dorjay Jigschat was kept over it, which still exist.

But in his valuable book *Tarikhe-Rashidi* published in 951 Hijri, Mirza Haider Gorgan has revealed in detail, which provide us the factual information. It is much important that history of Ladakh had been linked with the foreign countries after this event, which continued further and there is possibility of comparing and criticizing the events.

Whatever the learned author has written about the events of Kashmir and Ladakh that is very interesting and important on historical point of view, which throws light on the cultural, social and geographical condition of present time. I present the translation before the readers; the unnecessary lengthy portions have been deleted and the gist of the text has been narrated in my own language. Mirza Haider has mentioned two rulers in Maryul (Ladakh) one Lata Chokdan and another Tashi Gon. The later is certainly Lahchhen Tashi Gon king of Tingmogang, who is called "Namgyal" in Ladakhi chronicles. But according to the events this title was granted to King Tsewang Namgyal, after the unification of the two governments. Lata Chokdan is a Persian pronounce and calligraphy but by copying again and again, its original spelling has lost. Thus due to similarity of words it is very much clear that Lotus Chhogdan is the King of Shay. At that time, the two were the rulers of Maryul (Ladakh) who used to attend Mirza's court.

MIRZA HAIDER'S INVASION TO BLOOR (DARDISTAN)

Mirza's Ladakh expedition started with the invasion of Bloor. I am of the opinion, that as per the present geography, Mirza's Bloor is the regions, which are known as Kafiristan, Chitral, and Dardistan (Gilgit). Since Kafiristan has been annexed with Afghanistan and renamed as Nooristan. However, Mirza Haider writes as under:

Sultan Sayeed Khan issued order to me and Rashid Sultan to invade Bloor. Bloor is a country of infidels. Most of the people are "Khail". These people have no religion and never abstain from anything. They do whatever they like. In the east of Blooristan are Kashgar and Yarkend, in the north is Badakhshan, and in the west Kabul, Nagman and Lumghan and in the south is Kashmir. It takes four months to reach between Mabeen and its surroundings. The whole country is full of mountains, hills and passes. The life is so hard that one can say without exaggeration, that a "farsakh" of land is not plain in the whole Bloor. Though, their population is very high but there is no harmony between the villages, there is chaos and crisis in the country. They fight with one another. Such are the conditions that the women remain busy in agricultural work whereas the men are in the battle fields. While a woman prepares the food at home, she comes in between and says, "It's lunch time, so you should not fight with each other". They disburse and go to their respective home, take their food and again busy themselves in quarrels, till the time of "Asar". Sometimes the women interfere and make the compromise between the men. Surprisingly these men sometimes quarrel the whole night. The pastures and meadows are very few, there is the paucity of cattle's and camels, goats and sheep are limited, so less that they can't afford to use their wools as dress to keep them warm. But cows are in a large number giving them enough milk and butter to survive, making these limited cattle's their assets for survival because they have nothing else to lose. Their dialects are different in every region and they don't know other languages because the chaos, crisis and quarrels are always there to make them enemies to each other. Many people have not seen other places except their own village. There are very good orchards in Bloor and all kinds of fruits are available there, especially the pomegranates are found of good qualities and they are in good numbers. There is a kind of pomegranate in Bloor; its pimples are white, sweet, juicy and very tasty. I spent my winters in Bloor, a fierce battle took place and we were victorious.

In summer we returned safe and sound with the booties, it's "Khumus" (5% tax) was 1000 barda. In the beginning of the summer in 934, Hijri according to the 1527 AD, I reached back in the court of Khan.

SULTAN SAYEED KHAN'S TIBET EXPEDITION THROUGH MIRZA HAIDER

After this, the Ladakh expedition starts, but before narrating about the invasion the author has revealed the social and geographical conditions of Tibet, as follows:

In 938, Hijri according to the 1531 AD, Sultan Sayeed Khan issued orders for Tibet expedition to Rashid Khan and me. Tibet is such a place with such conditions, where very few people are expected to arrive, due to different kind of hardships. The mountains, hills, passes and routes are full of dangers. It is awfully cold and there is scarcity of grass and water. People have no skills and are ill-tempered. Because of the fear of dacoit and robbery no tourist or travelers visit there. That is why, nobody knows about the factual conditions of this country. The length of this country (Tibet) from north-west to south-east takes eight months to reach, and its width extends up to one month journey, and in many places it totals up to ten days.

Bloor is in the north-west and Ursang is in the south-east, which is under China. It has been mentioned in the mountain ranges of Mogulistan and Kashgar in which the actual mountain range of Mogulistan, starts from the north of Kashgar and via west of Kashgar goes towards the south of Kashgar. It has been also mentioned that the country of "Fargana" is situated on the west of Kashgar, and the mountains are located in between the two countries. The country which is in between the Kashgar and Fargana is called "Balai" and is located on the west of Badakhshan and Yarkend. This is also the same mountain range in the middle which is called "Pamir". At some places the width of this country is about eight day's journey. When we go ahead, there are the Balai valleys like Raskam and Tagdumbash, just adjacent to the Bloor and Yarkend. After crossing these valleys we reach Tibet. Badakhshan is situated on the north of Yarkend towards "Tabistani" and Kashmir is on the west "Zimistani" and the said mountains are in the middle. Whatever is in between Yarkend and Kashmir, it's Tibet. There is region in Tibet which is called Balti [now BALTISTAN]. In this country the width of the mountains are much wider than upper Pamir. In Balti the width is about 20 "Padao". From Yarkend the ascending route is Sanju pass and towards Kashmir the descending route is called Skardo pass. The distances of these two passes are about 20 "Padao". Similarly on the west of Khutan, towards Ziministani, there are some provinces of India, like Lahore, Sultanpur, and Wabajawara, and whatever is between Khotan and these places, they are the provinces of Tibet like Rudok, Kugay and Spiti. Here it is to be noted that these mountain range ends in China. India is on the west-south of this range and the provinces right from Bhera, Lahore and Bengal are situated under the foot of these mountains range.

All the rivers of northern India follow from this range. Most of the sources of these rivers are in Tibet. In the east and north of Tibet, there are Yarkend, Khotan, Jarjan, Lob, Kang, and Sarig Alinoor and the border of the desert of Habas like Qamjo and Sakjoway are connected with China. From the mountains of Tibet towards the west-south, the Indian rivers follow; they are Neelab (Indus), Aabe Bhera (Jhelum), Aabe Chinab, Aabe Lahore (Ravi), Aabe Sultanpur (Beas) Aabe Bajwara (Sutllj). These all rivers annex with Indus. The rivers like Ganga and others which fall in the Bay of Bengal come from the north-east of Tibet mountains. The river of Yarkend Aaqash, Garba, and Jar Jan, etc., falls in the Koknadar lake. Koknadar is a lake in this desert. Some Mughals who had seen this lake, says, that it takes three months durations to have a full round of this lake, and a great river follows from this lake, called Qara Noorane Khatai. These events reveal that Tibet is a high altitude place, because its water follows to all directions. If a man wants to go Tibet has to ascend upwards and there is no chance of descending downwards. On the top and some places in the way there are plains. Tibet is a coldest place. Therefore except turnip nothing is available in some villages. The barley of Tibet is ripped in 40 days. If it fails to ripe within this days than it began to fade because of coldness and the pimples are very small. In most of the villages the green grass are seen for two months only. Similarly, there are some villages in Tibet where the summer season is only for 40 days. During these 40 days too, the water in the canals freeze at night. Because of awfully cold neither the trees nor the grass grow high.

In Tibet, The cow dung and the waist of cattle's are being used as fuel.

Now the area is not so cold, besides turnip many other vegetables are grown in great and little Tibet (i.e. Ladakh and Baltistan) Barley grow in the coldest region. Kohl's not freeze in summer and one crop can have easily. It indicates that the temperature is improving day by day, and the seasons have changed as compare to the past. If the present condition of the seasons continues, than within next 100 or 200 years one can have two crops instead of one crop, than rice and maze will began to grow in all parts of Baltistan and Ladakh.

The people have divided in two kinds: one is the "Yulpa" or Inhabitants and the second are the "Changpa" or Nomads. Both the types are under one rule of Tibet. The lives of the Tibetan Nomads are very interesting and funny which not match with any other tribe. First, mostly they eat meat and uncooked food. There is no system of cooking food (It is not so yet). Secondly, instead of grass the horses are provided with mutton. Thirdly, the transportations are being done through sheep. Approximately a sheep has to carry 12 Man Sharyi (One mand sharyi = Five pao English) for this purpose they have prepared a double sided bag called "Khorjun". And it is kept throught day and night and in all seasons, over the back of the sheep and removed only when it has to consume.

The activities of the Nomads or the Changpa tribes are like this; during winter they come down towards the hills of west-south, where India is situated. They bring from Tibet the Chinese goods, salt, borax, yak, gold and pashmina and sold to the Indian Hindus of the hilly region. From India they purchase the Indian goods like cloths, gudh, sugar, sweets, rice and load them over the back of sheep and go back to Tibet in summer. Further they take the goods of Tibet which are useful in China and continue their slow journey. Finally they reach in China in winter and exchange the Indian and Tibetan goods with the Chinese goods. In the next summer they used to come back Tibet with the Chinese goods and in winter go to India. The Chinese goods loaded over the back of the sheep in summer are being unloaded on reaching India during the winter. Similarly, the goods loaded in India are unloaded in China. They pass one winter in India and another in China. All the Changpa's keep moving throughout their life. There are some Changpas who are having ten thousands loaded sheep and every sheep carry "12 Man Sharyi" or 15 kgs. Thus one can calculate the total numbers. These goods are unloaded once in a year either in China or in India. The rest of the year it remains on the back of the sheep, unless the sheep remains healthy. The Changpas are in a large number, one of their tribe is called "Dolpa" these people are more than fifty thousands family. But we know through reliable sources, that the quantity of this tribe does not siege the number of other tribes.

Those who are called "Yulpa" are consisting of regions; Balti is one of the regions of Tibet. In Baltistan there are some other regions; like Purig, Khapulo, Shigar, and Skardo.

Every region has their own forts, inhabitants and towns. In Tibet most of the regions have been captured by me with force, and some were ready for compromise. Some of the regions of Tibet are; Zangskar, Maryul, Rudok, Kugay, Lo, Boras, Rongo, Mankab, Zairso, Karanga, Nisan, Ham, Allalai Bonka, Tok, Labok and Skabrak. I like Skabrak very much. From Skabrak to Bengal it is the journey of 24 days, and Ursang or Lhasa which is on the east of Skabrak and Bengal on the south. Ursang is considered the religious headquarters of China and Tibet; here is a great temple which is the educational centre of China and Tibet and the residence of ascetics.

Whatever I have tried to observe these people closely and explain but failed. However the wonderful thing which I have seen is the gold mines in most of the villages. Two mines are very astonishing; one is in the region which is called "Alto Anji Tibet" here few branches of the Dolpa tribes works in the mine. But due to awfully cold they could not work beyond 40 days in a year. They dig and make the hole on the earth, and the men enter in the hole. There are large numbers of holes and they are inter connected. It is said that the members of about thirty thousand families always remains under these holes. Some Mughal invaders who saw them from the distance, when the Mughal reached nearer, they disappeared. No body can entrap them. Except the fat of the sheep nothing can be used in these mines for lightening purposes, probably it is less polluted. People bring the dust from these holes and wash in the water. It is said that sometime one can extract 4 masha of gold, out of full sieve of dust from this mine. A man dug the earth, bring the dust out and wash the dust himself. A man procures 20 sieves of dust a day. Most of the Tibetans revealed me the same, and after confirmation I have written the events. The second mine is in Kugay region. It is consisting of 22 forts and towns. The length is about 3 padao. Gold is everywhere. Wherever digging is made, its dust is being scattered on skin sheets and gold is recovered. The gold dust are very small, the big one's are like a pimple of a pulse of mysoor or mash. It is said that sometimes one can have gold equalient to the liver of a sheep. I fixed the tax on the mine of Kugay. The local nobles narrated me that a person was plaguing his field. Suddenly his plough was trapped at a place. He tried his best but could not remove it. Finally he removed the dust and cleared the spot. He was astonished to see that the plough was trapped in a big piece of gold between two stones. He immediately went to the ruler and informed him. People gathered and crashed the stone, and they found 150 "Misqal" of pure gold from the spot.

(One Tibetan Misqal = one and half Misqal), God has created such gold in Kugay which is pure. After extracting from the dust, give heat and make the ornament as you like. After heating on the fire there is no such change in the weight. These are the wonders of Tibet.

A respiration problem, which is called "Dam-giri" in Hindi, is felt in the whole Tibet, but it is less in the towns and forts. This made a person very uncomfortable, whether a man walks, sits or rests on the bed, in all conditions he feels breathing problems like that of a man runs carrying a heavy load. Hence, a man cannot sleep with ease. When a man sleeps, suddenly woke up because of the breathing problem and feels pain in the lungs, and sometime becomes senseless, and began to speak nonsense and silly words. Sometime one could not speak a word. Hands feet and the face began to swallow. If these happens a man die, within a day. Sometime a man remains senseless for a long time. During the illness, if he reaches in a town or fort he can be saved, otherwise his death is certain. Only the foreigners has to face this problems otherwise the local Tibetans have no problems. Their physicians don't know the cause why the foreigners are facing these problems, and what is the remedy. The more the air becomes cold this problem increase. It is not confine to the human beings only but the animals also face the respiration problems. The horses also face the same problem. One day we have to move fast, in the morning we found that more than one thousand horses have died and the quantity has reduced. There were twenty four special horses for my personnel use, they mostly walks unride. On that fateful night twenty-one of them were dead. The horses feel more breathing problems.

The scholars of Tibet are called Lama, but every Lama has got the name according to his skill and knowledge, as it is a tradition in our own society. They use to call "Tongpa and Kajuwa" to the Imam and Mujtahid. I inquired this through translators, but the problem is that they could not explain properly and the purpose is not achieved. Whatever I know about their belief is as follows:

It is said that at the time of beginning the universe, the Almighty God created the souls and instructed individually to all the sprits, how to get the nearness to God, enter the paradise and avoid the hell. He, according to His wishes, brought down the souls and mixed with the dust, thus the power of nourishment and botanical were included in it through dust. Because the sprit came downwards to this world from the holy place, and could not retain the purity. And instead of purity and cleanliness, thoughtlessness and senselessness dominated it, since it is mixed up with the dust and entered in the body of human beings. Though, it is contaminated with dust and has entered in the body, thus it is a kind of elevation. It will enter in to different body as per one's devotion. If one attains the devotion because of good deeds than the sprit will migrate in to a better one. On the other hand, if lacks in devotion, than it will have a worst body. On the contrary, if the body has done evil deeds than the soul has to mix-up with the dust again. For many years it remains suspend there. Similarly it enters from one body to another and achieves higher status and gets the elevation and finally reaches in the body of a man. In the beginning it enters in the body of slaves and people of lower status but after passing through the different human status, it achieves greatness and enters in the body of a Lama. Here if he performs the good deeds then he remember all the actions of the past and he knows that what he did in different bodies, which became the cause of his elevation and which is the causes of his downfall. This decency and wisdom is the higher status. In this way because of much devotion, he achieves such a great status, that he remembers the eternal teachings. And whatever he had heard from the Almighty God, remembers in the heart. This is the highest status of prophesy, whatever heard from the Almighty God, it is taught to the people, this is the religion. This type of personalities has no death but eternal life, how long the body is strong soul remains with the body, whenever the strength of the body exust it perishes and only the soul remains. The person, whose spiritual power is resemblance to him, can see him, otherwise the eyes, placed on the head of the human beings can't see it. These are the faith of the "Sakyamuni" religion. Whole the China had the same faith. While in China; he is called "Sheghamuni" where as the Tibetan's called "Shaqsato" or "Shakyamuni". In the historical books of Shakamuni it has revealed that Shakamuni was among the Indian prophets. Some claims that he was a philosopher. They are of the belief that every person can't enter the heaven, just following a particular religion. But his good deeds help him to achieve this. If a Muslim do good deeds, he will go in the heaven otherwise he has to taste the bitterness in the hell. Same is the case with the infidels. No doubt they consider Prophet Muhammad (pbuh) a great scholar but do not consider it obligatory to enter in this religion. They used to say. For us our religion is right and for you, your religion. Whatever faith a man posses he must perform right actions. They are of the opinion, that Shakyamuni has said, "that 1,24,000 Prophets or Messenger of God will come on this universe after me. Among them the last one would be Jan Kasbah by name. He would be an orphan both from the paternal and maternal side. People will follow his religion all over the world. Whenever he appears, it is binding to all the people to follow his religion. Those would be the luckiest people, who follow his religion. My followers should remember the testament and should reveal the same from generation to generation, till his appearance. The feature of the Prophet will be similar to this. He gave a figure and advised the people to remember it, and said, "A statue of this figure will appear and all the human beings should submit to him". During that time this would be the real statue in all the temples which has to be kept in front of others and all other statues would be attentive and face towards him. This is the figure of Jan Kasbah.

Whatever they gave the definition of Jan Kasbah it comes true to the Prophet Muhammad (saw). I told them, whatever the Sakyamuni has said, and that is our Prophet. They replied that Sakyamuni has said, "That he will come after 1,240,000 Prophets. Out of them only few has come and most of them has not yet appeared. I tried to convince them that he has already appeared but they never agreed to me.

Rongo is considered, a popular province of Tibet. Where, "Mah Farfeen" is born.

I have seen the sign of Chinese King in Chinese alphabets, translated in Tibetan language in one corner, and Persian language on the other. It states; all the praises are for the Almighty God. Shakyamuni preached this religion about three thousand years before and explained such philosophical points which are beyond the reach of everybody. I remember only the above mentioned words the rest was about the repair and renovation of the temples. History also reveals that Shakyamuni was born three thousand years before. Date has been recorded on this sign but it is not Hijri and is not prevailing among us. But the sign indicates that it is not more than one hundred years old. I reached Rongo in the month of Rabiul-Awwal 940. Hijri, according to the 1533 AD.

Qitas Sahrai (which is called "Dong" in Tibetan) is such a fearful and harmful animal, if he attacks anybody, there is no chance of rescue. Whether struck with horns or legs, a man goes fly few yards in the air when comes down, he die. Sometimes he kills a man with his tongue. A Qitas is a load of twelfth horses. A man can not move its shoulder. I killed a Qitas and distributed the meat among seventy people everybody got lot of meat which were sufficient for four days. I have never seen this animal except on the soil of Tibet.

On Zilhajja 938 Hijri Khan invaded Tibet. As mentioned earlier that the boundary of north Tibet is "Balti". The country of Baltistan is connected with Bloor and Badakhsahan. The east Ziministani is the country of Yarkend, its west is Kashmir.

Khan deputed Sikandar Sultan with me on this expedition and he himself went via Khotan towards Altonji Tibet which is "Dolpa".

I started my journey in the last week of Zilhajja, reached at Nubra on 1st day of month of Safar. Nubra is a waste region of Tibet. General invitation was given in the region through a man. Most of the common people obeyed the invitation. But the nobles of Nubra rejected the offer and revolted. Everybody took the refuge in the forts. The Head of these nobles was Bu Rafstan (Probably Nurboo Raftan) who was staying in the fort of Hunder, which was the largest fort in the region, and fortified. I besieged the fort, and arranged the weapons like gun and "Tora" to capture the fort. When we attacked the fort on the appointed day, Bu Rafstan could not face us and his people fled to every direction. My soldiers followed them and nobody was spared. Bu Rafstan along with his courtiers was killed. Heads of those killed were piled up in the form of a pillar so as to scare and terrorize others. The rest of the forts were captured completely. From Nubra we preceded to "Maryul". There are two kings in Maryul. One Lata Chogdan (Lotus Chhogdan) and the second Tashi Gon. Both the kings attended my court. In the meantime the winter started. In winter season there is awfully cold in whole Tibet. If we compare the cold of Tibet with the Mughlistan, we can guess a little from our coldest period. The nobles began to whisper among themselves that which place is better in Tibet to spend the winter where there is less cold and the animals can have feeder. The people replied in negative. Finally it was decided that the winter should be spent in Kashmir. If captured well and good otherwise after staying in Kashmir during the winter we will come back in the beginning of summer. When it was decided, I collected a huge army from Maryul to increase my own army and proceeded towards Kashmir.

In the mean time Abdal Quli Yasadal, a close confidante of Khan reached with the news that Khan is also reaching here. He is badly suffering because of the hardship faced by him in the way. He is waiting for you. Therefore you should go immediately to see him. At the very movement I left leaving the army at the very place. It has been mentioned earlier that Khan was intending to move towards Dolpa via Khotan, and I was told to move towards Balti. It was summer. Khan reached here in the winter, covering the distance of one month, after crossing the Khotan Mountains. The experienced people who were aware of the hardships asked him that it is too late. Thereafter the river, streams and the canals will freeze. Even water will not be available. There is scarcity of fuel to melt the ice, so as to fetch water for the animals. If efforts are made one can have a small number of dung of the "Qitase Sahrai" (Dong) just to prepare the soup. In the past because of the said hardships some army perished in the way. However, knowing these problems, Khan said that the intention have made to capture Tibet. If it is not possible as right now, it is better to follow Mirza Haider and decide there about the expedition. Khan returned back from Khotan and opted the route for Tibet, which was used by me earlier. In the way Khan has to face many problems due to breathlessness, even he remained senseless for few days. There was no hope of recovery. The Physicians were using the "Taliniyat" and whenever came in the sense, he used to say to the nobles and friends. Since my health and strength has not favoured me for the expedition, but the purpose should not be discontinued. If I will depart from the company of the living people and go among the dead, I will be more contended that I have laid my life in the said way and remained determined. Till there is life in my body take me towards the battle field. If I die, than it is your choice.

Moreover, he was also inquiring about me during this period. Whenever, he came in the sense, he was repeating the same words. It is surprising that in spite of illness, he never stayed at a place. Since, in spite of chilled wind, scarcity of water, awfully cold and lack of feeder, it was not wise to stay in wilderness, because the patient will face more problems. So the efforts were made to reach such a place where the breathing problem can be solved. Wherever the breathing problem was controlled, he came in the sense. I met him, after shaking hands and inquiring my welfare he wept and said, "This time among all my friends and sons, I missed you much. It is the blessings of the God, that I have seen you. Now no desire has left in my mind and heart. Later, he recovered day by day when reached in Nubra, he was completely recovered. He came riding up to Nubra. Later on he ordered the nobles and officers to move from Nubra, because the people of Nubra have created chaos and crises in the area. So we came to Maryul. Tashi Gon showed some resistance; therefore after capturing one of his forts he was killed. Till I came back from Kashmir, he made the said place his capital.

SULTAN SAYEED KHAN'S INVASION OF BALTISTAN

Five thousands soldiers were accompanying Khan. In Maryul they could not be afforded with the facilities. They discussed what to do. Everybody gave their own suggestions. I came to know through reliable sources, that the Tibetans can not afford the facilities for not than one thousand man, and in the presence of one thousand soldiers no body can dare to attack. To accommodate rest of the soldiers, there is no suitable place except Kashmir. Since there are so many passes in the way of Kashmir, moreover Khan is not in a position to travel on this rout. It is better that Khan should invade Baltistan along with one thousand soldiers, where he will face no breathing problem, and no pass is there. And I may be allowed to precede Kashmir along with the additional soldiers, so as to stay in Kashmir during the winter. In summer we will reframe the plan and polices. Khan agreed my proposal. Four thousand soldiers were deputed with me to Kashmir. Mir

Dayim Ali, Baba Sariq Mirza and some other officers were with me.

Khan reached in Balti (Baltistan) during the winter. Bahram Cho subdued and attended in the court. The rest of the Rajas of Baltistan showed resistance. First captured the fort of Shigar with the cooperation of Bahram Cho, which is the capital of whole Baltistan. The men were killed and the women and wealth came under the control of the victors. Besides Khan captured all other hilly areas except the strong forts and the passes.

During winter there was no communication, due to heavy snow fall. Khan received no information from me, and was anxious. In the end of winter messengers were sent from Kashmir and received the good news of victory, and got relief. In the beginning of the summer Khan returned from Baltistan, but regarding the expedition of Nubra, their arrangement was made by me and was left to Khan. Later Khan assigned the duty to Qanbar Kokaldash. He destroyed the whole area, because these people showed great resistance, and went to their strongholds. Qanber Kokaldash captured all the forts.

MIRZA HAIDER'S INVASION OF KASHMIR

I marched from Nubra along with the new army and the officers, to whom Khan deputed with me, and reached in the vicinity of Maryul, where I met with my army. After taking them with myself I departed towards Kashmir. In the way to Kashmir the nobles of Tibet showed their loyalty and subdued, and came with their army to join our victors, and from the Balti Tibet some tribes, who are settled on the way of Kashmir, became our guide and introductory. In middle of autumn, in the month Jamidul-Sani 939 Hijri, according to 1532 AD, crossed the Zojila and entered in the vicinity of Kashmir. Prior to that the Rajas of Kashmir had have heard the news of our departure. They tried to block the narrow rout of Paragna Laar. When we crossed the pass, we selected 400 experienced and knowledgeable persons and send them in the advance party. Toman Bahadur Qaluji, whose name has mentioned in the Yasadale-Kashgar, was appointed as its leader. When reached at the narrow place the Army of Kashmir was there, and a group was stationed, on the other side of the narrow place as advance party of the Kashmiris. Early morning our advance party reached in front of the Kashmiries and out of fear they run away. And our army followed them. When this news reached to the Army of Kashmir, they could not do the arrangement to block the road, and they too run away. I also reached behind them and our army passed with ease, through the narrow way and captured the Kashmiries the next day. It is not out of place to mention here about Kashmir, their kings and administrators, so as to throw light on the factual condition of Kashmir. Kashmir is one of the great countries of the world, and it is famous in the world because of its different types of jokes and wonderful objects, and has been mentioned in different languages. Today in the month of Muharram-ul-haram 950 Hijri, according to the 1542 AD, I conquered whole the beautiful Valley of Kashmir. I have observed all the wonderful objects of this country, and have recorded whatever I have seen. The Valley of Kashmir is situated on the west of Ladakh.The length of the plain areas of the valley are about 100 "Karda", i.e. 33 "Farsakh" and the width at most of the places are 20 Karda and at limited number of places are 10 Karda. Within this limited area the agricultural lands are divided in four types; Aabi (Water), Barani (Rain), Bagh (orchards), and Banjar (Uncultivated) different kinds of beautiful flowers grow in the later type of uncultivated land. Because of humidity and moisture it is not fit for agriculture purposes, hence it has left uncultivated. It is the fineness of this country. During the summer, it is deliciousness in the air and there is no need of fan. Cool breezes always blows, which refresh the mind soul. In winter there is not so cold. In spite of heavy snowfall one feels no need of jacket. The coldness of the country makes one crave for the heat of beautiful summer. The sunshine has no heat. There are so many magnificent buildings in the city and surroundings. Some are five storey's high. In each storey there are rooms, drawing rooms and balconies. The balconies have slightly appeared outside, which looks very beautiful. Stones have been placed on the road of the Bazaars and the lane of the cities. But the styles of the Bazaars are not as per the norms of the cities. There are no shops except retail sellers and cloth merchants. The artists do their work in their own houses. The shops like grain seller, druggist, fruit seller, perfumer, cold drinks, tea stall and hotels are the beauty and ornaments of the Bazaar. There is no tradition of keeping them on the upper storey. The population of the city is equalient to the big cities.

Kashmir has different kinds of fruits like pears, mulberry, cheery, dried plum and all types of other fruits, but the apples are much better. In Kashmir the fruits are in abundance. There are mulberry trees in Kashmir; the silk worms are being feed on the leaves of this tree. Nobody eat it because it is considered vicious. The rest of the fruits are in abundance, but there is no system of buy and sell. The lands of orchards and the rest are equal. Most of the orchards are without walling because nobody stops the people by taking fruits from their orchards. Wonders of Kashmir are its temples. These are more than 150 in whole Kashmir. These have been constructed by keeping big boulders of stone on one another, and mud has not been used at all. Without lime powder, the big boulders of stone have been joined so beautifully, that a piece of paper cannot be pass through the joints. The length of each stone is about three yards to eight yards long and the width is one yard. It is very surprising, how these big boulders have been procured and how it has been placed over the buildings. Most of the temples have a square shaped compound the height of the wall at some places are about 30 yards. The total length of the compound will be approximately 300 yards. There are pillars inside and the top of the pillars have been made conical and square, and pillows have been placed over it. Most of the pillar and its top have been made with a piece of stone; the arches which are about 40 to 50 yards long have been prepared on two pillars. The side rooms have been constructed on four pillars of one piece each. This inner arch appears to be two halls from the outside. There is one piece or two pieces of stone over it as roof. The length of every hall is about 20 yards and the width is 7 to 8 yards. Paintings have been made on every parts of the building in such a beautiful way that cannot be explained.

Some figure laughs where as some weeps. A man wonders to watch them. In the centre there is a chair made by stone carving and a dome is over it, which is all stone. I am unable to admire or express properly about these things. Neither I have seen such a beautiful building in the world nor have I heard. Where as there are one hundred fifty such buildings. In the east Kashmir there is a province namely Barang. Here is a pier and a reservoir shaped tank is over it. A hole is in the bottom, which remains dry during the winter but in summer lots of water comes out with pressure. When the tank is full, it began to follow outside and ceased. Then every place is dry except the hole. After the summer is over, it remains dry whole the year. The hole was filled with mud of lime powder, but at the appointed time it makes its way and the water come out with pressure as before, and could not stop it. This spring still functions like the past. Its water is also being used for irrigation purposes. Here is a big village in Kashmir, called Magam. A long tree is there. If a man shoot arrow, it can't reach up to the top. In spite of such a greatness and glory, if we move it, by catching a thin branch, the whole tree begins to move. Devsar is a province of Kashmir. Here is a spring like that of a tank, which is a square of eight yards. In the surroundings, there are beautiful trees. The characteristic of the spring is, that one put rice in the pot, its passage is sealed, and the name of the person is recorded on the pot. Then the pot is put in to the spring, it goes down and some times it remains unmoved. After some time it comes out on the surface. There is no fixed time. When the lead is removed, the rice is cooked and warm. It is considered a good sign, but some times the color changes, it is mixed with dust and sand and is polluted, it is considered bad sign.

Here is a lake in Kashmir called "Dono" (Dal). Its radius is seven "Farsakh". The King of Kashmir Zain-ul-Aabedin has built a very magnificent building in the centre of the lake.

First he put the stones in the lake and a 200 square yards platform was prepared, which is about 10 yards high. Stone of very good qualities have used there. Over the platform, a very good and magnificent building has been constructed, and trees have been planted in a well planned manner. Really, this type of wonderful buildings would be very few in the world. The King Sultan Zain-ul-Aabedin has built a building in the city for himself, which the Kashmiries called "Rajdan." It is twelfth storey's high. There are fifty rooms, halls and balconies in some storey. No great and magnificent building of the world like that of "Koshak hashte behaist" of Sultan Yaqub Tabrez, Vinoshaq Baghe Zaghan, Baghe Safaid, and Baghe Shahar of Hirat, Kok Sarai, Duaq Sarai, Baghe Dilkasha, and Baghe Pola of Samarqand cannot compete this beautiful building, but whatever beauty, grace and delicacy are found in the above buildings are missing in the Kashmiri architecture.

Prior to the narration of the Wonders of Kashmir, I have revealed about my expedition that after crossing a narrow passage we reached in the city, and the Kashmiri soldiers fled to different directions. The city people leaving their houses and possessions left for mountains, lake and rivers. I stayed at Rajdhan (The old palace of Bud Shah). For days there was no response or reaction from any quarter. I stayed in the city for 24 days, that all my men and horses were feeling refreshed. The Army of Kashmir appeared at the distance of two "Farsakh" in the south of Kashmir. The nobles and officers advised me that we have to do nothing with the defense of the city; hence we should come out, so that we can have suitable opportunities to counter them. Since the Army of Kashmir is more in number, stronger and they have better weapons than us. We can defeat them only with good plan and policies, so we marched from the city in front of their army, towards the east and stayed at a place called "Baghla". From Jamidul-Awal to Shaban we were moving here and there. Hence, the Army of Kashmir became more bold and arrogant. When we had to move from a place the Kashmiries were following us. Finally a rumor of our triumph and victory among the masses helped us, and the enemy was not in a position to counter us. The Maliks of Kashmir, among them Malik Ali Chadori was a prominent one joined us along with other Maliks, and became loyal to us. So the prominent group was perished, and rest of the army went up on the top of a hill. At that time with the blessings of

God I became aware about the tricky plans and ill will of one Mirza Ali Taghai.

Mirza Ali advised that the group of soldiers who are at the top of the mountain must be very strong. It is foolishness to go on the top and attack. It is the better way to destroy the opponent that we should march towards Kashmir with their "Sarkoch" than their Koch has to come down to defend it. And join with their own "Sarkoch" thus only a few will remain on the top and their group will disburse and there would be no need of attack. He was playing trick and kept me away from the right track. Therefore I decided to go down in the early morning. Mir Daim Ali told me during the night that the enemies have been dispersed. Now, what is the purpose of leaving the station? I was astonished and stood up. Mirza Ali inquired the cause of standing up. I revealed him whatever Mir Daim Ali, explained me. Mirza Ali looked over me in a hypocritical way and said, it is childish to change the policy. Whatever has decided that should not be changed. The plan of Mir Dayim Ali was absolutely right, which I avoided while the proposal of Mirza Ali was a great mistake, which I opted. We departed from that place and reached in the vicinity of Magam. At the next "Padao"(destination) I was informed that there is no way to go forward. I stayed at Chadora village. Because of our march the Army of Kashmir got full time to reunite and consolidate them, and came down from the top of the mountain and reconsolidated them at a suitable place. This event took place during summer on 4th Shaban. Mirza Ali, because of his ill will, explained the people secretly, the drawbacks of the conquest of Kashmir. Even he diverted the mind and the heart of the soldiers from the invasion of Kashmir. Except Mir Dayim Ali, who did not came under his tricky influence, all other Mughal nobles approached Mir Daim Ali and expressed unanimously, that ask Mirza Haider that we are Mughals and always remains busy in Mughal events. We like the deserts where there are no inhabitants. We prefer the laugh of the owl of a desolate place over the song of the night angle of the garden. We had not built our houses in our country like the spider our companions are wild wolf and our opponents are wild pigs. The top of the mountains are our favourite shelters and the skin of dogs and other wild animals are our dress. The meat of wild animals and birds are our diet and the people of Kafirane Baiwash are our society. Kashmir is an exemplary of paradise. How can we stay here? Moreover there is a long distance between Kashmir to Kashghar. There is lot of hardships in the rout. Koch Dina and Gala Dariba are very far. Just staying far from the Gala we feel no taste in our lives. It is better to cancel the war and return to Khan. If Khan kills us, our men will take our body to our home land. We have no desire to go anywhere except Mughlistan. I was astonished to see their attitude and behaviour.

I told to Mir Dayim Ali, if we show negligence and carelessness to maintain discipline and control in Kashmir, these people will commit such blunders that can shake the foundation of the government. Mir Daim Ali replied, Khan said, that Ali Taghai neglects the important affairs of administration. Considering his disability, he had been pardoned several times. He has repeated the mistakes this time also due to his past mistakes. Eliminate him through my son Sikandar Khan Khord. You should not waist the time. He has committed a great blunder, therefore, issue order to little Khan to execute him. Thereafter nobody will dare to do such blunders. The rest of the part of Kashmir which has still not occupied by the Mughal Khan's will surrender, thus you will gain name and fame in the world. I replied, since last ten years the Khan has assigned the charge of expeditions and invasions to me. It is the blessing of God that till now I accomplished the expeditions in a very efficient manner. There is not a single case that one could raise the fingers. If such happens, I will be responsible for that and it is not good as per sharia and law of the land. When I had gone through the problems, there was no alternative but to accept the two options; either to execute Mirza Ali Talai and conquer of whole Kashmir or to spare him and depart from Kashmir. Finally I preferred to leave the Kashmir, and did compromise with the Malik's of Kashmir. I did mistake that I did not follow the advice of wise and confident men for which later, I have to pay the price. After

Malik Ali was killed Kashmir was ruled by Mohammad Shah. Besides, there were Malik Abdal Magray, Hasan Chak, Lohar Magray, and Regi Chak. A meeting was held with them for compromise and they never took it otherwise, because after conquering a country it is one's foolishness to restore it. However "Khutba" was read and coin was struck in the name of Khan. All the possessions captured from Kashmir by the Mughals were restored to them. A Kashmiri princes of Mohammad Shah was brought with us to marry IsKanders Sultan. Friendship was developed, as per Mughal traditions, with the Kashmiri nobles. Mir Daim Ali met and maintained friendship with Abdal Magray, Mirza Ali Tagai with Lohar Margay, Baba Sidique Mirza with Kaji Chak and my cousin brother Mehmood Mirza with Regi Chak. And also exchanged valuable presents and gifts.

On the last day of Shawal, we returned from the same way of Laar, wherefrom we came in Kashmir. When we reached in the vicinity of Tibet they welcomed us and presented gifts. But the people of Kartsey, which is a province of Tibet, showed coldness and never paid the tribute. Therefore at the time of Nimaze Zuhar we arrived there. All the soldiers kept ready their arms during the night and early in the morning we attacked them. A fierce battle took place. We have to face lot of problems, because they created obstructions in the way 100 times by throwing big boulders towards us, and we have to stay back. Finally the Islamic soldiers destroyed the powerful Army of Kartsey. Most of them were killed, and their possessions came under the control of Islamic soldiers. Because of the fear and terror they brought and presented their belongings to the Mughals at Purig. Which I distributed equally, among the soldiers, but spared some beautiful and valuable goods for Khan. Purig is also a province of Tibet. Later, we left for Maryul. After conquering many countries I came to the Khan as a victor. He was highly excited to see me, and I was encouraged by hugging and shaking hands. He inquired in detail about the different events and was much delighted to know about the expeditions and honored me. Prior to that, among the Mughal Khan's right from Changez to present date nobody could conquer Kashmir. You have accomplished this great task and the name of Khan is being called from the "Menbar" (Chair) of the mosques of Kashmir. Because of this great task it is the duty of the Mughal Khan's to respect and regards you. I came ahead of the army to meet Khan. The rest of the army, the nobles and Sikander Sultan reached next day before the Khan, and presented the valuable goods of Kashmir and some gold and silver coins on which the name of Khan was inscribed. Khan accepted all these things and as per the tradition distributed among the soldiers. After his address to the soldiers, he convened the Mughal officers and the nobles in the court, and asked to give their remarks regarding the expedition. After hearing their statement, Khan told me, "You know that my intention was good after accomplishing these expeditions, I wanted to attack the great temple of Ursang, which is a place of respect and reverence in the whole China".

Among the Muslim Kings nobody has interfered and capture it, even no Muslim has passed through that country till today. Now I am old enough and weak. You should left me in the custody of God and do efforts on behalf of me to capture this temple. Where as I will return to my country. I am handing over all the affairs to you. I and your uncle both are old enough. Keep us busy in prayers and keep continue the expeditions for this government. We will pray for your success and you should help us with good deeds. He issued an order authorising me to choose the people as per my choice. When the royal order was issued. I permitted all the elder and senior members to return home, except brother Abdullah Mirza and cousin brother Mehmood Mirza, and Hataka Mirza and Barka Mirza, about whom have had mentioned in "Yasale Kashgar" were appointed as officers in the army. I selected one thousand soldiers out of the army, and proceeded for the expedition. On 7th Zilhajja, it was the day of departure, when Khan called me at Takhlia and offered me some of the valuable dresses which he possesses. He also gave us some horses. Khan also offered me a beautiful and valuable sheath, wrapped in a cloth, which was prepared by him in a very efficient manner, and said, "it is my handicraft, I hand it over to you as a memory. When you will come back safe and sound, return it to me." He further said, "That in all conditions, one should always trust in God. Go in the name of Allah and he will protect you and hope that you will come back safe and sound to see me. Moreover you will do your best efforts to accomplish this task, and the name and fame which you have gained after the triumph in Kashmir, will further improve. It is my duty to respect you. Similarly, we have had lot of discussion. Finally he permitted me to leave and himself went for Yarkend."

SULTAN SAYEED KHAN'S RETURN FROM LADAKH AND DEATH

When the Khan assigned me the expedition of Ursang and left Maryul (Tibet) for Yarkend. I also went up to the next destination to send him off and took the leave of him. After four days I got a letter of his own hand writing, stating "that while crossing the Sagri pass, he felt some weakness, and after the prayer of Eid-ul-Azha will go ahead." Since after the prayer of Eid-ul-Azha Khan crossed the Morazat pass and due to icy cold and chilly winds, Khan suffered from exposure. The place from where the breathing problems start is eight day's destination. The nobles decided unanimously that the fast and slow journey both are injurious for him. Hence efforts should be made to reach the place where there is no breathing problem. Among the nobles there were some ill willed persons, whose leader was Mirza Ali Taghai, who made the horse of the Khan run fast, in this critical condition. The eight day's destination was covered in four days. At the time of "Nimaze Zuhar" Khan reached three "Farsakh" down from the place where breathing problems is low, but because of exposure and the respiration problem he became very dull and weak. Thus the just, kind and the pious king passed away on 16th Zilhajja 939 Hijri, according to the 1532 AD (i.e. ten days after his departure from Taglai).

After this unfortunate event, the jealous and tricky people hatched the plots. Mirza Ali Taghai and Khauja Shah Mohammad, both were the mischievous people. They decided and deputed one Yadgar Mohammad, who was the son in law of Mirza Ali Tagai to Rashid Sultan at Afso, along with a fake letter, pretended to be the testament of late Khan. It states that it was not my intention to invade Tibet. The two Syed Mohammad Mirza and Mirza Haider provoked me to undertake this action. I will not be happy with my son Abdul Rashid, unless and until he kill them. As long as they remain alive you will not get the kingdom. Moreover they fabricated a bundle of lie of similar type, because of enmity and sent to Abdul Rashid Khan. Another man was deputed to my uncle with warning to follow the Khan's instructions strictly. My uncle, when he came to know about it came to Yarkend; he paid the condolence according to the Mughal tradition. Abdul Rashid Khan reached at Yarkend on the last day of Zilhajja. My uncle and other Mughal officers and nobles went to receive him and suggested that the last day of the month and year is inauspicious for public appearance. Hence you should come tomorrow on Thursday the Ist of Muharram 940 Hijri. Some of the nobles who went earlier, came to know that Mirza Tagai approached secretly with Rashid Khan, and has said to him, "that Syed Muhammad Mirza has decided with me and other nobles, that whenever Rashid Sultan arrive in Yarkend, should be got killed and Sikander Sultan who is in Tibet be appointed as Khan." In the morning Rashid Sultan went to the grave yard to recite "Fatiha" at the grave of his late father. Later my uncle and all other relatives were killed, because Mirza Ali Taghai became a very strong person. Without going in detail of this event, now I want to narrate Mirza's expedition of Ursang.

MIRZA HAIDER'S EXPEDITION TO URSANG (TIBETE KHAS)

When Khan returned back to his country Yarkend and I took the leave of him. After celebrating the Eid-ul-Azha at Maryul on 10th of Zilhajja, I went towards the temple of Ursang. When we traveled eight day's destination, no one was seen in the region, because the people has fortified themselves. The forts are on the top of the hills with narrow passage and are very strong. Due to these hardships it was useless to capture them. Therefore Sultan Sikander and brother Abdullah Mirza and my cousin brother Mehmood Mirza moved ahead very fast with strong animals for loading and riding. They arrived at Yarma on Ist Muharram and destroyed many villages of Tibet. They captured about three lakhs sheep, many horses and goods. On Ist of Safar 940 Hijri, we proceeded towards Rudok fort, and destroyed it. These people have managed 3,000, Indians from a neighbouring state for their help. Sikander Sultan and my brothers along with 200 soldiers proceeded towards the fort. Khan marched so fast that out of 200 men very few reached there. My brother Abdullah was a brave man, prior to that under the command of Khan he fought bravely in Balti (Baltistan) and he was conferred with awards and rewards. Because of it he became proud and without considering the strength of the army, he attacked one thousand Tibetan army, with only three soldiers, he was arrested. In the mean time my cousin brother Mohammad Mirza reached there along with four persons and brother Abdullah was rescued from their custody. Abdullah attacked them again and Mehmood Mirza came forward to help him. They were gheraoed. Five more persons joined them. They killed Abdullah Mirza and cut him into pieces. His armors were also cut into pieces and carried away but I took the full revenge with them. However I have to be contented with this great tragedy and stayed few days at the pasture. When the riding and transportation horses became strong we proceeded further towards Ursang, taking the booty along with 900 soldiers. After two month's journey from Maryul (Tibet) I reached at a place where a great lake is. Probably its length and width may be 40 "Farsakh". There is a fort on the bank of this lake, called Tog thog. Halted the night at the said place. In the morning I found that all the horses were dead. Those few who spared were ill. There were 27 spare horses with me all found dead. It happened because of breathing problem, as has mentioned earlier. When we moved further from here only 1/5th of the soldiers were having horses to ride the rest of the soldiers were walking on foot the next day captured a village (the name of the place has not been mentioned) the people of the village said, "that Bengal is only 24 days journey from here." Many people have been made prisoner her. Now only ninety good horses were left for the soldier. After four days journey we arrived at a place called Skabrak and captured it. Wherefrom, we got one lakh sheep, twenty thousand Yaks, and equal number of goats. The distance between Skabrak and Ursang was about eight day's journey, but all the horses of the soldiers were dead, hence wanted to undertake the return journey. After six days, collected the army and started the return journey. It was the 20th Rabil-ul-Awwal. However we reached at Maik on the last day of Jamid-ul-Awwal, which is 20 days journey from Maryul. The nobles of Kugay gathered and requesed that Kugay is the largest province of Tibet, hence religious toll should be imposed to all. After departure from Tamleek, we arrived at Kugay, and stayed there for three days. The people subdued and paid "Jazia" (tribute) the total amount of Jazia was three thousand Tibetan "misqal". Here one Tibetan misqal is equal to one and half Sharyi misqal. In the way we came to know about the destruction of the Mughal army, which are as follows:

> When Rashid Sultan became free from the killings of the nobles and sickness of his relatives, he dispatched two letters through his men to Tibet. One to his brother Sikander Mirza; the theme of the letter was like this, "I have bestowed the country of Tibet to you. Keep Mirza Haider and Mehmood Mirza there with you." The second was a warning letter in the name of group leaders; stating, anyone who is in Tibet, should depart himself from the army and reach Yarkend immediately, otherwise his family members would be sold to the Yarkendi nomads in exchange of horses. When the letter received, I was at Kugay, the soldiers because of fear and harassment, at once returned to Yarkend. Except a few confident loyalists Sultan Sikander and Mehmood Mirza also returned in hurry. I too returned after two days, along with one hundred soldiers. Most of them were Military Officers and was related to my family since their fore fathers. They took active parts in the battles. Some of them were my half brothers, who had got the title of "Kokaldash". There was no fear of disloyalty from these people. All these people run away, like that of

the stars disappear when the sun rises. All the confident disappeared like that of the stars.

Shah Mohammad Kokaldash was a group leader, who came to me with Khan Ahmad Joo my "Shire pidar" and other five persons. This helped me to reduce the bore ness and loneliness. Later Sikander Sultan and my cousin brother joined us along with fifty soldiers. I went towards Maryul with them and reached there after twenty five days. But due to chilly cold the hands, nose and feets of forty persons of the group were burnt.

MIRZA HAIDER REACHED LADAKH AFTER DESTRUCTION

The Rajas of Maryul Tashi Gon and Lata Chhogdan came to me and offered their assistance, in spite of the fact that they were harassed and warned by me. Here seems to be some misunderstanding. According to Mirza, if Tashi Gon was assassinated by Sultan Sayeed Khan, on his reaching Ladakh, then he cannot attend personally. Probably his successor might have come to see Mirza, or actually Tashi Gon was not killed but he was warned to be loyal. However, whatever has mentioned by Mirza has revealed and I could not criticize it. They came to apologies and said that since our fore fathers, we are your well wishers and supporters. The time of warning has gone. Previously, whatever we did, did it because of fear. Now we are supporting you sincerely on the basis of friendship, so as to judge our sincerity and character. It indicates that Mirza was still strong. However, Mirza has explained that the representative of the Kingdom of Maryul, its capital was Shay reached to see Mirza at Ney with presents. For the time being Mirza was contented that some people among the soldiers also joined him. Moulana Darvesh was one of them. He had been an employee of Makhdomi Khauja Yusuf and was a pious man. He was familiar with the Tibetan language and was having a good relation with the kings of Tibet (Ladakh). He was looking after the trade mission and was dealing with them in a very efficient manner. Among the Kashmiris, a person Haji by name also joined me. The soldiers, who run away towards Yarkend, have to face lot of difficulties in the way. It became very difficult to proceed ahead. All the goods were destroyed and one hundred-fifty soldiers died in the way and the rest reached at Yarkend in a half dead position. Moreover a group of soldiers came back to Maryul in a very awkward position. Thus my strength increased to five hundred. And ten thousand sheep were also gathered and the life began to pass in a smooth manner.

Before I arrived at Maryul I deputed Khan, Ahmad Angga and Shah Mohammad Kokaldash to Yarkend with some presents to Rashid Sultan to remind the old promise and friendship. Some signs which in the past, were exchanged by one another as a token of love and friendship, were also sent. When the winter was to end Rashid Sultan deputed his representative Hasan Devana along with my Kokaldash, Khan Ahmad Angga, seeking apology for his misdeeds. Saying that whatever has done because of ignorance and foolishness was a sin, and it should be pardoned. At present I am helpless to convene you back at Yarkend. However, I am deputing two hundred soldiers under the command of Moulana Qodash to you. I have no objection, if the employees who came back to Yarkend want to join you again. Besides, I received a horse and some gifts as a present. After this event, I was highly satisfied and got relief. Most of the Tibetans submitted and became obedient.

During that period, Moulana Qudash came to me, along with some of my confident employees. With the support of this group I went towards Balti. All the Balties paid their dues honestly. Suru is a region of Balti is a stronghold and keeps superiority in the area. Moulana Qudash seeks my permission to collect tributes from this area. I had not given the permission, because the infidels of Suru do not like it that the strangers may come and see their pass and the area. They apologized and promised to bring the dues at the proper place and need not to come in their region but whatever the Almighty God has proposed cannot be evaded. Every body has to taste the death. Qudash went to Suru with humble request, but the people of Suru got killed twenty four of my confident men, at a narrow passage in Suru without battle. Though there were seven soldiers with me but due to lack of arms and facilities could not take the revenge and from Balti proceeded towards Tibet Zangskar with high depression. In Zangskar the crop was not yet ready and we have to wait there for the tribute. In the mean time a helper Balti youth whose name was Tanki Skab, came to me and informed that the time has come to take revenge with the murderer of Qudash. The men should be killed and women and children should be imprisoned. Hence, the people who were weak and coward were sent back to Maryul and I proceeded to Suru along with some strong and brave people. Here I deputed my cousin brother Mehmood Mirza to observe the activities of the required persons, who were just one "padao" ahead of us. He arrived there at night. Since, it was a danger place, so at night he kept the horse nearer to him. When he was asleep, the horse came near to his head in drowsiness. He hit the horse with a stick, to keep it away, but the horse struck his leg on the forehead of Mirza. As a result the bone of the forehead was broken. The next day he came to me. I observed his wound and suggested medicines according to the Mughal surgery and informed Tanki Skab about this accident. He replied that knowing about us fear has created in the area. Hence, if you depute some more persons, we would be able to capture Suru and the booty will be sent to you. This will be my service to you. From Zangskar where I stationed, towards Suru, at the five day's destination is situated Tanki Skab's house. I deputed Moulana Darvesh Mohammad Qarabagh and his disciple Noor Ali Devana along with seventy people.

Two months passed but the wound of Mehmood could not be cured and it was expended over his face. Now it became impossible for him to stay at Zangskar, because of chilly cold, so I sent him to Maryul along with some attendants and I stayed at Zagskar, with the intention, if Mehmood arrive safely at Maryul and wounds is cured then I will turn towards Suru, so as to acquire some livelihood. When Mehmood reached the place where the horse kicked him, he stayed the night there. In the morning he made open the bandage to put some ointment. The chilly wind penetrated in to the wounds, drowsiness came over him and he was fainted. At the time of "Nimaze-Zuhar" people informed me. I marched immediately and reached there at midnight. He was senseless and the next day he came in sense and looks cheerful and remained in sense the next day too. On the third day he again became senseless and passed away at midnight.

In the mean time, a man was caught among the people, to whom I deputed Suru. He hatched a plot against the Mughals with the collaboration of Noor Ali Devana and his companions and arrested Moulana Mohammad Darvesh Qarabagh, and handed him over to Baghan. Bhaghan was the ruler of that region, which was once conquered by Moulana Mohammad Darvesh and was, killed many people. These cruel people handed the Muslim over to the infidel ruler of the area and after taking his permission went to Yarkend. The said Moulana was given a terrible punishment by the infidels. His mouth was sealed with thread and got killed. Thus, the Suru expedition was totally unsuccessful. I brought the dead of Mehmood to Maryul where from it was sent to Kashgar to his ancestor's grave yard. This happened during the winter season in Tibet, when I reached in Maryul. I have to face lot of difficulties due to chilly cold of winter when the summer came; I along with seventy people went to Atlok pasture, so as to get good grass for the horses. The Atlok pasture is very famous in whole the Tibet, where we hunted the wild Yak (Dong) and other wild animals to overcome the rationing problems. Later came back to Maryul. I had left Sikander Sultan at Maryul with a group of people. When all the people came together and the horses became stronger. Suddenly they proceeded to Yarkend. Only fifty people among them remained with me. In the meantime Jan Ahmad Anggah, who was deputed by me earlier to Rashid Sultan during the return of our army from Ursang came back to me from Yarkend and brought the message that I should not stay anymore in Tibet. The main cause of my staying in Tibet was the fulfillment of the promise. If I would have moved without his order, then I have to be blamed. Now, when I got the clear order, I at once started my journey to Badakhshan with Jam Ahmad Anggah.

RETURN OF MIRZA HAIDER FROM LADAKH

Since, the invasions of Sultan Sayeed Khan Mughal over Tibet, Kashmir, and Lhasa became unsuccessful, despite the victory. His able, energetic, sincere and brilliant General has to leave the conquered region, in a helpless condition, in spite of great achievements. The author narrates the same as under:

> As mentioned earlier that out of seven-hundred soldiers only fifty remained with me. The rest of the army fled to Yarkend. It has also been mentioned that on the way in Tibet there is lack of fuel, pasture, food and lodging, and horse shoes which is urgently required in the hilly routs and there is abundance of chilly cold in the region. To cross the passes on a less number of horses was another problem, moreover. Moreover the rout from Tibet to Badakhshan without touching Kashghar had not seen by anybody. I had heard from a person that a rout from Taga Tak, via Pamir goes to Badakhshan. So I traveled on this unseen rout. Some of my men stayed at Tibet. Only twenty-seven persons traveled with me. We have to face lot of difficulties in the way because of awfully cold and lack of facilities. Sikander Sultan could not bear these problems and compelled me to allow him to go to Rashid Sultan. May be because of home sick and love of his brother but I was not happy with this proposal but he was totally disgusted with the topography and difficulties of Tibet. He did not agree my suggestion and finally went to Yarkend via Karakuram pass along with four persons and I continued my journey, along with twenty-three persons. In the way hunted the wild animals to supplement the food. On the third day after depart from Sikander Sultan we reached in a nomad village called Raskam and provided us every facilities they have got. The distance from Raskam to Pamir was five days journey. These people escorted me up to Pamir in seven days and after taking leave of them we reached in Badakhshan. Suleiman Shah Mirza was there. He was my maternal uncle and provided me all sort of facilities. I spent the whole winter in Badakhshan and in summer I

arrived in Kabul along with my supporters, wherefrom we went to Hindustan. I reached in Lahore, where Kamiran Mirza son of King Babar was the provincial ruler. He gave full regards and respect to me and I was appointed as administrator of Lahore province. The author was the employee of King Humayun and the king was defeated by Sher Khan. Thus, the Mughal army had no alternative but to run away from Hindustan. Mirza Haider suggested the king to conquer Kashmir. The king allowed Mirza Haider to precede Kashmir along with four-hundred soldiers. Thereby Mirza once again invaded Kashmir.

MIRZA ONCE AGAIN CONQUERED KASHMIR FROM LAHORE SIDE

At that time the opponents were very strong in Kashmir. The Maliks of Kashmir had become slaves of the nobles. They had expelled Kaji Chak, Abdal Magray, and Regi Chak from Kashmir. These people were wandering helplessly in the Himalayan belt. They requested me and a person Haji whose reference has given ahead came to me as mediator. Finally, it was decided to precede Kashmir. I decided with the King Humayun, that first I will go to Nowshahra along with some persons. When the Maliks of Kashmir may come to cooperate me, then Sikander Topchi should come to see me at Nowshahra. When I reach at the pass, then Amir Khauja Kala should come at Nowshahra. When I reach at Kashmir, then Amir Khauja Kala should come below the pass and the king should enter in the Nowshahra. After making this decision I proceeded further and met the Maliks of Kashmir at Nowshahra. Sikander Topchi came at Nowshahra in one day, and Amir Khauja Kala reached at Siyalkot. On the day when I send a message to Sikander Topchi, I came to know that all the persons had left Lahore. I went quickly and reached at the pass of Kashmir. Kaji Chak went from one way and myself from another one and reached without any obstruction but the news of destruction of Lahore came to Sikander Topchi and Amir Khauja Kala. Sikander Topchi went towards Sarangpur. Sarangpur is a hilly station in India. After returning from Siyalkot, Amir Kaka joined the rebellions. The king tried to come towards Kashmir, but nobody was ready to assist him. Handal Mirza and Yadgar Nasir Mirza, etc. took away the king towards Tana.

I proceeded from Lahore, and crossed the pass of Kashmir on 22, Rajab. It was winter and because of snowfall the whole area was looking like a white floor. Kaji Chak went to Sher Khan and returned back with the reinforcement. In the meantime Malik Abdal passed away and the expedition had to control by Regi Chak. When I observed the situation, I left the family at the fort of Inderkot and I went to counter the enemy's army. About three months we created obstruction for them. Finally Kaji Chak with the support of the Sher Khan's Army marched over the conquered territories and the Army of Kashmiries went to different directions. The Mughal Army had no opinion of any attack on that day, so they were wandering here and there. We were having about two-hundred and fifty soldiers, besides some Kashmiries also joined with us. Now we were having three hundred soldiers as compare to enemy's five-thousand riders and two different armies of foot soldiers. The enemy's were having more foot soldiers than that of riders. They ambushed us and came from the back side and were busy in destructions. I had to face lot of difficulties in this battle which I don't want to mention here. Finally on Monday the eight Rabbi-ul-sani 948 Hijri, according to the 1541 AD, at noon the Quranic verses "Alam tara kaifa Faala Rabbica bi ashabe feel"[1] came true to the enemies and the Almighty God helped us with the Quranic verses "Nasrun minallahi wa fathun qarib".[2] Since, the three hundred soldiers defeated the huge army of five thousand riders and much mora foot soldiers. After that Mirza Haider ruled over Kashmir for ten years, in a very successful and efficient manner. Later, he was killed by an arrow shooter because of mistake. His grave is still in the compound of Mazare-Salateen at Kashnir. Col. Moorcraft has got repaired it in 1823 AD and his achievements, were recorded on a slab of stone, has placed over his grave.

Verses from Holy *Quran*:

(1) Did you not see how your lord dealt with the companions of the elephant?

(2) May God help and bestow upon success!

PEDEGREE TABLE OF THE NAMGYAL DYNESTY LADAKH

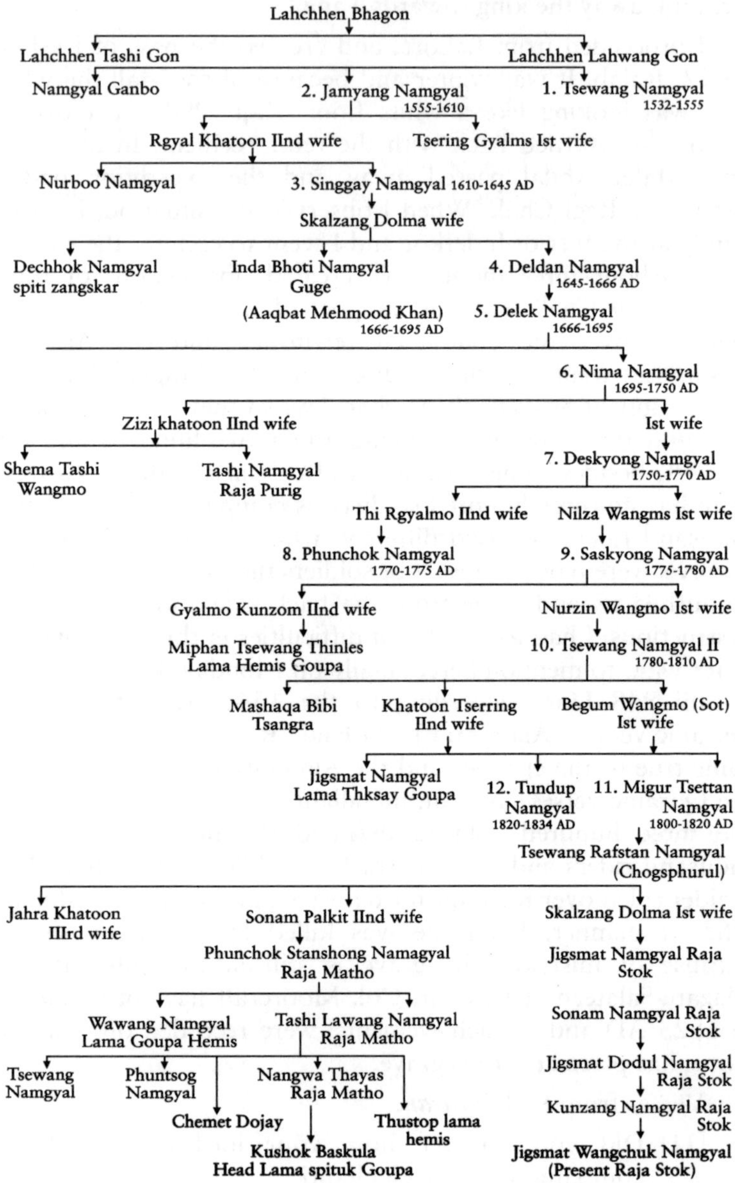

4

Namgyal Dynesty of Ladakh

Actually Takpa Bum is the founder of this new dynasty. He founded his new kingdom at Tingmogang, in spite of the fact that his elder brother Tak Bum Ldey was ruling over Ladakh from Shay as its capital. But he was not successful to conquer the whole Ladakh.

Neither his son and successor Lahchhen Bhara, nor his grandson Lahchhen Bhagon and great grandson Lahchhen Tashi Gon were able to conquer the whole Ladakh, but finally Tashi Gon's nephew and successor Lahchhen Tsewang Gon fulfilled the desire of his great grand father. He with the collaboration of the people of Shay hatched a plot against the King Lotus Chhogdan and got killed the king and his brothers. Or after the death of the king, he got killed his brothers and captured the whole Ladakh and just to hide the evil deeds he took the surname of "Namgyal" which means "Victor".

These events have been twisted in the Ladakhi chronicles, just to hide the factual information about the invasion of Sultan Sayeed Khan. Besides the authenticity of local events also seems to be suspicious. Since, after the death of Lotus Chhogdan, Lahchhen Bhagon has shown as ruler of the whole Ladakh. Whereas, there were two separate government at Shay and Tingmogang, during his invasion. Moreover, the Rulers of Ladakh, Lotus Chhogdan and Tashi Gon used to come in the court of Mirza Haider the General of Mughal Army. While, Tashi Gon was assassinated by the order of Sultan Sayeed

Khan for his disloyalty. After he was killed, his successor, whose name has mentioned wrongly as Tashi Gon by Mirza Haider, has attended his court along with Lotus Chhogdan, when he came back from Ursang. It indicates that till the return of Mirza Haider from Ladakh, Lotus Chhogdan was alive and was ruling over the Stot Maryul (Ladakh) and also there was a separate government in Sham Maryul. There is no alternative but to guess about the further events. If we analyze the Ladakhi chronicles with the history of Mirza Haider we come to the conclusion that the events regarding the annexation of the two governments of Shay and Tingmogang has referred towards Lahchhen Bhagon (Tashi Gon). Actually it was the achievements of Tashi Gon's nephew Gyalpo Tsewang Namgyal, who became his successor after the assassination of Tashi Gon. After the return of Mirza Haider either he got killed Lotus Chhogdan along with his brothers or after his death he killed his brothers Labstan Tashi and Tonagpa Ali and captured his kingdom (at that time he should be very old and weak). Since, Tingmogang was an inconvenient place and Shay being the capital of the old regime he disliked it. Therefore in the north of Leh town he got built a place on the hill top called Namgyal Tsemo and made it his new capital.

TSEWANG NAMGYAL 1532-1555 AD

History reveals that in 940 AH, according to the 1532 AD, Tashi Gon was assassinated by the order of Sultan Sayeed Khan. After the event his blind elder brother Lahwang Gon along with his wife and two sons were released from the prison. The blind man was not made the king because of his disability, instead his elder son Tsewang was appointed as Raja of Tingmogang. Though, he was very young but had learnt lot of experience, because of being in prison. He proved himself a far-sighted person and provided full honors and royal facilities to his blind father, throughout his life. Tsewang Namgyal was a witty and courageous king. He built the first royal palace at Leh, on the top of the Namgyal Tsemo hill, and below it the hamlet of Chhubi, which has become a part of the town now. The Namgyal Tsemo place is now in ruins but some of its ancient walls still remain, which indicates the dignity of this king. He also erected a temple on the same hill and has placed a very big clay statue of Buddha inside it, which is still in tact. The walls of the temple have decorated with paintings of the God and Goddesses and the court of the king in a very beautiful manner. I was surprised to see the paintings of the court, since there was turban on the head of the courtiers. It indicates that in the past the Ladakhi nobles use to wear turban. Along with the men there are the paintings of the women, as the queen in the centre, but the "Naslan" (lamb's skin) was missing only "perak" is there. It indicates that the "Naslan' was invented at the later stage. On the top of this temple, there is a small temple and some small rooms. There are one "Chhorten" and some small statues inside it. Probably, the small temple and the rooms were for his personal use. These are the memories of King Tsewang Namgyal, which indicates the dignity and greatness of the king. He was an ambitious king. When quite a young man, he invaded eastern provinces like Kugay and Purang and conquered them. He also captured low and Namrang and extended the boundary of his kingdom just near to Lhasa. In the south he got subdued the provinces of Nyungti and Zom-Lding. In the west he conquered Shigar and Kharko, etc., and ruled over Baltistan. Besides he was intending to invade Yarkend to take the revenge of Mughal invasion to Ladakh and the assassination of his uncle Tashi Gon, but the people of Nubra valley petitioned him to abstain from the war, so that the trade of Yarkend may not be harmed and he desisted.

Those vassal-chiefs, who subdued were restored their governments. However, he got appointed his representatives in their court and the chiefs and nobles were brought in his court as surety and they were not deprived of their government. The tribute which came to Ladakh during his days was very great. He used to receive 900 grammes of gold annually from Kugay. From Rudok came 780 grammes of gold annually, and in addition 100 goats, one riding horse, 10 skin bags of "Shahtosh" and the proceeds from the royal domains of other regions. King Tsewang Namgyal took interest to improve the communication system in the country. He got constructed two roads; one on the road to Baltistan, near the Hanu Gorge, the other on the way to Zangskar, at Hanupata. Besides he got constructed the bridges over the streams and Nalahs at many places.

Regarding Gautam Buddha, they are of the opinion, that he took the reincarnation in an elephant. It has mentioned in a Tibetan religious book that about 500 people got astray in an Indian forest. They wandered in the jungle for few days, without food and water. At last they met an elephant, who guided them the way. According to the book, the animal asked them, that at a certain place you will find a dead body of an elephant, eat the flesh to save your life, since you will find nothing except it in the jungle. Thus, the elephant parted and went on a separate way, but before they arrive at the place, he threw himself on the ground and killed. When the people saw the dead animal, they began to eat the flesh. Meanwhile they recognized that it is the same animal, who guided them in the way. They believed that it is the reincarnation of Buddha. In the course of time, King Tashi Gon got a piece of bone of the said elephant from a person. He got built a temple to keep the sacred gift, but there was a defect in the structure, that people could not have a round around it. Therefore his nephew, King Tsewang Namgyal desired to construct a temple at the plain, on the style of Rasad Tholing Gonpa, so as to facilitate the people to perform the "Tawaf" easily. But he died earlier and could not fulfill his desire. Moreover he could not have a chance to rule over Ladakh for a long time, and expired in his youth without having an issue. After his death his younger brother Jamyang Namgyal ascended the throne. Nothing is known in the Ladakhi chronicles about his elder brother Namgyal Gonbo, that why he was deprived of the Government. Probably he might have died before this event.

JAMYANG NAMGYAL (1555-1610 AD)

Jamyang Namgyal could not find an opportunity to rule over Ladakh with ease. Ali Sher Khan the crown prince of Raja Skardo captured the two provinces of Ladakh, i.e. Kartaksha and Parkuta. The Ladakhi Governor who is called "Kharpon", run away from Kartaksha. Though the Ladakhi army resisted at Parkuta and Kartaksha but could not stop the Baltis. Most of the people were killed and the remaining army fled towards Ladakh.

Ali Sher Khan followed them upto Morol and Ganokh. Here he came to know about the crises in Chiktan and Sot. The two brothers Rgyal Malik of Sot and Tsering Malik of Chiktan were quarreling with one another and there was chaos and crises in the whole Purig. Probably Raja Tsering Malik might have prayed him for his assistance. Considering it a golden opportunity, Ali Sher Khan invaded Sot and captured the whole area. Later he restored Chiktan to Tsering Malik and in return annexed the Bodh Kharboo area in his kingdom. He appointed a Governor and kept a small number of his army in the Bodh Kharboo fort and after looting some of the villages of the Ladakhi territories, he went back to Skardo. When King Jamyang Namgyal came to know about the activities of Ali Sher Khan, he became very angry and wanted to take the revenge. Finally, with the intention of capturing Bodh Kehrboo and to warn the people of Sot, he decided to attack Bodh Kharboo. But the Bodhi new year was approaching nearer. The Ministers and Courteen advised him to be present at the capital on this auspicious occasion, and it was not considered lucky to start before having celebrate the New Year's festival. However, to wait for the New Year would have meant a delay of two months. Therefore, Jamyang decided to celebrate the New Year's festival two month's earlier on the 1st day of the Boddhi eleventh month which almost falls around 6th Feb. Ever since, New Year has been celebrated in the 1st week of December, about two month's earlier in Ladakh than in Central Tibet. However, after celebrating the festival, King Jamyang Namgyal marched towards Purig in the 1st week of December. As soon as he crossed the Fotola pass, captured the Bodh Kharboo fort tactfully, with the inner support of the local people. Some of the Balti soldiers were killed while some fled to Skardo to tell the sad story to their master. After capturing Bodh Kharboo he conquered Wakha. Finally he was busy in war with the Mulbe. Meanwhile, the situation changed. The king has to come back to Ladakh to defend his own home, leaving the invasion of Purig incomplete.

During this period Ali Sher Khan Anchan was already preparing for the expedition of Ladakh. He had united under his sway the forces of all Baltistan like Shigar and Khapulo. Meanwhile, those who run away from Bodh Kharboo reached in his court to tell the story of their destruction. Ali Sher Khan Anchan immediately invaded Ladakh. As soon as the Ladakhi Army had crossed the passes towards Purig and Jamyang was fighting the war in the vicinity of Mulbe. Ali Sher Khan kept him busy there and immediately reached his capital at Leh. There was no one to oppose or obstruct him. Though some of the officers of Jamyang resisted but could not stay in the way of the Balti forces. Thus, Ali Sher Khan captured his kingdom and ruled over whole Ladakh.

The detail of this war has not been mentioned in the Ladakhi chronicles. However, it has been stated, that the Baltis captured whole Ladakh. They looted everywhere, burnt the religious books and some were thrown in the river. Besides, they spoiled the temples and then went back to their own country. The fact is, when King Jamyang Namgyal came to know about the invasion of Ali Sher Khan, he leaving the expedition of Sot incomplete, returned back to Leh to defend his own kingdom, but before his arrival in Leh, Ali Sher Khan had captured whole Ladakh. When Jamyang Namgyal reached in Leh, the situation was reverse and nobody was ready to support him. Later he was imprisoned by Ali Sher Khan. Jamyang prayed for compromise. Ali Sher Khan agreed easily, because it was not his intention to rule over Ladakh. According to the agreement Ghota-Matchho (Nalah Gurgura) was declared as boundary between the Government of Skardo and Leh. And the village of Ghanokh and Nallah Gurgura and region of Kartaksha were annexed with the Government of Skardo. Jamyang Namgyal got married his daughter Mendok Gyalmo with Ali Sher Khan. In spite of these arrangements, he never freed Jamyang and after making a temporary arrangement in Ladakh, he along with his father in law and

Ladakhi princes' Mendok Gyalmo returned back to Skardo. According to agreement Raja Ali Sher Khan, kept the Bodh-Kharboo area with the Kingdom of Ladakh and in return the Ladakhi Government has to pay an annual tribute to the Government of Skardo. A Lama of Lamayuru Gonpa was appointed as collector, who has to attend the court of Skardo annually, along with the tributes and presents. This has mentioned in the chronicles of Lamayuru Gonpa, but the detail has not been recorded. According to Lama Gonbo, who was "Lopon" or Head-Lama of the Gonpa, states that the payment of the tribute continued till the conquest of Ladakh by the Dogra's. Whereas, after the victory Ali Sher Khan got collected lot of wealth from Ladakh and returned back to Skardo, along with his Ladakhi queen and father in law. Before departure he made a temporary arrangement in Ladakh. When they reached in Skardo, the Raja of Saling-Khar (Khapulo), Yapgo Sher Ali Meer Ghazi approached them and in order to maintain a better relation with the Government of Ladakh he got married his daughter Rgyal Khatoon with Jamyang Namgyal. Besides it was decided that the offsprings of Rgyal Khatoon would be the successor of the crown, instead of his children from the former queen. Since, Jamyang Namgyal had already married with Tsering Gyalmo, the daughter of Jigstain Wangchuk and had two sons Lahwang Namgyal and Stanzin Namgyal by name. After the second marriage the two princes were deprived of their rights and disinherited. Rgyal Khatoon gave birth to Singgay Namgyal, who became the successor of Jamyang Namgyal. After this arrangement Yapgo Sher Ali Ghazi, approached Ali Meer Anchan and tactfully got restored the Kingdom of Ladakh to Jamyang Namgyal and returned him back to Ladakh.

Zakaullah has mentioned this event in his book *Tarikhe-Hindusten, Iqbal-Nama Akbari*. That, in 1005 Hijri, according to 1556 AD, when the king was in Kashmir, he desired to send the army to conquer Tibet but due to famine in the country, it was very difficult to arrange the ration for the army, for forty days. So the king decided to depute his representatives to Tibet. Thus, he deputed Umaid Ali Holik, Talib Isfihani and

Mohammad Quli to little Tibet in the court of Raja Ali Rai and Ayub Beg, Salim Kashghari, Abdul Karim Kashmiri and Kokaltash were deputed to the Raja of Great Tibet. The general and the minister of the Great Tibet Raju Rai showed some resistance. So, the king confiscated his property and the minister was highly depressed. During this period Ali Rai (Ali Sher Khan Anchan) was in hostile activities against the Raja of Great Tibet and due to weakness of his ministers. Overpowered him and after capturing his palace, he was imprisoned. When he came to know about the arrival of the king's army, he appointed a local person as governor and returned.

When Ali Rai conquered the great Tibet and collected lot of wealth. He became arrogant and created crises in the vicinity of Kashmir. The king ordered Qalij Khan Subedar Lahore, to depute a group of soldiers to assist Mohammad Quli the administrator of Kashmir, so as to crush the proudy person. As per the order, Qalij Khan deputed three thousand horse riders and five hundred super fast under the command of Saifullah Khan, to assist Mohammad Quli beg. Saifullah was his son. Ali Rai runs away, without facing the challenge. King's army followed the enemy on horse back as far as the horse can move and returned back. It happened in 1112 Hijri, according to the 1603 AD.

Though the name of the ruler of Great Tibet has not been mentioned in this history, but the conquest of Ladakh by Ali Rai ruler of Little Tibet indicates that this should be the period of Jamyang Namgya. Moreover the Raja's of Little and Great Tibet was of the similar age of King Akbar.

When Jamyang Namgyal returned back to Ladakh from Baltistan, the people gave him a warm reception. Though the Government of Ladakh was restored to Jamyang Namgyal, due to the tactic and diplomatic policy of Raja Yapgo Ali Sher Ghazi (father in law of Jamyang) but the size of the empire was now smaller that it had ever been. The whole Purig region got the freedom, and the region ahead of Tangtse also became free. As a result his empire was confined between Lamayuru and Tangtsey and he was content over it. Now instead of attacking other countries, he began to consolidate his own country. The invaders brought enough crises and destruction in the country and showed disregards to the religious institutions. The condition of the people was miserable. Therefore he exempted the public from the tax and reliefs were sanctioned to the needy people. To set an example to his subjects, Jamyang Namgyal sent a deputation with costly presents to the statue of Cho-Rinpochhe and principal Central Tibetan monasteries and Lamas. He also got copied the Buddhist religious books like *Kargyut Sethang* in gold, silver and copper. Because he would have much liked to rebuild and present anew whatsoever had been destroyed by the Baltis; but his life being short, he died before he had been able to accomplish his purpose.

Jamyang Namgyal had two sons with his previous queen. He deputed them to Lhasa with the above mentioned presents to the principal monasteries. They stayed in Lhasa and began to receive religious education from the great scholars of Tibet. Later the elder son Lahwang Namgyal became the Head Lama of Lahol. Jamyang also had two sons with his second queen Rgayal Khatoon. The elder son was named Singgay Namgyal as per the desire of his father in law Yabgo Sher Ali Ghazi and the younger was Nurboo Namgyal. It is said about Rgyal Khatoon in Ladakh, that in spite of her marriage in a Buddhist royal family, she continued to be a Muslim till her last breath. When I visited Nubra, I found a grave in a deplorable condition inside a garden at Hunder. I was astonished and inquired, and came to know that it was the grave of Queen Rgayal Khatoon. There was a platform just adjacent to the grave, and I have been told by the locals, that it was the mosque of the queen. It is said that both the monuments were in a good condition in the past but now the ruins are there. Nobody could tell me the name of the queen. There are two beautiful "Mane-walls" along the road, which were in good condition. I have been told that the "Mane-walls" have been constructed by the same queen, whose grave and mosque are there in a ruined condition. I closely observed both the "Mane-walls" but could not find an inscription or writing over it, so as to throw light about its construction. On observing closely, I am of the opinion about these two monuments, that after the death of Jamyang Namgyal, his Queen Rgyal Khatoon preferred to stay at the royal palace of Hunder. Moreover the grave and the mosque, both are in a deplorable condition are the memory of the poor princess, who being a princess of Khapulo was got married in Leh, just to fulfil the political aims of her ambitious father. Now the monuments are in a deplorable condition, not to speak of lightening a lamp or offering flowers, even dust and grass are not found over her grave. It was ready to fall but I got it repaired. Later, I invited the attention of her offsprings at Leh and Khapulo, so as to take care of it. As far as the Mane-walls are concerned, I suppose that Queen Rgyal Khatoon had built them in memory of her late husband, as per the Buddhist's faith and rites, so as to rest the departed soul in peace. Being a Buddhist religious structure, the local people repaired the Mane-walls from time to time and took care of them. These are in a proper condition and reveals the faith and dignity if its founder. Since, there is no Muslim population in this village, hence because of the lack of repair, the Muslim monuments were in a ruined condition. When I arrived in Leh, I inquired from Raja Sonam Namgyal and he confirmed that really it is the grave of their great grand mother Queen Rgyal Khatoon, the mother of Singgay Namgyal and the two Mane-walls were also constructed by her. Further the king told me that in the beginning a beautiful tomb was built there and there was a golden umbrella over the tomb and the mosque was also in a proper condition. But with the passage of time, there was no care taker of these monuments and is in a ruined condition. Only the name of the queen remains. Later in 1830 AD, I came to know that Munshi Jamshed son of late Mr. Johnson, who now resides at Hunder, has got repaired both the monuments. But I have not seen personally. I came to know later, when I inquired about the condition of Khapulo that after the death of Queen Rgyal Khatoon, two mounds of "Phuli" (Soda) and twelfth mounds of salt were paid to Raja Khapulo, for a long period as tax of her possessions in Nubra. But during the period of Mr. Johnson it was reaffixed as thirty-two "Khal" of grain and one sheep. Later, the payment was ceased. Phuli is a kind of soda, which is found in a field of Nubra. It is being collected through Government agency and sold. But after the availability of soda its use has minimized.

SINGGAY NAMGYAL 1610-1645 AD

Singgay Namgyal ascended the throne of Ladakh after the death of his father Jamyang Namgyal. In spite of his Muslim mother, the king does not appear to have had any liking for Islam, but had inherited the warlike sprit of his grandfather Yabgo Sher Ali. From his childhood he was very strong, and clever at wrestling, running, jumping, and arrow shooting as well as matchlock, and riding. When yet a youth, he made a war against the back steppes of Kugay to re-conquer that lost province for his kingdom and carried away ponies, yaks, goats and sheep, even so far as from the northern slopes of Kailash. Sometime later he made war against the central provinces of Kugay also. A farce battle took place at Shadang and Janey and many people were got killed and brought a large number of cattle and wealth to Ladakh. He was married to Skalzang Dolma a lady of a noble family of Rupsho and had three sons; Deldan Namgyal, Indaboti Namgyal and Dechhok Namgyal. Being the son of a Buddhist father and Muslim mother Singgay Namgyal was too much interested and inclined towards the upliftment of Buddhism. To perform the religious activities, he got the full cooperation of Lama Stag Tsang Raspa. Basically the saint was an inhabitant of Lhasa, but during his youth he went to India and got religious education at Ujjain. He visited all the holy places of Buddhism in India and later came to Zangakar via Kullu, where he met with Jamyang Namgyal, who provided him all sort of facilities. Jamyang requested the saint to visit Ladakh and said that my son is the ruler there, he will certainly help you. The saint replied that once I have to go back to India and during my return journey I will certainly go to Ladakh. Hence, he returned back to India from Zagskar. Finally the saint came to Ladakh via Kashmir. At that time Singgay Namgyal was married and was inclined towards religious activities. His visit proved a blessing in disguise for Singgay Namgyal. He gave full regards and respect to the saint and both jointly did a wonderful job for the promotion of Buddhism in Ladakh.

Stagtsang Raspa was a Sanskrit scholar and a pious man. He was a man of simple living and high thinking. He would have never thought even in a dream, that his followers would be in such a great number. According to Buddhist faith there is another world which is called "Shambala" like that of Paradise in Islam. Stagtsang Raspa has written a book, *The Journey to Shambala* which is very popular in Lhasa and Ladakh. He got constructed magnificent Gonpas at Hemis, Chemray, Anlay and Tashigang. Hemis Gonpa is considered famous among the Ladakhi Gonpas, because of its educational, economical and political status in the region. Singgay Namgyal granted the income of Hemis, Chemray, and Anlay villages to these Gonpas. Many "Mane-walls" have been constructed during this period along the roadside. A Mane-wall is a room five yards wide and hundred to six hundred yards long and slab of stones have been placed over the roof, inscribed "Om mane padme hong", Avalokiteshrara, kindly bestow the precious Jewel of enlightenment to librate all living beings verses from the religious books, sketch of the great saints or sacred religious signs. There is a Mane-wall at Lingshed, where a slab of stone has placed, with the words, that it has been erected by Singgay Namgyal. There is a Mane-wall between Nemo and Bazgo, which is very wide, long and high and still is in a good condition. It is said that it has been constructed by Lama Stagtsang Raspa. There was a harmonious relation, love, regards and respect between the King Singgay Namgyal and Lama Stagtsang Raspa. Stag means tiger and singgay, lion, and the fame of the "tiger-Lama" and the "lion-king" are still remembered and the chronicles have the following passage on the two. The king governed over all his dominions according to the ten virtues, and thus it came to pass concerning the kingdom of this world that the king was like the lion, and the Lama like the tiger, and their united fame encompassed the face of the earth as "the lord and the Lama" "Sun and moon" a pair.

The king erected a gold coated bronze statue of Buddha, equallent to the size of a eight years boy. He also got copied the five volumes of the religious books *Chamchhos Danya Pothi* and got appointed five Lamas to enlighten the lamps to the sacred books. After Tsongkhapa, there were two groups of Lamas in Lhasa. The leader of the first group was called "Gyalwa" who is now called "Dalai Lama" and the leader of the second group was called "Pan Chhen". Who is now called "Tashi Lama". The headquarters of the later is Shakartsey. Pan has been derived from the Sanskrit word pandita and "Chhen" means great in the Tibetan language. Since, the founder of this sect was a very great scholar. Hence, he was called "Pan Chhen". Gradually his reincarnated disciples who sat on the throne also called "Pan Chhen". The King Singgay Namgyal sent costly offerings of silk, gold, silver, corals, pearls, amber, etc., to the Panchhen Chhosgi Gyalson in Tibet, so that the departed soul of his mother may rest in peace.

When he was old, bethought himself: "My uncle Tsewang Namgyal certainly did rule over all the country as far as Ngamring in the east; but he did not live long, and during the reign of my father all the vassal-princess again rose and made themselves independent."

In order to restore the position he collected an army and invaded Purig. Though there is no mention of it in the Ladakhi chronicles but the Purgis confirm it. Moreover it has been mentioned in the *Tareekh-e-hind*. Since, the Raja of Sot, Mirza Sultan ill treated with the Raja of Chiktan Tsangkhan Malik and his sons, pretending to take revenge from Raja of Sot, Singgay Namgyal made an attack on Sot. At that time Adam Malik and Choszang Malik were ruling over Pashkum and Chiktan and Bodh Kharbu and Tikchay had already been conquered by Jamyang Namgyal. Therefore Singgay Namgyal straightly reached Wakha passing over Chiktan and Bodh Kharbu. Raja Geeldey was only a Raja of a village and he didn't have the strength to fight against Singgay Namgyal and without showing any resistance he bowed to the will of the King. At the border of Mulbe Goritham and his brothers and Dubla Singgay, Raja Phokar and his sons fought jointly against the King but got defeated. Dubla Singgay was imprisoned but the rest got killed. Mulbe and Phokar came under the control of Singgay Namgyal. He appointed Kalon Rafstan and Kalon Sonam Tundup as Kharpon of Mulbe and Phokar respectively. Later he invaded Kartsey. At that time Sultan Kungga Namgyal was the Raja of Kartsey. He countered but defeated and was imprisoned. After consolidating his position there, Singgay Namgyal was intending to attack Sot, but the scenario changed. Mohammad Sultan was ruling over Sot at that time, he, with the collaboration of Raja of Skardo, plotted against Singgay Namgyal right from the day when he entered Bodh-Kharbu. But there was not a brave man (a lion) like Ali Sher Khan Anchan, to prey at once, on seeing the animal. Instead, the Raja of Skardo, contacted the Subedar of Kashmir of Delhi administration, and motivated him to send an army against to stop the advances of Singgay Namgyal. It is said that even Singgay Namgyal was yet to move from Kartsey towards Sot, the Mughal army arrived from Kashmir and a farce battle took place at Karpo Khar. Singgay Namgyal was defeated and run away from the battle field. Later to save his own skin, he deputed his envoy to the Mughal Officer of the royal army, to settle the dispute and make the compromise. He fixed the ransom, which had to be sent in the court of the Delhi King. Thus, the vassal kings of both Sot and Kartsey were saved from the paws of Singgay Namgyal and Ladakh came under the rule of the Mughal King. Mulbe and Phokar remained under the Kingdom of Ladakh and were ruled through the Kalon's and this system continued till the Dogra's invasion to Ladakh.

Zaka-ullah writes in his book *Tarikhe-Hind* that in 1048 Hijri, according to 1638 AD, the Mughal Army captured little Tibet (Baltistan) and Abdal the second son of Ali Sher Khan Anchan, who was ruling over Baltistan at that time was imprisoned and the administration of the land was assigned to Adam Khan, the younger brother of Abdal (see the chronicles of little Tibet, i.e. Baltistan)

When Ali Mardan Khan came in Kashmir as Governor, at that time Adam Khan the Raja of little Tibet, complained against the Singgay Namgyal the Raja of great Tibet (Ladakh) about his invasion of Purig and the surroundings. Ali Mardan Khan deputed his relative Hassan Beg, with the Mughal army. On 25th of Rabbi-ul-sani 1048 Hijri, a farce battle took place between Singgay Namgyal and Mughal army in the surroundings of Karpo Khar. He was defeated and fled away. Considering that his capital is very far from the battle field, he deputed his envoy in the camp of Hassan Khan to make the compromise. Hassan Khan agreed, he fixed the ransom and advised to send it in the court of the King at Delhi. Later he invaded in the east but his luck did not favors him and his army was routed at Shirikarmo. This place is situated on the right bank of the Charta River (Brahamputra) near its source. After the defeat there was no alternative but to make the compromise with the Tibetans. Upon this there arrived a envoy from Tibet, and it was agreed, that the frontier should remain as before and the river Naw was earmarked as border. This river is situated just adjacent to the Shrikarmo. Here from he returned to Ladakh and during the course of his journey, he died at Hanle.

Before this campaign Singgay Namgyal had entered, in co-operation with Lama Stagtsang Raspa, on a great scheme of grand building enterprises. The best known of these buildings is the Leh castle, called Lehchhen Spalkhar. It is a magnificent building of nine stories, above the Leh town on a hill. It is said that the building was completed in three years. It has big rooms, drawing rooms, royal resting rooms and magnificent balconies. All these reflect the architectural test of the king. This palace is still in a good condition. The external portion of the building looks very beautiful, but internally, being old it has damaged. Some rooms of the top storey have already fallen and the whole building needs to be repaired. I came to know later, that the State Government has got repaired the historical building and when I visited Ladakh as a tourist in 1830 AD, I found it in a good condition. Another remarkable building is the Maitreya monastery at Basgo, above the ruins of the ancient fort. Here the gold coated bronze statue of Buddha is two storey's high, which is worth seeing. Lama Stagtsang

Raspa got constructed the "Gonpas" at Himis, Chemray, Hanle, and Tashigang; these were completed because of the financial assistance of the king. The king got constructed a bridge over river Indus just near Alchi, which presently not exist there. A new bridge has been constructed just two kilometer ahead of the old site, which is a source of communication between Alchi and Saspol.

DELDAN NAMGYAL 1645-1666 AD

After the death of Singgay Namgyal, his son Deldan Namgyal set on the throne. He ruled over Ladakh from 1645 to 1666 AD. But failed to keep the vassal kings under his rule, who were the subject of his father. Inda Boti Namgyal, who became a Lama at the hand of Lama Rigzin, later became a principal disciple of Lama Stangtsang Raspa and acted as Superintendent at the erection of the Hemis and Chemrey Gonpas. He achieved a higher status among the great Lamas of the Gonpas and became the ruler of Kugay. Dechhog Namgyal, the youngest, was made vassal King of Zangskar and Spiti under the patronage of his elder brother. When Deldan Namgyal ascended the throne, his government was right from Purig to Maryumla. This hilly range goes along the Mansarowar lake towards Lhasa. It was his desire, which the honour and dignity of the Ladakhi army should be restored again and the Sultan's of Purig have to be made his subordinate. Moreover it was his intention to take revenge from the Balti Rajas. But his Plans could not be matured and has to postpone from time to time and he could not have an opportunity to fulfill his desires before his old age. Finally he was able to conquer these regions and the dignity, power and authority of the Ladakhi kingdom, during his rule was so remarkable like that of his ancestors.

Deldan Namgyal was not only a brave general but an able administrator. He was taking keen interest for the welfare of his subject. Therefore he was very popular in the country and everybody young and old in the country used to praise him.

During the summer Deldan used to stay in Rudok but in winter in Ladakh. He constructed mostly religious structures only. In order to rest in peace the soul of his father, he built a very magnificent bronze statue of Lord Buddha at Shay and it was gold coated. This statue is two storeys high in the sitting position. He also got constructed a beautiful "Chorten" which is five storey high. Both these monuments are in a good condition. Moreover to rest in peace the soul of his mother he constructed a long "Mane-wall" in the south-east of Leh town on the Lhasa road and built two beautiful "Chortens" at the beginning and end of the "Mane-wall". The lengths of the Mane-wall including the two chortens are about 800 yards. In the Leh palace he got constructed two storey high, bronze and gold statue of Lord Buddha and Chinrazig and two storey high silver chorten. Except the last three structures, the rest are still in a good condition. The statue of Lord Buddha at Shay was got repaired by Lama Tsultim Neema and looks very new and beautiful. Moreover he deployed 100 lamas each at Nubra, Zanskar, Bazgo and Tingmogang, to recite the Buddist prayer "Om mane padme hong", so as to rest the soul of his mother in peace. One hundred lamas can recite this prayer, with a good number of ten crore a year. The present royal palace of Shay, was also got constructed by this king, instead of the old palace. This is a small, but a very beautiful palace its rooms are still in a good condition except a few, which has damaged because of negligence.

During the reign of Raja Deldan Namgyal of Ladakh, Raja Hatam Khan was ruling over Sarling Khar, i.e. lower Khapulo and Raja Babar and Yaqub (The nephews of Shah Murad Raja of Skardo) were ruling over Thursay-Khar, i.e. the upper Khapulo. Hatam Khan Raja of Thursay-Khar wanted to annex the Sarling and rest of Khapulo with his government, so as to expand the country. Thus because of his family relation with the Raja of Ladakh, he plotted against the Kingdom of Thursay-Khar and jointly invaded. Babar and Yaqub failed to counter the attack and were arrested. The Raja of Ladakh took them along with their mother and imprisoned them at the Bodh-Kharboo fort. He annexed all the region of Chorbat, ahead of Poyon with the Kingdom of Ladakh and rest of the region of Thursay Khar was given to Raja Hatam Khan. Thus,

Hatam Khan fulfilled his desire by eliminating the rulers of Thursay Khar, and he ruled over the entire region of Khapulo.

To take the revenge, the Raja of Skardo Shah Murad Khan, with the collaboration of Imam Quli Khan Raja Shigar invaded Bodh-Kharboo. When Raja Deldan Namgyal came to know about the invasion, he deployed the Ladakhi Army to counter the attack. A firce battla took place at Bodh-Kharboo. Finally the Ladakhi Army left the battle field and fled towards the Bodh-Kharboo fort. The Army of Skardo followed the Ladakhies and stopped their way to the fort. Nine-hundred Ladakhi soldiers were arrested, about fifty soldiers fled away and the rest were killed in the battle field. Thus, Shah Aalam conquered Bodh-Kharboo and captured the fort.

The fifty soldiers reached Ladakh, to tell the sad story to the king and Deldan Namgyal became very sad. He was planning how to release the prisoner of war from Bodh-Kharboo. Finally it was decided, that the sister of Shah Murad and her two sons are in the prison with us. We will release them from the prison and hand them over to Shah Murad, so as to release the prisoner of war of Bodh-Kharboo. Shah Murad easily agreed the proposal of exchange. So, Babar and Yaqub along with their mother reached at Bodh-Kharboo and Shah Murad released all the Ladakhi prisoners. Later he got restored the Kingdom of Babar and Yaqub. Therefore the plan of Hatam Khan and Deldan Namgyal were failed. The incidents have been revealed in detail in the history of Khapulo and Skardo. Because of the interference of Deldan Namgyal in the affairs of Thursay-Khar, the attention of King Aurangzeb Aalamgir was invited towards the activities of Deldan Namgyal. Which have been narrated by Zakaullah in his book *Tarikhe-Hind* volume 8th.

Badshah Nama Aalamgiri, in the following words; "During the reign of King Aalamgir, Nawab Saif Khan was the Governor of Kashmir for the first time from 1075 Hijri to 1078 Hijri, according to 1664-67 AD. During his rule over Kashmir, the Raja of Tibet Deldan Namgyal revolted. Hence, the King ordered Saif Khan to depute a confident representative to Ladakh, to advice the Raja to mend his ways and accept the sovereignty of the King Aalamgir and recite the "Khutba" and release the royal coin. He has to construct a mosque in Leh and should choose the right path, and consider himself as subordinate of the King Aalamgir. Otherwise invade the country and crash them. The copy of the letter was sent to Deldan Namgyal, the Raja of Tibet (in the past Ladakh was known as Tibet). Saif Khan deputed Mohammad Shafi, the royal representative to Ladakh along with the royal order. At first he refused to comply the royal order but at once he realized the consequences and thought it better to obey the order of the King Aalamgir. He convened the citizens outside the city on the very first Friday. And recite the "Khutba" in the name of King Mohiuddin Aurangzeb Aalamgir Ghazi. Moreover golden and silver flowers were offered to the "Khatib" along with a shawl and a mosque was constructed. The drawing of the Mosque, two thousand Ashrafi, and nine-thousand fresh coins, bearing the name of Aalamgir and the gifts were sent in the court of King Aalamgir. The application, along with the reply of the royal order, indicating faithfulness and obedience were handed over to Mohammad Shafi, to present before the king. Beside Mohammad Shafi and his companion were treated well by Deldan Namgyal, during their stay at Leh.

It is not out of place to mention here, the brief description of Zakaullah made about Tibet.

In Tibet there are barren lands and desert, which are not able to cultivate. Hence, the production and income is nil. In the length except Bejapur, no other province can compete it. It takes 4 to 5 months to cover the journey. The distance of the breadth is about one month's journey and at some places it is one and half months. There is no province in India equivalent to it. But the income is so less, that it cannot compete even a block of other province. Hence, the region is profitless. Therefore, no king has preferred to establish their kingdom, recite "Khutba" or release the coin. In Ladakh, I got two "Farmans" of King Aalamgir, in the name of Raja Deldan Namgyal. First; dated; 2nd Shawal Sana 1075 Hijri according to 1661 AD. With the following contents:

The 2nd was dated; 19 Shawal, but the year could not be read. The contents are; "I got your application and came to know that you have already recite the Khutba and has released the coin in your country, with our name. Moreover, you had started the construction of the mosque. Since, Saif Khan has already confirmed it. Hence, you are offered with a shawl and sword as a token. These two "Farmans" confirms the above events and it is clear, that the foundation of the mosque in the Leh Bazar was laid by Raja Deldan Namgyal in the year 1661-64 AD. Later with the expansion, it was repaired and renovated.

5

Namgyal Dynesty of Ladakh
(Continued)

DELEK NAMGYAL ALIAS AAQIBAT MEHMOOD KHAN (1666-1695) AD

After Deldan Namgyal, his son Delek Namgyal set on the throne (1666-1695). Prior to that, there was a disturbance between the Lamas of old and new faith in Tibet. Each sect was trying to destroy one another. The internal conflict became so complicated, that each sect approached the King of Mongolia, one after another for Military aid. Because of this internal disturbances, the external interference increased, and both the sects lost their independent and the Mongol ruler Goshri Khan captured all Lhasa. Since he was against the Lamas of red sect and came to Lhasa to assist the yellow sect. Hence, the influence of the Lamas of yellow sect was increased in the administration.

During this period, there was a conflict between Bhutan and Tibet. The Head Lama of Bhutan was the "Guru" of the King of Ladakh. King Delek Namgyal warned the rulers of Lhasa, not to interfere in the affairs of Bhutan. Otherwise, the Government of Ladakh is ready to take weapon in favor of the Bhutan. In response to the warning, the Government of Lhasa immediately invaded Ladakh. The General of the Tibetan Army was a Lama of the Galdan Gonpa, namely Galdan Tsewang. He was a Lama of Mongol race and was considered a very clever and able administrator. After the departure from the Gonpa along with the Tibetan Army, he entered inside the border of Ladakh within few days.

Delek Namgyal became very anxious to hear this news. He hurriedly prepared an army and deputed to counter the Tibeto-Mongolian invasion, under the command of Gyalson Tundup Shay Lonpo. Both the army met at Jamarding, which is in between Tashigang and Gar. A fierce battle took place and the Ladakhies were defeated. The Tibetan Army continuously marched towards Ladakh. When the Tibetan Army reached near Leh, the king left the capital Leh and proceeded to Bazgo and was busy in consolidating the Bazgo fort. When the Tibetan Army marched towards Bazgo, the King Delek Namgyal was fortified in the Tingmogang fort. Then, the Tibetan commander Galdan Tsewang besieged the Bazgo fort. The Bazgo fort was very strong. There was suitable and good arrangement of supply and water inside the fort. The Tibetan Army could not capture the fort. However, the Ladakhi army could not counter the invaders. Different historians have revealed, different opinion about this invasion. Some reveals that the fortification continued for three years, while others are of the opinion, that it was ended after six months. The Tibetan Army looted the people, during their stay in Ladakh. The Ladakhi people are mostly dependent on agriculture, if the agriculturist fails to cultivate their lands for a year; they have to face lot of difficulties to make both ends meet. Hence, the second report seems to be more correct.

When Delek Namgyal found it very difficult to withdraw the Tibetan Army from Ladakh. Because of compulsion he approached Ibrahim Khan the Governor of Kashmir and requested for help. King Aalamgir detailed the soldiers of Kabul and Kashmir to fight the invaders. He deployed Fidai Khan Son of Ibrahim Khan to Tibet, along with the Khans of Kabul, as a general. When the Tibeto-Mongol Army came to know about the advance of the Mughal Army, they withdrawn the fortification and took the position at the Chargyal-Thang. This is between Bazgo and Nemo. Here a fierce battle took place and finally the Tibeto-Mongol Army was ruined and withdrew back. They left lot of weapons like armour, arrow and bow, etc., in the battle field. The Kashmiri Army followed them up to village Spituk. The Mongol Army never stopped anywhere and run away up to Tashigang. Later the Kashmiri Army did not follow them. When the Tibetan Army satisfied, that none is following them, they stayed at Tashigang and strengthened their position and turned the Gonpa into a fort. They dug the pit around the Gonpa and filled it with water and stayed inside the fort comfortably. They were also watching the activities of the Kashmiri Soldiers. The fort of Tashigang is still in the shape of a Gonpa.

After performing the military service, the Kashmiri Army returned from Pituk. Gyalpo Delek Namgyal also came out from the Tingmogang palace, and paid sincere gratitude to the Commander of the Kashmiri Army. The Kashmiri historians are of the opinion, that Delek Namgyal accepted Islam at this occasion, and his Islamic name was Aaqibat Mehmood Khan. But nothing has been mentioned about this in the Ladakhi Buddhist history. Moreover the prominent personalities of Ladakh, totally deny the statement. However, the Government of Delhi has mentioned the said name in the official documents. Hence, one can't say, that the statement is false. Thereafter, Gyalpo Delek Namgyal accepted the suzerainty of the Shahinshahe Hind over Ladakh, and agreed to pay the following annual tribute to the Mughal king, but according to some it was after every three years.

Ablaq horses 18, Mushk nafa 18, Yak tail 18. In return the Nawab of Kashmir allotted land to the Gyalpo of Ladakh at Now-Shahra, wherefrom, the income for the Ladakhi Raja was 500 bags of Kashmiri rice. It continued as long as Kashmir remained a province of Government of Delhi. After making the arrangements, Fidai Khan took Jigspal, the son of Gyalpo Delek Namgyal and some prominent personalities as captive and returned to Kashmir with a handsome booty. This happened in 1094 Hijri, according to the 1683 AD.

Hereafter, King Aalamgir got the full authority over the Kingdom of Tibet, i.e. Ladakh.

Since, Gyalpo Delek Namgyal developed relations with the outsiders and provided them chances to interfere in the affairs of Ladakh. This was disliked by the Government of Lhasa. In order to abstain him in doing so, the Government of Lhasa, i.e. the Dalai Lama deputed, the Head Lama of Drukpa sect, Kushok Lama Mipham Wangpo as his representative to settle the issues with Delak Namgyal. Lama Mipham Wangpo reached at Tingmogang along with some prominent members of Lhasa. Being the Head Lama of Drukpa sect and Guru of Ladakhi King, he advised the Gyalpo and said, "We are sharing same race and religion and the Kashmiri are Muslims and outsiders, if you allow the outsiders to interfere in the affairs of the country, it is feared that we will also suffer in the long run. Hence, it is better to abstain from these activities. Forget, what has happened in the past, we promise that there will be no war with Ladakh in future." In return the Gyalpo of Ladakh should take the responsibility to defend the border of Kashmir. The Gyalpo agreed to stop the Kashmiri invaders, if and when they enter the country.

As far as the trade of pashmina wool is concerned, Kushok Mipham Wangpo assured the Ladakhi King, on behalf of the Government of Lhasa, that the Pashmina of Changthang is to be sold to no country but to the traders of Ladakh. The rate was fixed rupees two for 80 "Nyagha" (6 Nyagha is equal to 1 kg). Whenever the Tibetan people will sell the pashmina to the Ladakhi traders, the balance will be in the hand of Ladakhies. But the Ladakhi traders have no right to reject the Tibetan pashmina on the pretext of wetness and dust, etc. In the Rudok area, no other traders will be allowed to purchase the pashmina, except the traders of Ladakhi Raja. The Kashmiri pashmina traders will not be allowed to proceed Changthang ahead of Spituk. They have to return back to Kashmir after the purchase of pashmina at Spituk. Those Ladakhi traders, who had gone to Changthang to purchase pashmina, will not be allowed to proceed Kashmir to sell their pashmina; instead they have to sell their pashmina to the Kashmir traders in Ladakh.

Because of the religious pressure of the Lama, the Ladakhi king has to hand over all the region of "Naris Korsum" to the Government of Lhasa. And it was assured that this will be a gift on behalf of the Raja, for lightening the Gonpas of Lhasa. In the name of religion, he has to bear the losses of territories. However, he kept the Manesar area with Ladakh and said that it is binding for him to enlighten the butter lamp at Kailash and Mansarowar Lake. The Lama agreed the proposal. The Lahri hill which is adjacent to the village Demjok was fixed as new border, between Ladakh and Lhasa.

As far as the trade relation between the two countries are concerned, it was decided, that the traders "Jungtsong" of the Government of Lhasa will come to Ladakh annually. They will bring 200 horse load of Chinese tea. The "Jungtsong" will sell this tea to only the Ladakhi traders, and will not import to the foreign countries. Moreover they will offer the following presents to the Gyalpo of Ladakh.

Chinese green tea 22 damo, Chinese silk cloth 7 than, Woolen cloth of Lhasa 2 than, Khatak on behalf of the Head Lamas of Lhasa (Khatak is offered to the VIPs to welcome him). On the other hand the Ladakhi Gyalpo will depute his representative, in the court of the Government of Lhasa, to pay homage, after every three years, called "Lobchhak". Through the Lobchhak the following articles will be sent to the Government of Lhasa as presents:

Gold 3-¼ tola, saffron 35 tola, Yarkendi cloth 6 than, Punjabi cotton cloth 1 than.

The Lobchhak will get free accommodation from the Government of Lhasa, during his stay in Lhasa, and during the travel of and within the territory of Lhasa, he will get 200 animals, ten yaks and 15 horses for transportation of goods. Moreover he will be provided with three servants, grass for his own horses, boat to cross the river and tent at every destination on free of cost. The transporters have to go from one province capital to another, so that the Lobchhak may not suffer, during the travel, for want of transport. Similar arrangements have to be made by the Ladakhi King, during the travel of "Jungtsong" within his territory. After getting signed the agreement, Kushok Mipham Wangpo returned back to Lhasa. The Government of Lhasa appreciated his political services and granted him three villages as "Jaghir", which is still in possession of the Gonpa of which he was the Head Lama.

Thus Gyalpo Delek Namgyal was under the influence of two big powers. He also managed both the powers, till the decline of Mughal Kingdom. Later the relation of the Ladakhi Kingdom with Kashmir ceased, but the relation with the Government of Lhasa continued, till the decline of the Ladakhi Kingdom. The said agreement was renewed by Dewan Hari Chand, on behalf of Maharaja Gulab Singh on 2 Asoj 1899 Bikrami. And with a minor difference the cost of the pashmina is still the same.

NEEMA NAMGYAL (1695-1750 AD)

King Delek Namgyal had five sons. After his death his elder son Neema Namgyal set on the throne (1695-1750). He was a very intelligent king. During his reign, the able and honest persons were elevated and the diligent people, who use to take the advantage of their cleverness, were ruined. He appointed Nambardar in every village. He use to take the advice of senior and experienced people during the hearing of cases. He was deadly against the partiality. He use to issue the decree based on justice. That is why, everybody in the country was happy with him. I got a copy of an order of King Aalamgir, with the content, issued in his name (but the date could not be read) the month of Jamidul-Aakher, 1107 Hijri, according to 1697AD. I came to know that your grand father Raja Aaqibat Mehmood Khan has expired. Hence, you are conferred with Khallate-Fakhira (shawl and certificate) and the status of one thousand soldiers, one thousand horseman and five hundred riders with two horses. Don't allow the "Qalmak" sect to enter and interfere in your country. Try to keep the subjects, happy and prosperous. And keep busy for the promotion of Islam".

Another order, issued by Abul Fateh Nasiruddin Mohammad Shah, King of Delhi, in the name of Raja Mehmood Khan (Delek Namgyal) dated 6 Rajab, 1147 Hijri according to 1735, AD, was seen by me with the following contents:

> "I got your application, in which, you have mentioned, that you are following the Islamic faith with sincerity. Hence, you are conferred with "Khallate-Fakhera" (Probably shawl and certificate) and sword. It is binding upon you, to be grateful, loyal and firm in serving my Government." As per the Ladakhi traditions, when Gyalpo Delek Namgyal retired, he handed over the Kingdom of Ladakh to his son Nima Namgyal. Perhaps he must have submitted the application to the Mughal king during this period and in response to the application the said order, in his name must have been issued. Even though King Nima Namgyal was already ruling over Ladakh, as the letter of confirmation of succession in his name, was issued by King Aalamghir, 38 years earlier, as mentioned above.

Gyalpo Nima Namgyal managed to send gold, for coating of the statues of gonpa Samyas and other great Gonpas of Lhasa. Paid the expenses, for lightening the lamps. Alms were sent to the Head Lamas of every sect and parties were arranged for common Lamas. He also got prepared many statues of gold and silver in proper Ladakh. He got constructed a Mane-wall just ahead of Choglamsar bridge, which still exist. Though the length is good enough but the structure is inferior or has damaged due to lack of repair. He introduced the printing press for the first time in the country, and it helped to propagate the religion. It is surprised that its use is restricted only for religious purposes and only the religious personalities use it. The verses from the religious books which are being kept inside the statues got engraved on wooden tablets and the instruments were imported from Lhasa. Thereafter, it became a tradition in Ladakh. This printing press is still in existence at Gonpa soma in Leh town. There is also a paper making factory just adjacent to the press where paper is being prepared, which is soft but the surface is coarse and rough. The local people easily write over it with the help of bamboo's pen. This type of printing press is in existence in every big Gonpas, but its use are restricted only for religious purposes, as already has mentioned above. Both these factories are in use like that of initial stage, when it reached in this country. Where as the priest of the Moravian missionary brought the Litho press in this country, which also being used for religious purposes. Gyalpo Nima Namgyal got copied the religious book *Kangure* which consist of 108 volumes. Moreover, he distributed many religious books among the Lamas and common people. He introduced small handy prayer wheel of gold, silver and bronze. Above all, he tried his best to modify the morality of the masses. He eliminated theft, dacoit, and telling a lie, from the society, and he use to advice the people regarding the above mentioned evils very gently and affectionately, like that of parents use to do so for their children. The most famous construction of King Nima Namgyal is the royal palace of Nubra, situated at Charasa. A major portion of the palace is still in a good condition. Though, it is empty for a long time and nobody use it.

During the reign of this king, two important events occurred and both the events have not been mentioned in the Ladakhi chronicles. The first event is the arrival of two Italian priests, Epolito Desideri resident of pastoya and Emanuel Friary of Rome, in Leh on 20th June, 1715 AD via Gova, Agra, Delhi, and Srinagar. Their intention was to precede Lhasa. Father Desideri has revealed in his travel note of Kashmir and Ladakh. It will be more interesting and useful. If it is compared with the travel notes of Mirza Haider, 1531 AD. For that very reason both the notes have been translated and added in this book.

After the end of very beautiful, greenery and fertile hilly land of Kashmir, we reached on 29th of May, 1515 AD, under the foot-hill of a very high, terrible and frightful mountain called "Kantal". It is the border of Kashmir and Baltistan. On 30th May, we started to climb the mountain (Probably Zoojila). In the evening, we arrived on the other side of the Kantal mountain, the first inhabitation of little Tibet called Matain. But Friary has mentioned in his travel note, that they rested in a cave during the night and the next morning they reached in a village. Though the language is different from the Tibetan language, but there seems to be too much of similarities. Except villages, there is no town or cities and the first floor of the residential houses are under ground. The productions of the area are grain, some vegetables and apricot. The religion of the people of the area was like that of Ladakh, but due to being a part of the "Chogtai" Kingdom; the total populations are now Muslim. These regions are being ruled by the ruler of Kashmir, through governors and other officers. Since, the regions are small (probably it is Daras and Baltistan). A few days later, we entered in the territory of Ladakh. Here a nodal Raja was ruling over the region, under the Ladakh Kingdom. He is a Muslim and is a subordinate of independent kingdom of Ladakh. His palace is situated on the top of a hill (probably it is the Sot palace). When we reached near the fort, we submitted the letter of identification to the Raja, and requested him to allow us to proceed further through his territories without interruption. The Raja invited us the next day for a meeting. When we arrived in the palace, he gave a good reception to us. We were invited for lunch. The next day, he came for a meeting and he took us with himself to witness the Polo game. On the other day, before our departure, he not only gave the road permit to us, for which we have applied but also presented a valuable gift to us and gave money for our employees. Moreover, he deputed his own men to guide us, so as to help us to cross the bridge. We reached at a place, where we found that the rout on the left hill is inaccessible and there is no rout. Later we found that the rout is on the opposite hill. There is a stream between the two hills, which neither a man can cross on foot nor can swim. The only alternative is to cross the stream through a trolley. The trolley is fastened with the help of two ropes made of willow branches from one hill-top to another. The ropes are fastened at a distance of four feet from one another. Moreover, there are small willow ropes hanging downwards at a distance of half yard each. Now one has to move through the trolley by holding tightly the upper ropes and keeping the feet on the hanging ropes. At every step the trolley move towards left and right and only one man can sit on it at a time. Moreover, the trolley is open from every side. It is so high from the river, that while crossing the stream one feels giddy and the eyes are dazzled. However, we crossed the stream through the trolley and our guide went back. We kept continue our journey (since, Desideri has not mentioned the name of the place (probably it is Nallah Kanji near Hanasku). After few days we reached in a town. It was the capital of the province. Where the Governor was the son of Prime-Minister of Ladakh (Probably it is either Khalsay or Tingmogang) When he heard about our arrival, he invited us at the palace and gave a warm reception. He presented some gift during our departure and also gave a letter in the name of his father. We reached in the Leh city (Ladakh) on 20th June 1715, AD. It is the capital of Little Tibet. It takes 40 days to travel from Srinager to Leh. One can travel on the foot only and the rout is so narrow, that only one man can pass through the rout at a time. And some places the rout pass through the foot of high and terrible mountains. It was damaged at many places due to heavy rainfall and avalanches. It was very difficult at such places to put the foot straightly. So our guide uses to cut the snow with, an axe, so as to keep our foot over it. He also helped us in moving forward by catching our hands, and began to make the space for the 2nd step. Even we reached at a narrow rout and the hills at rest of the places were covered with snow or ice. It was a great danger to travel over here. If anybody slips, there was no alternative but to fell into the gorge. Among the Kashmiri traders who use to come Ladakh, to purchase 'pashmina' many people lost their lives or injured (they never cross the Zoojila during the month of June, but wait to melt the snow). The length of the Ladakh region is two month's journey. In the north it touches the boundaries of Yarkend and Kashgar, in the south the Government of Lahore, in the west Baltistan and in the east, the desert of Nari-Jongar (probably Changthang). All are hilly region and is not cultivable. On seeing the hilly area, one feels fear in mind. Where, there is a habitants, they grow wheat and barley and apricot is also grown at some places.

Plants and trees are very few so there is scarcity of fuel. There are many high-breed sheep. The meat of the sheep is very tasty and the wools are fine. The musk bags are also available. The people draw out the gold dust from the bank of the rivers. It found in dust and not in pimples. People use to take the "Sattu" of meat and barley and drinks "Chhang". It is a kind of wine, which prepare from barley. It will be revealed later, in detail. They use to wear woolen clothes. The people are not arrogant; instead they are faithful, obedient, compassionate and cheerful. The language is similar to the Tibetans. Moreover the religion and the religious books of both the countries are similar. There are many Gonpas and Lamas. The Head Lama controls them. To become a lama one has to seek religious education from an institution in Lhasa, so as to get a high degree and status. Many Kashmiri traders, who deal with pashmina are permanently settled here. They have got freedom to construct the mosques and pray according to their faith. Some time many traders use to come here from Chinese Turkistan. They bring superior horses, cotton cloth and other articles. Some traders use to come here from Lhasa via Changthang. They bring tea, tobacco, silk, and other goods of China. Except Leh, the rest of the inhabitants are villages. The Head Lama and the independent king reside here. Leh city is situated in a vast area and is surrounded by mountains. There are villages everywhere. The inhabitants of Leh city are under the foothill, and have spread upwards towards the resident of Head Lama and the royal palace. Both these buildings are very beautiful. There is a fort above these buildings on the top of the hill. For the security of the town, it has been fortified. The houses are built strong and are wide. These are very good as per the local environment. As soon as we reached Leh, the king had already got the news of our arrival. Before we could submit our identification letter, he convened us for a meeting. He treated us well, because we had come from a very far country, and that we were the scholars of our own religion. He greeted us and without confirming our letter he assured us, for our safety and security. Moreover, the Head Lama, Prime Minister and other ministers treated us well sympathecally. Later they presented us gift. Even when we met for the first time, the king was already on the throne. And his ministers and officials of the palace were present there, but later on during our two month's stay in Leh, he use to casually call us to his palace very often. Since, we were meeting the

Raja and his courtiers frequently, hence the Kashmiri traders became jealous and began to made rumors against us. That we are pretending to be religious scholars, actually we are rich traders, who have brought pearls, jewels, and other valuable antiquates for sell, from our own country. When the Raja came to know about the rumor, he sent a message through one of his minister, that the goods should not be sold to anyone except the Raja, he wants to purchase it and assured to pay the due price. We replied that whosoever has informed the king, it is nothing but a rumor and misinformation. Our valuable belongings are the principles and preaching of the true religion which leads us towards heaven and salvation.

The Raja was not satisfied, he thought, that our answer of being religious scholars are nothing but a pretext and we are misleading him. The ministers again came to us with the assurance that the Raja will pay the full price of the goods and should not bother for any kind of loss and ill-treatment. Even we will not have any chance of complaint.

When we saw that the Raja is not satisfied with our reply. We asked the ministers to check all the goods physically. He replied obediently, that your statement is enough. But we again insisted him to search. Finally he checked all the goods and found nothing, except some books, written documents, some clothes and utensils, and money for the travel expenses. He went back to the Raja and narrated the whole storey what he has seen and assured the king, that we are true of our word and the storey of jewels and other valuable things are false and fabricated. The Raja is a just and kind person. He issued order immediately, that the Kashmiri traders neither should be allowed to enter the court, nor should they come near the palace. Moreover, the Raja sent the message to bring some of our goods to show him at the palace. When we reached at the palace, he apologize us for his persistency for the sale of the jewels and had a look on the prayer books, religious photos, medals, and other religious articles with great interest. He said, "Despite having the jewels and other valuable antiques, I enjoyed much to see these sacred relics". We had a long meeting with the Raja and parted with us, with the presentation of gift. During our meeting the Raja and the minister wished us to stay at Leh itself and to start religious preaching. I can't reveal that we were getting such a great opportunity, to start the propagation of our religion. We prayed the Almighty God, and after mutual consultation we decided to continue our journey to Lhasa. Since, Lhasa is the centre of this religion. Besides, Priest Antanewdy Andraway and the preachers of our religious group have already stayed there for propagation of religion, so we thought it reasonable to proceed there and started to make the arrangements for the journey. The Raja ordered his men to help us properly in purchasing horses and other articles for the journey. When we took the leave of the Raja, he not only presented us with more gifts but also give us road permits in the name of his officers and the Head Lama and Administrator of Tashigang.

On 7th September 1715 AD, we reached at Tashigang. It is situated between Leh city and the border of Lhasa. It has been fortified and a deep ditch has been made around the fort. Such movable bridges have been constructed over the ditch that it can be withdrawn in emergencies. The Prime Minister and the administrators, along with the army reside inside the fort, because it is a border region. Especially it has been constructed to defend from the Mongol invasion. They are brave, tactful, trustless and deceiveciable people. Because of the identity letter of the Raja of Ladakh, the Lama, Prime Minister and administrator of the fort gave great respect to us.

It is not out of place to mention here, about the activities of other priest, which Father Desideri has mentioned in his travel notes. It reveals the relation of foreigners with the Government of Lhasa and other neighbouring states. One Priest Antanewdi Andrade from Portugal established the missionary centre at Agra. Here he came to know that a religion similar to Christianity is exists in Lhasa. So, he decided to establish a mission in Tibet. He left for Tibet via Srinager Garhwal, in March 1624 AD, along with brother Emanuel Marx and reached at Chhabrang in Kugay. Here he came to know, that whatever he heard in Agra about the religion in Tibet was false. But the Raja and Rani of Kugay and other members of the royal family showed great respect and regards to him. Even they allowed propagating the Christianity and constructing church. Father Andrade promised them to start the work, after getting the approval from the higher authorities and came back to Agra on 17th June 1625 AD. Father Gonsil Desouza, along with two Tibetan youths whom he brought from Kugay, during the first visit, again went back to Kugay.

These people reached at Chhabrang on 28th August 1626 AD. On the day of Easter 1626, they laid the foundation stone of the church in presence of the Raja. In the meantime the priests had started propagation of Christianity, among the members of the royal family and other persons. Priest Estive Kachila, Priest Joao Gabriel, and Brother Bartolomio Fantabona, who were working at Malabar mission, were asked to proceed from china to Ursang, the capital of Lhasa for propagation of Christianity. They stayed at Mon province (Tawang of Arunachal Pradesh) adjacent to Gyantse city in the north-west of Bhutan. They constructed a church in the city with the consent of the Raja and Kharpon in 1627 AD, and made many people to follow the faith of Christianity. Another preacher from Chhabrang mission was deputed to Gyantsey, on the request and expenses of the Raja. In this very year Priest Judi Aluvera, Priest Elanodi Angels, and Priest Entano Perera came to Kugay and joined with Priest Entaniodi Andradey. They baptized twelve persons and many more people were kept ready for baptism. Gyalmo and her niece, who was the daughter of the Raja of Lhasa, accepted to be baptize. At this occasion the Raja donated a huge amount to establish the mission and got construct the church. He also got constructed the houses to accommodate the priest and granted annual honorarium for the missionaries.

The year 1629-30 AD proved to be very harmful for the mission. In the beginning Priest Emanoildias passed away at Mordang. This place is in between Sikkim and Nepal. Later the Raja of Kugay and other members of the royal family were imprisoned and no one was there to protect and look after the priests. In this very year two priest of Ursang, who were under the patronage of the king, passed away. And above all, father

Estivio Kachela who was the head of the mission, died at Gyantse. During the period the Raja requested priest Joao Gabriel to come back to Gyantse. Beside some more priests were sent from Bengal to Chhabrang, because there were about 400 new Christians in Chhabrang, Rudok, and Kugay. During this period the Ladakh King invaded the area and arrested the Christians and took them to capital Leh as slaves. Moreover two priest of Rudok were also arrested and imprisoned at Leh. Later the Raja of Leh released them.

Luckily, in the year 1631 AD some more priest arrived for their assistance. Priest Entanio Prera, Sopareir, Frasiscodi Azeodo, Dominco Kapichay and Frasisco Morendo left for Chhabrang from Goa on 14 February 1631 AD. Where Father Antonio Enradey was the provincial. Priest Francisco Azeodo and Jaode elivebera left Chhabrang and reached Leh within 20 days. And got the permission to built Churches at Ladakh, Rudok, Kugay and other places and to propagate Christianity in the region. But the effect of the recent disturbances was still continuing. In 1632 AD five Priests was under arrest in the palace of "Kharpon" of Kugay. Nothing can be sent to them inside or receive outside, without the inspection of the authorities.

In 1635 AD Father Fonokorsama was deputed from Goa, along with six companions, so as to start the mission again. Among his companions were Priest Caldera Pedadi Fretas and Brother Fasteno Barpros. But because of the famine in India, Tibet and Srinagar Garhwal and followed by influenza, the five priests died before reaching in Tibet. The travel expenditure from Surat to Tibet comes to ₹3,000. In spite of these hardships, the quantity of the Christians increased day by day. The "Kharpon" of Chhabrang in a letter to the of Raja of Srinager Garhwal, has mentioned that Father Elanode Angeles died in 1636 AD and has complained, that those priest, who were convened to Chhabrang, were detained at Srinagar.

Later, after four years in 1640 AD Father Thomade Yarus was sent to Agra, wherefrom he proceeded to Tibet along with three companions, but nothing is known about the result. Later the name of many priests have been mentioned, who worked in

Tibet for the propagation of Christanity. In 1641-42 AD, Brother Emanoil Marx and Priest Stenslao Plachi were busy in missionary work in Chhabrang. After completing the tenure of provincial in St. Pal College Goa, Father Entanewde Andrade was making arrangement to go back to Tibet, but he died. Later Priest Embroso Curia, Bout Godeno and many other priests worked in Tibet under the Christian missionaries, where numbers of the Christians were very high, and was increasing day by day. The name of more than 30 priest and brothers have been mentioned, who performed their missionary services in Tibet in those days. Thereafter Father Desideri reveals about the Capuchin missionaries. That in 1704 AD Roman migrants was sent to Tibet as missionaries. These people came to Bengal in 1708 via Turkey, Babul and Arab. Among them Priest Joseph Diskoli and Francais of Toris reached Lhasa, but Francais returned immediately and died at Patna, and Joseph Diskoli stayed back in Lhasa till 1710 AD. Even when Father Dominaco Dafano reached Lhasa, Joseph returned from Lhasa and died at Patna. In 1711 AD, Jhony Dafalow joined father Dominique and both of them decided to quit the mission and returned to Bengal, therefore none of the Capuchin priest was left in Lhasa. Till 1715 AD when Father Desideri reached Lhasa, none of the missionaries were sent there. Father Amanuel Freddy was appointed from Delhi to accompany Father Desideri, but he returned back soon after reaching Lhasa. Father Dominique Dafano went back to Rome via Bengal, wherefrom he was sent back to Lhasa again along with Cappuccino priest. He reached Bengal in 1715 AD, and entered Lhasa in 1716 AD. Father Orazio Vilapina and Father Francisco Cassumbronay were with him. All three of them went to the house of Desideri and convinced him that they have written in Roman that Tibet is under the influence of Capuchin missionaries and no other missionary should be allowed to operate there. To which he replied that he will go by the edict of the Pope. Therefore, they stayed in harmony with Desideri and in 1721 Father Desideri returned back from Lhasa.

It is clear from the above-mentioned events, that the Christian missionaries have scarified their lives for the sake of religion. As long as, when Tibet was not under the influence of China, there was no system of isolating the country from rest of the world. This is the strategy of the Government of China that they banned the entry of the outsiders in the country of Tibet, which is still continuing and is strictly in force. The second significant event which occurred during the reign of Nima Namgyal was that of he was adopted by Thi Sultan. It is said that when Mohammad Thi Sultan, the Raja of Suru Kartse grew old and he was having no issue and was worried about his kinship and wanted to adopt some one as his son. One of his ministers was a Buddhist; he suggested that Nima Namgyal should be adopted as his son. The Queen of Mohammad Thi Sultan, Rgyal Bi, was deadly against this proposal, but she failed to change his decision and finally Thi Sultan declared Nima Namgyal as his adopted son. Because of this decision of the Raja, his Queen was depressed and committed suicide, but Thi Sultan didn't change his decision. After Nima Namgyal was adopted he deputed Kalon Raftan to pay homage to Thi Sultan, his adopted father. Even after the completion of these formalities Mohammad Thi Sultan continued to rule over Suru Kartse, and after his death Raja Nima Nmagyal as adopted son start to rule over Kartse and appointed his middle son Tashi Namgyal as King of Suru Kartse. Since that time Suru Kartse remained a part of Ladakh till Dogra's invasion. The task which the ancestors of Nima Namgyal could not accomplish even after fighting two wars was fulfilled by Nima Namgyal sitting at home without any effort. Tashi Namgyal ruled over Kartse for a very few days and became a Lama and the region was ruled through Kharpons; which ended during the war by Zorawar Singh.

The long period of rule by this king was mostly peaceful and no war was fought in this region. Though during his old age, the dispute of succession over the throne arose among his son in his lifetime. He got married twice; the first Queen was from Shey, with whom he had a son Deshkyong Namgyal. She died after the birth of their fist son because of natural death.

Later Nima Namgyal got married to the princess of Purig, Zizi Khatoon. From this marriage he had two children, a son and a daughter, Tashi Namgyal and Tashi Wangmo. When Nima Namgyla grew old he handed over the reign to his elder son Deskyong Namgyal as per the traditions. But this was not acceptable to Zizi Khatoon as she didn't wanted his son Tashi Namgyal to remain crown less while as Deshkyong would rule the country. Since Deshkyong was brought up by Zizi Khatoon and Deshkyong used to regard her as his own mother. Zizi easily got Deshkyong agreed to pass on Purig to Tashi Namgyal. But she failed to convince the courtiers on this issue. In spite of the fact that Nima Namgyal had deputed Tashi Namgyal to Suru Kartse to rule over there but the ministers objected to the division of the kingdom and insisted that either as per the traditions Tashi should become Lama or should be contended with Tingmogang. When Nima Namgyal realized that the dispute is growing, he took over the reign in his own hands and ruled over Ladakh for a long time. With this Tashi Namgyal was left with no option and had to become Lama.

DESKYONG NAMGYAL (1750-1770 AD)

Deskyong Namgyal was the son of Nima Namgyal. He set on the throne after his father during 1750-1770 AD. But he was an insignificant ruler and all power of the government was in the hand of his stepmother queen Zizi Khatoon. Tashi Namgyal became Raja of Mulbe and Phokar and made Mulbe his capital. Here he built a palace on the top of the hill, called "Mendok-Khar". Now the palace is ruined, but only the Gonpa is in a good condition. I got a letter (Farman) of the great King of China Sohangdi, in the name of this king, dated 8th of 2nd month. The translation is as under:

> The order is issued in the name of Deskyong Namgyal Raja of Ladakh.

The king looks after and treats equally to the rulers under the sky and creatures. Earlier, your father Nima Namgyal has helped my representative Khanchen. You are also directed to help my representative Pali Folada. I also like my respected king father conferred you with certificate and "Khallat", i.e.

the rope of honor. You should be grateful to us. After hearing the important news and observing the situation, inform immediately to my representative Pali Folada. Really, it was your duty to present the gifts to me and to request for the certificate from a very far country. In future too, you should loyal to us like your father Nima Namgyal and promote religious activities. Don't delay in supporting my representative Pali Folada and get benefited by the status granted by me. The following articles are hereby sent to you as a gift:

Glass plates: Yellow 1 pair, Red 1 pair, Blue 1 pair. Clothes all kind, 200 roll.

Flower vase of white glass 1 pair, Chinese cup 1 pair. Glass cups with kettle 1 pair.

It could not be find out; who is the Khanchen and Pali Folada, whose mention have been made in the above edict. Because nothing has been mentioned in the Ladakhi chronicles about them. Probably, after the deputation and made the treaty with Kushok Mipham Wangpo, one of the Chinese officers might have deployed , like that of the British Resident, and the Raja have been asked to act according to their advice.

The marriage of Shema Tashi Wangmo, the daughter of Zizi Khatoon was proposed with the Raja of Kishtawar, during the life time of Raja Nima Namgyal. Though the elites of Ladakh were against this marriage, they were of the opinion that the princes should not be married in such an environment, whose caste, religion and language is different from us. But the queen never agreed their request and said that the parents have the right think about their daughter. Consequently, she was married and sent to Kishtawar, escorted by Tingmo Gaphel and other royal employees. Later people complained that the princes is always busy in domestic work and she has no time to stay out in the sun. When the news came it was decided that Tashi Wangmo should be convened back from Kishtawar. When the Ladakhies reached at Kishtawar to bring her back, because of love and affection, her husband desired to accompany her to Ladakh. When Zizi Khatoon came to know that her son in law is also coming to Leh along with her daughter. She thought that he will create problems by interfering in the affairs of the administration of Tashi Namgyal. Thus, she secretly deputed one of her loyal person with the instruction to eliminate him in the way, whenever get a chance. It is said that while crossing a bridge over a river between Kishtawar and Padar, the man of Zizi Khatoon pushed the husband from the bridge and got killed. This accident brought a very bad name for Zizi Khatoon in the country. Later Shema Tashi Wangmo was married in Khapulo.

There is no mention of this event in the history of Kishtawar. Hence, the Raja of Kishtawar whose marriage, according to Ladakhi chronicles was solemnized with Shema Tashi Wangmo is difficult to trace. However, the death of Prithi Singh the adapted son of Maher Singh Raja of Kishtawar seems to be similar as mentioned above, but the difference is that as per the history of Kishtawar he was pushed down from a bridge in the Chinab River near Bhandarkot, by his cousin brother Ajit Singh. The period is also matching with Prithi Singh. Most probably the unfortunate person might be Raja Prithi Singh. Deskyoing Namgyal married with Nilza wangmo, who was from Low Pato adjacent to Darjeeling. After the marriage he set on the throne. The queen gave birth to a son called Saskyong Namgyal. But there was a dispute between the couple and the queen went back to her native land. Later he married again with Thri Gyalmo, who gave birth to Phuntsog Namgyal. Nothing has been mentioned about the achievements of this king, except that he was the Ist ruler of divided Kingdom of Ladakh.

PHUNTSOG NAMGYAL (1770-1775 AD)

Though after Deskyong his elder son Saskyong Namgyal was the true successor of the throne but due to interfere of the queen in the administration, she made tactfully her own son Phuntsog Namgyal the ruler of the kingdom (1770-1775 AD). And the elder son was sent to Hemis Gonpa to become a Lama. Since Phuntsog Namgyal became king against the local tradition, due to the cunningness of her mother but he could not have a benefit from the kingdom. His Uncle Tashi Namgyal was the ruler of Purig and Phuntsog Namgyal was the king of proper Ladakh. In the meantime, Tashi Namgyal ill-treated his own subjects and the pashmina traders of Kashmir. Raja Phuntsog Namgyal asked him to abstain from such activities but Tashi Namgyal took it very seriously and it harmed the mutual relation, which gradually became very serious. The elites of Ladakh were very anxious, that if the situation continue the same, it is feared, the Kashmiri rulers will attack Ladakh. Hence, they submitted a detail report to the Government of Lhasa. Consequently, Dalai Lama deputed Kathog Rigzin Chhenpo Tsewang Nurboo to Ladakh, who was a great Buddhist scholar and was busy in Nepal in the repair and renovation of a "Chorten" to resolve the dispute amicably. Therefore, he directly came to Ladakh from Nepal. When he reached at Ghar, Tashi Namgyal and other elites decided to depute the Lonpo of Zanskar to greet him. He informed the Lama about the overall situation of Ladakh. The Governor of Ghar also kept his representatives with the Lama. Now he marched towards Ladakh. Both the rulers of Purig and Ladakh along with the ministers and courtiers attended the Lama. Both the party unanimously decided to agree the decision of the Lama without any objection. Lama ordered that there should be no dispute in future in the case of succession. The elder son of the Raja would be the successor. All the younger brothers should become Lamas in the Gonpas of Spituk and Thiksay, The kingdom should not be divided among the two brothers and the younger brother should not make the king by ignoring the elder. Lama made the decision impartially but made some leniency in the enforcement. Since Zanskar is a border area and to defend the country, an administrator should always remain there. Hence, it is better to keep him continue. He will be responsible to defend the border. About the Raja of Hinasko he said, it is a small area and should not be interfered. Nothing has been mentioned in detail about Tashi Namgyal, but it is said that he remained the Raja of Purig till his death. May be the elite might have objected that a person who ruled over Purig through out his life, is not good to humiliate him in the old age. So, he should be kept continue. As a result he remained the Raja of Purig through out his life. Since he was issueless; therefore the region of Purig was annexed with Ladakhi kingdom after his death.

SASKYONG NAMGYAL (1775-1780 AD)

The Lama got no point about Phuntsog to pretend and the unfortunate king has to scarify his government on the decision of the Lama. His elder brother Saskyong was called back from Hemis and made the King of Ladakh (1775-1780 AD). The deposed king and his mother divided all the assets of the palace equally among themselves and both settled at the Sakti palace. The first wife of Saskyong, Queen Nurzin Wangmo was from low. Who gave birth to Tsewang Namgyal. Later, nothing is known about this queen in the history of Ladakh. Queen Kunzom was the second wife of Saskyong Namgyal. When he has to take refuge at the Himis Gonpa, this queen was with him. His son Galosh's Mipham Tsewang Thinles was born here, and was made the Lama of this Gonpa. As a Lama his name was Mipham Tsephel Thustobs Dorje. He made the developmental works in the Gonpa and benefited the Gonpa in every field. There was another brother of him, who got mastery in medicine, and died in Lhasa. He was also having a sister who was married in Lhasa.

Because of the justice of Lama Rigzin, Saskyong was elevated from a Lama to a king on the throne of the Kingdom of Ladakh, but he could not have a long time to rule. Lama Rigzin Chhenpo was still in Leh when a representative of Nawabe Kashmir arrived here. The Lama was very famous in his generosity and miracles, so he was intending to taste the Lama. And to say that the vast area between Spituk and Leh should be brought under water, so as to irrigate the area. He came to the Lama. The Lama was the royal guest at the Shay palace, at that time. Many people were gathered there. When he saw the Kashmiri representative, he understood his intention. He got brought tea in a small tea pot and all the audience present there were served with the tea. On seeing this, Kashmiri representative convinced with the Lama's miracle he went back without expressing his desire. People will surprise to know why he failed to get the benefits of his miracles. Otherwise, Ladakh would really be a city today. There is no mention of this representative in the history of Kashmir or Hindustan. Either it seems to be a myth or he was an ordinary person who came to Ladakh because of his own business. And hearing about the miracles of the Lama, he went to see him. Lama Rigzin Chhenpo submitted the copies of the agreement to the Rajas of Ladakh, Mulbe, and Zanskar and a copy were also deposited in the Hemis Gonpa. Later he went back to Lhasa.

TSEWANG NAMGYAL (1780-1810 AD)

After the brief rule of Raja Saskyong Namgyal his elder son Tsewang Namgyal set on the throne (1780-1810 AD). His father died when he was young; hence, he fell into bad habits. Regarding his marriage messengers had been sent to Zangla to ask one of the princes to become Tsewang's wife. The chronicles say, "The evil one entered his mind" before the queen reach in Ladakh Tsewang had fallen in love with a low caste woman of Tsangra, Kartse called Mashoqa Bibi. She was very famous for her beauty. Tsewang married her and convened her in the palace. When the princes of Zangla, who arrived soon after, became disgusted to see the situation, she was angry and returned at once to her parental home. Later she married with the Raja of Zanskar.

This Raja did many unpleasant works. He kept 500 horses in his stable along with the grooms. As a result the expenditure increased. He used to check the accounts of the domestic records daily. The low profile men were elevated to the higher posts. The noble men had no approach in the court. These attitudes of the Raja were disliked by the people, and every Tom, Dick, and Harry began to criticize the king. Finally, the elites and nobles gathered and asked Raja Tsewang Namgyal to discontinue the relation with the low caste woman; otherwise you have to face problems. It was very difficult for the Raja to oppose the public opinion, and because of compulsion he has to disassociate with his beloved Mashoqa Bibi and Prime Minister Stokpa Kalon. Later, he married with the princess of Sod Begum Wangmo, who gave birth to three daughters and two sons. His elder son was Migur Tsettan Namgyal and the younger was Migur Tundup Namgyal. He was having another queen called Khatoon Tsering, who gave birth to Jigsmat Namgyal.

These two events have been explained differently in the Tibetan chronicles. The fact is when the marriage proposal of Tsewang Namgyal with the Zangla princes came to an end, he married with Begum Wangmo. She is known in Ladakh as Kunzom Wangmo. In spite of the presence of Begum Wangmo, he was having a luxuries life. He fell in love with a low caste woman Mashoqa Bibi of Tsangra, married and called her in the palace. The system of administration was paralyzed. Consequently, he was compelled to step down and asked to stay in Chemday Gonpa in isolation, and his elder son Tsettan Namgyal was appointed as the new king. I got a written document in Ladakh, regarding the events is as under:

> When Raja Tsewang Namgyal married with Kunzom Wangmo, he began to ill treat with his subject. As a result there was a gap and disunity between the Raja and the public. Since, at the time of accession to the throne, the Raja promised to rule over the country with justice and as per the laws of the land. His subjects also promised to be loyal to the king, but the Raja failed to fulfill the promise and he ill treated the people. The Raja came under the influence of one Mirza Malik. He use to offer valuable presents and horses, etc., to the raja and there was a good relation between the two. He also married a low caste woman and kept her in the palace and under the influence of one conspirator Beda Karpo, both Kalon Kungyap and Tongspon Skit Tundup were assassinated. The elites and the nobles were punished by penalties; it was against the law of the land. The low caste people were elevated on high posts. He showed disrespect to his own religion and was taking interest in other religions. Kalon Wangyal of Stok also came under the bad influence and was assisting the Raja in performing the evil deeds. People became deadly against the Kalon Wangyal and tried to arrest him. But both Kushok Gyalrsas of Himis Gonpa and Chhagzot Tashi convinced the people and because of their intervention people abstained themselves from the crises and the public convinced to agree the decision of the Kushok.

> Finally it was decided that Raja Tsewang Namgyal should step down and become a Lama and the prince has to ascend the throne. Kalon Wangyal has to be expelled to Lhasa. According to the agreement, Prince Tsettan Namgyal ascended the throne, so as to run the administration of the country. Moreover the public has to be loyal to the new king. The deposed Raja has no right to interfere in the affairs of the government. He has to stay at Chemray Gonpa in isolation, and was granted agriculture land and pasture at village Saboo and Stok.

Looking at the kings of this period, the thought cannot be avoided that the dynasty was on the decline. Government and ability are two different things which cannot be gathered in a single man. No one of the kings of this period was great as a warrior, as a politician or as organizer. They lived debauched lives, and women became occasionally the ruler of the state, and the expected result was there after a few days.

TSETTAN NAMGYAL (1800-1820 AD)

Tsettan Namgyal, like his father was still not arrived at the prime youth that he has to took over the reign of the government because of the dismissal of his father. The Head Lama of Hemis Gonpa Kyapgon Gyalrsas and the nobles of Ladakh amicably decided to marry him with the daughter of the Raja of Pashkum, and he was ascended on the throne. His younger brother Tsepel Tundup Namgyal became Lama at Hemis Gonpa. Beside Jigsmet Namgyal the son of Khatoon Tsering, entered as a Lama in Thiksay Gonpa. Among the daughters, the first was married in Pashkum, second married with Kalon Tsewang Tundup and the third one died a natural death. After seeing the beginning of Tsettan's administration, it appeared as if the dynasty was making a new start. Since Tsettan was more of a character than many of the kings before him. The chronicles described him as a great king. He was a diligent, and obtained proficiency in Tibetan grammar and mathematics, Persian letters and speech, Kashmiri speech, and other such languages. He also knew well how to govern. He was devout, and knew the duties of kings. He was genius and witty and the senior ministers of the government was helpless before him. In memory of his father he built a mane wall, just above the mane wall of Raja Deldan Namgyal towards Leh town, on the Leh-Lhasa road, with magnificent Chhortens at either end. Its length is about 700 steps. It is the beautiful and largest mane wall next to Chargyal and Deldan's mane wall. It is known as new mane wall and is still in a good condition.

He was very popular among his subjects because of his good governance, but he could not have a chance to serve his people. Because of ill luck. He died at Karzoo Bagh in his youth. At that time Drugpa Thaamschad Khenpa was the Chief Lama of Hemis, he performed the funeral rites of the Raja in grand style.

TUNDUP NAMGYAL (1820-1834 AD)

Tsettan died without leaving any children, though the queen was pregnant, who gave birth to Tsewang Rafstan whose religious name was Chhogsphurul. Therefore, his brother Tsepel Tundup Namgyal about 1820-1834 AD, who was a Lama at Hemis Gonpa, was induced to turn layman and was invested with royal power. He inherited from his brother not only the kingdom but also his wife. Tsewang Rafstan was born during the period when her mother was the wife of Tundup Namgyal. Therefore, some historian has referred his parentage to Tundup Namgyal, while some has mentioned Tsewang Rafstan and Chhgsphurul as two different personalities, which is not correct. Raja Tundup Namgyal was the opposite in character to his elder brother Tsettan. He loved an easy life, and was lazy in every respect. He never went to battle, although he had plenty of opportunity to do so. In judgment, he regarded the faces of the influential and riches of men. Besides, he seems to have inherited the taint of madness from his father; for many strange things are told about him. The private servants in the palace had to promise daily not to sleep at night. The king also did not sleep at night, and use to sleep when the sun rises, and rose when the sun grew hot. In the morning, when washing his hands, he required twelve basins of water, and uses one pack of "Soda" with each basin of water, which had harmed the skin of his hands. When he traveled about in the provinces he went at night, and then with lamps and torches. He never trusted the senior and old courtiers. Kalon Tsewang Tundup was the former Prime Minister who was popular for his ability and wisdom. People like him very much. He maintained a very good relation with the neighboring states and established the system of keeping envoy. He use to exchanging the presents with these countries off and on Raja Tundup Namgyal neither considered in veiw, his past services to the kingdom nor the relation of being his brother-in-law. He took the privy seal from him to his own palace and directly issued the orders in the name of administrators and village Headmen, consequently the Ministers and nobles became disgusted. The Raja of Zangskar and Kalon of Purig were arrested and kept them in prison at Leh and his domestic employees have been elevated as Kharpons. Besides, he dismissed all the senior, experienced, able and loyal officers and appointed new and low profile persons on the high posts. The previous edicts, decrees and agreements were kept aside; he gave more stress and emphasis on the personal matters than that of state affairs. In short by ignoring the sincere services of the loyal officers, he tried to establish a new system of administration and its result was very bad.

During the rule of this Raja, Col. Moorcroft visited Ladakh, 1820-1822 AD. This event is described in the Ladakhi chronicles in this manner. At that time two Englishmen came to Ladakh via Sultanpur Kullu. They were called the great lord (Barah Sahib) and little lord (Chota Sahib). They gave all sorts of rich presents to the noblemen of Ladakh and expressed their desire to meet the king. But the Raja ignored them for a long time, because he feared that the result of the meeting will be negative. Finally, they got the opportunity for a meeting. They presented to the Raja Tundup Namgyal a knife, scissors, and a gun, and other wonderful things and gave suggestion with good intention that the system of administration of your government, and the functions of your noblemen and ministers indicate that one day this country will slip from your hand. So, it is better to construct a tower at this place. It will be useful for you, whenever required. But this suggestion was not agreed by the Raja and his Advisors. They feared that the tower will harm them. After few days the two Britons returned back, by handing a box and a letter to the Raja and said that one day this will required by you. A few days later the Army of Kullu, Sultanpur invaded Spiti, and after having destroyed the village, and carried away all the property, they returned home. The people of Spiti petitioned Raja Tundup Namgyal that he should wage a war of revenge, but he said; "you have not tried your best" and are responsible for the losses and punished them. Later on the Kullu, Karja and Khunu all the three kingdoms jointly attacked Zangskar. They destroyed the castles and looted the Gonpas. They stole ponies and yaks and whatever there was of value, and again returned home. Later the Raja of Padar Rattan Sher Khan invaded Zangskar, via Omasila, and the villages right from Atang to Padum have been destroyed. This time the people of Zangskar fought the enemy courageously at Karsha and stopped their advances. Finally, the war was ended on a compromise. Rattan Sher Khan along his army returned back. But Raja Tundup Namgyal was not satisfied with the bravery of these people of Zangskar, instead he discouraged them and blamed that you have not fulfilled your duties properly. How the invaders crossed the border of Zangskar. Consequently, he punished them. One year later, the people of Mande and Waran (from Kishtawar) came via Rangdum and devastated Zangskar, up to Dung-ring. They burnt the villages with fire, whatever of wealth and cattle they got they carried back with them. Although the land had suffer so much, the Raja did not perceive it, he took an interest only in what concerned his pocket, as history reveals. Because of this continuous invasion Raja Tundup Namgyal's position became very awkward. And the overall condition of the country became worse. But he never cared for it. He did nothing for the welfare of his subjects. He was very selfish and was taking interest in his own affairs. At that time the royal treasure had increased so much, so he thought that something had to be done with it. Instead of using the money for the defense of the country, as urgently required at that time, he decided to use the money for building purposes. The first work he undertook was the new palace of

Stok, a village opposite to Leh on the left side of the Indus River. Now the same has been granted by the Government of Jammu and Kashmir to the nominated Raja Sonam Namgyal, and he resides there. Later, Raja Tundup Namgyal built a palace at Karzoo Bagh Leh, now it is the residential quarter of British Joint Commissioner. Previously, it was a magnificent palace of Ladakhi type but now it has been modified in to a European bungalow. The Raja proposed the marriage of his crown prince Tsewang Rafstan with the daughter of the Raja of Lhagyari province of Lhasa. He built a palace for the crown prince at Leh, just above the Chanraszigs monastery. He deputed his men to Lhasa to bring the princes but the proposal could not be finalized because of the unknown reason. This place is not in existence now.

Later, the Raja devoted himself towards the religious affairs. He got erected an idol of Vajrapani (Chhagdor) of silver of the same size of the king and a "Chhorten" of silver. He also got built a statue of the saint Guru Padma Otbar with thirteen maunds of silver. At Shay palace a statue of Tsepakmed was made with seven maunds of silver. And he got erected a statue of white Tara Dolma, who since the days of Rgyal Khatoon was supposed to be incarnated in the Ladakhi queens at Stok palace with nine maunds of silver. Nothing has left now among these monuments.

During this period a great Lama of Lhasa, namely Eshay Duba Yangzin discovered, that Gyalrsas Tsewang Rafstan is the reincarnation of Lama Bhulwa Dorje, who had flourished during the reign of Tsewang Namgyal II. Tsewang Rafstan was kept at the Gonpas of Chemray and Hemis for a test, after the disclosure. Tsewang Rafstan was a furious person. Having thus become so important a personage; he found it difficult to obey the parents. Raja Tundup Namgyal has to go Nubra and Purig usually, in connection with the administrative affairs, the prince traveled about with him and passed the time, mostly with dancing and singing because of ill luck, the queen was not heeding the word of the Raja, she was under the influence of one domestic servant Chhagzot Sonam Wangchuk, and use to take the advice from him. However, the queen was very close and intimate with her son Chhogsphurul. In short, the life of Raja Tundup Namgyal was very restless and helpless, neither the domestic environment was good nor was he contented with the external affairs. When the Prince Tsewang Namgyal was old enough the Ministers persuaded him to marry but he replied, "I have to be at Hemis and would not marry." But as there was no successor of the throne, and Tsewang Rafstan has to attend the affairs of the kingdom. Therefore, the Ministers Steward Sonam Wangchuk, and the Head Lama of Gonpa Hemis interceded with him. Finally, Chhogsphurul consented and married with Skalzang Dolma, the daughter of Kalon Tsewang Tundup. Within one year of marriage, when it proved fruitful and having once tasted the sweetness of matrimony, he married yet another lady Sonam Palkit of Pankhapa Kalon Chemray and yet a third lady Zahra Khatoon daughter of Raja Pashkum. He married with these three princes within a year. The mismanagement and anarchy of the Raja and luxurious life of the crown prince provided a chance to the neighboring states to interfere in the affairs of Ladakhi Kingdom. Probably, the marriages were performed in the year 1834 AD and it was the same year that Wazir Zorawar Singh Kalohria, with the Dogra Army, arrived at Suru-Kartse.

6

Dogra's Ladakh Expedition Nos. 1 and 2 Under the Command of Wazir Zorawar Singh Kalohria, General Forientier Region Government of Jammu Conquest of Purig, Ladakh, Zangskar and Padar

When Raja Gulab Singh conquered Kishtawar and consolidated the newly conquered provinces, thereafter he turned his attention towards Ladakh. During this period East India Company was strengthening its position in India. Whereas Maharaja Ranjit Singh was ruling over Punjab. He was a far-sighted and talented administrator. He never missed the golden chance, he ever had. Before preparation for the Ladakh expedition, he approached the East India Company, to know whether they have any objection and also got the consent of Maharaja Ranjit Singh.

At that time the governor of the provinces of Reasi, Arnas and Kishtawar was Wazir Zorawar Singh Kalohria. He got the promotion to this position in the rule of Maharaja Gulab Singh, from a very ordinary employee and he was a trusted man of the Raja. And because of his sacrifice and loyalty to the kingdom, he deserved this promotion. Because he did everything for the welfare of the state, instead of his personal mottos. He was entrusted the job of commander in chief for the Ladakh expedition. Later, he proved himself that he was the fittest person for the job, and almost, he was having all the qualities of a warrior. The cause of the motivation for this war was that the Rajas of Sod and Pashkyum were trying to expel the Raja of Tambis Gyapa-cho Chhagdor Namgyal from the area. He complained against the Raja of Sod and Pashkyum, to the Raja of Ladakh. Since Raja of Pashkyum was a nearest relative of Raja Ladakh, hence, he took no action against them. And because of compulsion, Raja Tambis secretly approached the ruler of Kishtawar and requested him for assistance.

Finally in the beginning of 1890 Proshta, according to 1832 AD, about 4/5 thousands Dogra army was arranged for the invasion, under the command of Wazir Zorawar Singh. The following were the prominent officers of the Dogra army:

> 1. Mia Rai Singh, 2. Mehta Basti Ram Kishtawaria, 3. Mirza Rasool Beg Udpanpuria, Doda, 4. Rana Jalim Singh Arnoda, 5. Sangay Mankotia, 6. Mia Tota, 7. Sardar Utam Singh Padhyar Kishtawaria, 8. Wazir Khoja Bhonja Kishtawaria, 9. Imam Malik Mudhwa, 10. Sayed Madin Shah, and 11. Sardar Samad Khan.

Wazir marched from Doda, the capital of Kishtawar, along with a huge army and reached at Suru in Ladakh via Bhotokol. The region was under the kingdom of Raja of Ladakh, due to adaptation by Thri Sultan and his death without an issue. The Mulbe Kalon Tsewang Namgyal was the Governor of Mulbe, Kartse and Suru and under him one Tashi Wangchuk of Saboo was the Kharpon of Suru-Kartse. When he came to know about the activities of the Dogra army in Suru area, informed the Raja of Ladakh immediately. There was no system of keeping a regular army in Ladakh, but at the time of emergencies every household has to provide one man as soldier. These people have to manage the weapon and food by themselves. When the news of Dogra's invasion reached in Ladakh. Raja mobilized in haste an army of about 5,000 men from the neighboring villages and placed them under the command of Kalon Dorje Namgyal of Stok and deployed towards Suru-Kartse. Dorje Namgyal was a young, brave and fearless man. He was hardly 15 or 18 years old at that time.

Wazir Zorawar Singh along with a huge army reached Suru without any opposition. The people of Mande and Waran guided them along the way and via Maryumla, which is now called Bhotokol and Nallah Chilung, the army finally entered Suru. It was autumn at that time. Wazir stayed at Suru for a week's time. The crop in the area was ready. Wazir tactfully asked his soldiers not to damage the standing crop. As a result the people of the area submitted to the Dogra ruler. Zorawar charged four rupees per household as property tax. People happily agreed to pay the amount. He laid the foundation of the present fort of Suru and deployed some people there so as to continue the construction work, and after making the arrangement, wazir along with the army proceeded towards lower Suru. The Kharpon of Kartse, Tashi Wangchuk was deployed at Karpo Khar fort along with some Ladakhi soldiers. He bravely fought with the Dogra soldiers. The fort is situated on the top of a cliff and naturally it was strong, but the Ladakhi soldiers were having very inferior weapons and were ignorant about the norms of the war. It was very difficult for them to counter the Dogra army. The war continued through out the day. Both Tashi Wangchuk and his son got killed and many other Ladakhi soldiers also died. Finally, the fort was captured towards the evening. Almost every soldier of the fort died in this battle and those who were left were arrested. Some of the Ladakhi soldiers were at Kartse Khar. After hearing the news of the defeat they fled away via Rusila towards Shargol. In this battle around six, seven Dogra soldiers got killed. Later on, Wazir Zorawar singh captured Kartse Khar as Ladakhi soldiers had fled away from and no one was left behind. This fort is situated on the other bank of the River Suru below Karpo Khar. This way both the forts of Suru Kartse came under the control of Dogra rulers. In this area also Wazir imposed property tax on the inhabitants in comparison with Suru. And after getting the assurance of loyalty from public they moved further. After the departure of Kalon Dorjey

Namgial, Gyalpo Tundup Namgial mobilized four thousand soldiers from rest of the villages for reinforcement and deputed them under the command of Leh Lonpo Murup Stanzin. Soldiers of both the army had reached Lankarchay near the Astana; they got the news that Kartse Khar got conquered by Dogras. Therefore, the army decided to stay back and strengthen the posts under their control. When the Wazir came to know about this, he marched towards Lankarchay with full preparation. Ladakhi soldiers constructed a strong post on the narrow plateau on top of the cliff with a river on its foot, this area was between Astana and Bema Khumbu and it was fully consolidated. When the Wazir arrived Bema Khumbu after crossing the Lankarchay Nallah, he realized that there was no route ahead; Ladakhis attacked the Dogras from their posts with full force. Though they couldn't do much harm to the Dogras because of their inferior weapon, yet they didn't let the Dogras move ahead. The fight continued for two days, but it seemed impossible for the Dogras to win over the post. Finally, Nidhan Singh took the risk of his life accompanied by just one soldier surreptitiously entered the post. By Chance Kalon Dorjey Namgial who was on a white horse was near the post, he instantly killed Kalon Namgial there. The attention of Ladakhi soldiers got diverted towards Nidhan Singh, Wazir without missing this opportunity entered the Ladakhi post and hand to hand fight started between the two soldiers. Ladakhis fought courageously but for them to compete with the Dogras with superior weapons was next to impossible and ultimately all the Ladakhi soldiers got killed. When the Ladakhi Soldiers got disappointed and helpless they started fleeing and the Dogras chased them away. Murup Stanzin got arrested along with one thousand soldiers and about fifteen hundred Ladakhi soldiers fled the scene. This fight was a decisive one in the defeat of Ladakhi soldiers and the victory of Dogra army. After this the Ladakhi soldiers lost hope forever and never got the courage to fight back Dorgas. Ladakhi soldiers kept moving back and Dogras continued moving ahead.

The fugitives not even thought of breaking the Indo Bridge, after crossing it. During those days, there was not any alternative bridge over the Suru River in the Kargil town. The travelers from Kashmir and Kartse had to pass through Indo Bridge to reach Ladakh. This bridge was adjacent to the upper portion of village Baroo. Later on, Nidhan Singh, by the order of Wazir Zorawar Singh, constructed the present bridge adjacent to the Kargil town, but the Indo Bridge was still in use. After many years of this event the bridge was damaged partially because of the flood in the Suru River and it was not repaired. Finally, the historical bridge was demolished.

After the departure of the army under Mourup Stanzun, Raja Tundup Namgyal mobilized and deployed the re-enforcement under the command of Kalon Pankhapa, but this army failed to part takes with the previous army. The quantity of this army is not known, however it was not much than that of one or two thousand. Kalon Pankhapa along with his soldiers was staying at Pashkyum, when he came to know that Wazir Zorawar Singh has reached at Indo Bridge. It is said that on hearing the news, he was so frightened, that he immediately ride on the back of the horse and forget to open the rope of the horse. He made the efforts to move the horse fastened with a rope. That is why the word "Pankhapa's horse" is very popular in Pashkyum like a proverb. Finally, Pankhapa returned back along with his army and met with the fugitives of Lankertsey at Mulbe.

Wazir marched from Saileskot and Minji and passed through the Indo Bridge and reached Pashkyum. Nobody was there to counter them, because the Ladakhies had returned back to Mulbe. The castle of Pashkyum was empty, as the chief had fled to the castle of Yurbaltik in Sod. Now the Wazir did efforts to capture the fort of Sod. He fixed the guns towards the fort, though there was a battle for few days but could not capture the fort. Finally, Wazir deployed 500 soldiers under the command of Mehta Basti Ram to attack the fort heavily. Mehta Basti Ram attacked the fort at the dawn and it was captured till morning and many people were made captives. But the winter began and the Dogra army was not habitual of it, they were very upset now. But Wazir could not discontinue the expedition and return. So he levied taxes on the peasants of

Pashkyum at the rate of 4 rupees per household annually, like that of Suru-Kartse, and then sent an envoy to Ladakh to negotiate with them. The locally available reliable sources differ as far as conditions are concerned and after analysis one came to the conclusion, that Wazir wished that the Raja of Ladakh fully submit to the Kingdom of Jammu, to prove he should agree to pay rupees nine thousand annually as tribute. Besides have to pay rupees fifteen thousand immediately as war compensation. Since the Ladakhi army had already discouraged to see the weapons and boldness of the Dogras. They overjoyed to know about this proposal. They immediately deputed a messenger to Leh, to get the consent of the king. It was also said, if the king is not ready to pay the amount from the government treasury, the public will contribute six "Jau" (Ladakhi coin) from each house annually. Though Raja Tundup Namgyal and his courtiers agreed the proposal gladly and ordered to pay the amount from the treasury. (Ten pillars room) but the queen interfered and objected, and said that we should preserve our independent and should not waste the money, like that of money thrown away in the river. Most of the nobles agreed with her proposal. Thus, the Raja sent a letter through the messenger to his commander-in-chief, directing him to bring the head of the commander in chief of the Dogra's army; otherwise you would loss your head. When the Ladakhi army got the order beyond their expectation, they became very upset. But Kalon Pangkhapa tactfully encouraged them and made them ready for the war as a result, when the Dogra's envoy reached in the Ladakhi camp, to receive the money as per the promise. But they were treacherously seized and thrown away from the Darket Bridge into Nallah Wakha.

When Zorawar observed the courages of the opponent and awfully cold in the region, he thought to return back the army at Kartsey to spend the winter months. Thus, he deployed about 500 soldiers at Pashkyum and the rulers of Sod and Pashkyum were held responsible for supply of essential commodities. He took rest of the army with himself and went back to Sankoo, and remained there during the whole winter season. Mourup Stanzin was with him and performed best political services for the Dogras. He arranged the essential commodities and ponies, etc., for loading purposes and motivated the people to be loyal and submit to the Dogra rulers.

Neither the Ladakhies followed the Dogras, nor did they attack them during the whole winter. Some of the Dogra soldiers stationed at Pashkyum and the rest at Sankoo. Where as the Ladakhies were taking rests at Mulbe. However, they recruited some more soldiers.

Wazir Zorawar Singh, got completed the construction of Suru fort during the winter and kept the soldiers at different locations. Now the winter was almost over and Dogras marched towards Ladakh, under the guidance of Mourup Stanzin. Since the Ladakhies never attacked the Dogras during the winter period; now in summer it was impossible for the Ladakhies to counter them. When the Ladakhi army came to know at Mulbe that Zorawar Singh along with his army has reached at Pashkyum, they left Mulbe and reached at Bodh-Kharbu. After consolidating the region of Sod and Pashkyum, Wazir marched towards Mulbe. Here the Kalon of Mulbe Tsewang Namgyal and Raja Azam Khan of Wakha tried to create obstruction but they could not stop the Dogra army. Wazir left Mulbe and reached at Bodh-Kharboo, where as the Ladakhi army returned to Leh. Usually, like an introducer of the Dogras the Ladakhies marched ahead of two halting places. When the Dogra army reached at Bodh-Kharboo, there was a terror in the mind of the Ladakhies. Some people from Lamayuru came to the Wazir along with a horse and some money as tribute and to express the loyalty to the Dogra ruler. Wazir was overjoyed and a soldier was deployed with them in advance for security. When Wazir arrived at Lamayuru, some people from Tingmogang came to the Wazir to express their loyality along with two horses and some money as tribute. They were also provided with a soldier for their security. It is not out of place to mention here that the following rulers were ruling over little Tibet, i.e. Baltistan, during this period.

1. Skardo Raja Ahmad Shah Maghpon.
2. Parkuta Raja Ghulam Shah Maghpon.
3. Tolti Raja Ahmad Khan Maghpon.
4. Kartaksha Raja Ali Sher Khan Maghpon.
5. Khapulo Raja Doulat Ali Khan Yabgo.
6. Keres Raja Khurram Khan Yabgo.
7. Shighar Raja Haider Khan Amacha
8. Rongdo Raja Ali Khan Maghpon.
9. Astor Raja Jabbar Khan Maghpon.

Raja Ali Sher Khan was the nephew and son-in-law of Raja Ahmad Shah, but there was a political difference between the two rulers. As a result for his own existence, Raja Ahmad Shah invaded Kharmang. He mobilized a huge army from the whole Baltistan and invaded Kharmang under the command of his elder son and crown prince Shah Murad. Ali Sher Khan was badly defeated, he left the Kartakhsha palace and during the night he run away lonely towards Ladakh. Shah Murad captured the fort and occupied all the valuable goods possessed by Shah Murad. Since the wife of Raja Ali Sher Khan was the real sister of Shah Murad, so he abstained to harm the queen or her children. There was a shrine inside the Kartaksha fort, where some of the goods was kept by Raja Ali Sher Khan. Because of greedness, Shah Murad removed all the goods from the shrine. It is said that Shah Murad fell ill in Kharmang itself, and died few days after arrival in Skardo. The religious minded Balties consider it the injustice and disgrace showed by Shah Murad towards the shrine, but its impact was not restricted to Shah Murad only, and the great revolution, which occurred in the whole Baltistan was the result of this event. Since Raja Ali Sher Khan arrived at Leh and requested Raja Tundup Namgyal for military assistance. The request was under consideration, when the news of the Dogras arrival at Suru, under the command of Wazir Zorawar Singh was heard, and the situation changed. The political strategy of Raja Ali Sher Khan is praiseworthy. He wanted to have an agreement with Wazir Zorawar Singh. Therefore, he deputed his half brother, Wazir

Nagtalupa Ghulam Hussain and his Personal Assistant Akhon Fazle Ali to Purig, to meet the Wazir, thereby; he developed a relation with the Government of Jammu from that very day. This event has not been mentioned in the Ladakhi chronicles, but Raja Ali Sher Khan has mentioned it in detail, in his autobiography. According to him, the Wazir replied positively, and said, "From today onwards, you are a trustworthy person of the Government of Jammu." If possible, depute the Raja of Ladakh to greet us. Those events which are revealed later, probably is due to the inter mediation of Raja Ali Sher Khan, but could not be ascertain and verified. Since a page of the book is missing.

It is also not known that what were the conditions with regards to military assistance, between the Wazir and Ali Sher Khan, and when he returned to Kharmang from Ladakh.

However, it is expected that the accord, between the Wazir and Raja Ali Sher Khan, for the conquest of Baltistan wase executed at this occasion. It is to be revealed in detail.

Wazir was at Lamayuru, when the messenger of Ladakh Raja arrived there, with a letter.

Revealing that for last eight months we were trying to defend our sovereignty, but we failed. Now if the Wazir give the assurance that he will not interfere unnecessarily in the administration of the Raja. Then he will personally come to the Wazir to finalize the conditions of the agreement. Wazir agreed the proposal immediately, and replied that the Raja should not worry. Our main purpose is that the Raja should submit to the Government of Jammu and arrange to pay a fixed amount as tribute.

When the Wazir had got as far as Nyurla, he met the representatives from the villages of Alchi, Likir, and Nemo, who all brought presents and did homage to Zorawar and he promised to protect them in the mean time Raja Tundup Namgyal arrived at Bazgo, and wished to meet the Wazir. Wazir came to the Raja along with Mehta Basti Ram and hundred Dogra soldiers. The Raja greeted the Wazir whole-heartedly. Later all the Dogra soldiers came here and stayed here for 10 days. The peace negotiation had been formally approved by both the parties. Then it was decided, that Wazir along with some soldiers should come to Leh to finalize the negotiation there on reaching Leh, Wazir went to the palace to meet the Raja. At the time of the meeting the crown prince Tsewang Rafstan was also there. Wazir made a present of 100 rupees to the crown prince Gyalshas, which he swung round the young man's head. Chhogsphurul was about seventeen years old at that time; he was ignorant by this tradition, so he mistook this act of goodwill for an attack and humiliation and drew his sword on seeing this companion of Gyalshas also drew their sword. Then also the by standing Dogra soldiers also drew their swords. The Raja became frightened to see the situation and requested the Wazir with folded hands, that you should not mind for the misbehavior of the boy. He at once removed Gyalshas and his companions from the scene. Consequently, all the Dogra soldiers arrived at Leh, the next morning.

After a long discussion, it was finally decided that the Raja will pay a sum of rupees 50,000 as war expenses, besides an annual tribute of rupees 9,000 has to pay to the Kingdom of Jammu. As so much money could not possibly be procured in Leh, it was arranged that only 37,000 rupees were to be paid at once in cash and jewels, 6000 rupees after one year and 7,000 rupees after four months. On the above conditions, the kingdom of Ladakh was restored to Raja Tundup Namgyal and Wazir returned back from Ladakh.

All the Ladakhi war prisoners, including Mourup Stanzin, who were arrested earlier, were released conditionally, that they would be loyal to the Dogras. The Wazir, neither built a fort in Ladakh nor deployed any army. He appointed Munshi Daya Ram as representative of Jammu kingdom in the court of the Raja of Ladakh, and he along with the all the army returned back. While returning he restored the territories of Pashkyum and Sod to the concern Rajas, where as they have to pay some tributes to the Dogras. After making these arrangements, Wazir went back in to the Suru valley. Here, keeping in view his past services to the Dogras, he restored all the areas from Tambis to Pharona to the Raja of Tambis

Gyapacho Chhagdor Namgyal. Hereafter, he got completed the construction of Suru fort and appointing Nidhan Singh as Kardar of Suru he went to Zangskar. Wazir Zorawar Singh had conquered Zangskar, before his Ladakh invasion and got constructed a fort there. He deployed a Thanedar along with some soldiers there. During the time when Wazir was busy in conquering Ladakh, the people of Zagskar revolted against the Dogras. Hence, when the Wazir did the arrangements in Suru, he turned towards Zangskar to suppress the rebbelion. Therefore, he decided to precede Jammu from Suru via Zangskar and Padar. Since Wazir had not been deployed an army at Ladakh. Therefore, after his departure from Ladakh, the Ladakhies did efforts to be independent. It is said that Raja Tundup Namgyal was against this proposal but his queen and crown prince Chhogsphurul were the instigator. Rani suggested to Kalon Pangkhapa that the annual tribute, as promised should not be paid at any cost, and after mobilizing the Ladakhi army should follow the Wazir. The properties were confiscated from doubtful people who were considered loyal to the Dogras. Munshi Daya Ram was also teased. He sent a secret message of the changed behaviour of the Ladakhies to the Wazir, through the Raja of Tambis Gyapacho Chhagdor Namgyal, who had been in Leh at that time. Wazir got the message at Rangdum. He became very upset to know the situation. He immediately reached at Zangskar and the crises were settled without any military struggle. He removed the Raja Zangskar from the government and granted him the estate of Zangla and established the Dogra rule in the country. Rupees three and half were imposed as tax to every household, which they accepted gladly.

The main purpose of Wazir to come Zagskar was the conquest of Padar a province of Chamba state. After its conquest he was having another rout from Jammu to Ladakh. Since Wazir had to go back to Ladakh, therefore he deputed Wazir Lakhpat along with a group of soldiers to accomplish this task and he himself returned back to Ladakh, after making the necessary arrangements of Zangskar. To travel Ladakh via Suru and Pashkyum was not so safe. First, it was a very long route and secondly, there was possible attack of the Ladakhies at the gorge of Lamayuru. Therefore, he was in search of a short cut rout, where there is no danger of attack from the Ladakhies. He was in a fix, when one local inhabitant Mipham Sata took the responsibility to guide through a safest route. Wazir gave him reward and promised to grant him an estate, if the rout found satisfactory. Under his guidance, Wazir marched for Ladakh, along with the army from Zangskar via Shon-Shadi. This we call as Ladakh expedition No. 2.

WAZIR ZORAWAR SINGH'S LADAKH EXPEDITION

Under these circumstances Wazir marched from Padum the capital of Zangskar and via Kharnak and Sang, he along with his army reached at Miroo on the 10th day. When the Ladakhies, beyond their expectation, came to know about this event, became very anxious. Raja Tundup Namgyal at that time was at village Shay, celebrating the "Shubla" (Harvest festival) along with the members of the royal family. Out of fear, he along with his courtiers and nobles reached at Chushot to greet the Wazir. In the meantime, Chhogsphurul, who was the instigator of these crises, left Shay along with his two queens Sonam Paklkit and Zahra Khatoon via Gyamtsa to Hunder Dok. His first queen Skalzang Dolma was pregnant, so she stayed at the royal palace of Shay. The mother queen runs away towards Tangtsey. Chhogsphurul reached at Tangtsey, via Nubra. Since Sonam palkit was pregnant; hence, she stayed at Tangtsey. Chhogsphurul, his mother and one of the Queen Zahra Khatoon proceeded to Anlay, where from they went to Spiti. It is said, that from Spiti, Chhogsphurul went to Shimla, and both the mother and son complained before the Nawab Governor General Bahadur Hind, against the Maharaja Jammu for capturing his country, and requested for the help. He replied that the King of Lahore is a friend of British Government. We can't provide help against him, the time will come, and that Ladakh will also be a part of British Government. At that time we will return your country to you. At the movement, wait and see. You will be provided with all facilities. But because of unfavorable acclimatization, Chhogsphurul died very soon. Later, his mother also died.

When Zahra Khatoon was alone, she returned back to Ladakh along with the ashes of her husband. Here at Matho, Queen Sonam Palkit has possessed 50 per cent of the estate. The rest 50 per cent was given to her. She occupied the estate for a long time. Later, she married and finally migrated to Pashkyum to his brother Mohammad Ali and died there.

When Raja Tundup Namgyal reached before the Wazir, he humbly bowed hand folded before Zorawar and expressed his sorrow for what had happened. The Wazir said, "You failed to fulfill the promise. Although we conquered your country with only 10,000 men, we did not place a single man of our own over your country; and never interfered in your sovereignty; and this is the way you show your gratitude!" The Raja was much ashamed, and requested, that I will be truly faithful and obedient in future. The next day the Dogra army accompanied by the Raja reached at Leh, where the balance of 13,000 rupees for the expenses of the war was demanded, and the additional expenses of the second expedition was also demanded. Raja did not possess any cash now. It was paid by taking the property of the royal families. But there were the additional expenses of the new war and to meet them Steward Gonbo offered all sort of things, like the utensils of gold and silver, tea and wool, etc., which were accepted by the Wazir, as nothing better could be got out of the country. After the crises, the Wazir had to arrange matters on a new principle. Tundup Namgyal could not be trusted with the government any longer; he was dismissed and the village of Stok was granted as estate for his personal maintenance, and the Stok palace for his residence. Under these circumstances, the Namgyal Kingdom of Ladakh was ended in 1834 AD. Then arose the question, who will take the place of Tundup Namgyal as Raja. There was no person in the royal family. Chhogsphurul was the rightful successor to the throne, but he fled away. His elder son was just few days old at that time. Leh Lonpo Mourup Stanzin was a relative of the deposed Raja, and before becoming the prisoner of war, he was a minister and trusted noble of the Raja. He had performed good services to the Dogras during the first expedition, as a prisoner, that is why; he was ill-treated by the deposed Raja. Wazir nominated him to rule over Ladakh, and Bazgo Kalon Tsewang Stobdan was appointed his prime minister. Eighteenth thousand rupees was fixed as annual tribute. He got constructed a fort at Skara on the bank of Nalah Sangto, and 300 soldiers were deployed there under the command of Dalil Singh Thanedar. Then he went to Jammu, taking along with him Mourup Stanzin's son and several other people as hostages.

When the plot of revolt was hatched in Ladakh, the idea was also transmitted to Purig. The people of Purig were assured that a huge army from Lahsa is moving towards Ladakh for military assistance. It will be difficult for the Wazir to counter them. The good hearted rulers and nobles of Purig never waited, to reach the Tibetan army in Ladakh; instead they revolted against the Dogras, as soon as the Wazir along with the Dogra army departed from Suru towards Zangskar. The Raja of Sod recaptured the fort of Pasri-Khar, and the Dogra soldiers posted there were assassinated. Beside, Choki Chhubar Khar was besieged. The people of Suru-Kartse also got killed the Dogra soldiers and besieged the fort. Wazir came to know about these events at Lama-Yuru. He hurriedly arrived at Pashkyum. The estates and administrative powers of all the Rajas of Purig were ceased. Thereby, Rahim Khjan Raja Tikche, Azam Khan Raja Wakha, Kalon Mulbe, Mohammad Ali Khan Raja Pashkyum, Salam Khan Raja Sod and Chhagdor Namgyal Raja Tambis were deposed, and Rahim Khan Brother of Mohammad Ali Khan was appointed as Kalon of the whole region from Fotola to Daras and Suru. This Rahim Khan performed his best services, during the 1st Ladakh expedition of Wazir and not participated in the revolt later. For this very reason he was honoured. After making the administrative arrangements up to Suru, Wazir went back to Jammu via Zangskar and Padar. In the meantime, Padar was already conquered by Wazir Lakhpat on the way, he made the suitable arrangement of Padar and reached Jammu.

On his arrival at Jammu, Raja Gulab Singh gave a good respect and encouraged him. Deputed his "Dewan" (prime minister) to receive him. When he arrived in the court, he was hugged and honored. He ordered that Wazir should be treated like the members of the royal family and the royal salute "Jai Deva" should be used for him. It is true, that because of his victorious services, he was due for such honors. Wazir remained in Jammu for five years and later he again came to Ladakh, which is revealed in the next chapter.

7

Wazir Zorawar Singh's Expedition No. 3 Annexation of Ladakh and Purig and Conquest of Baltistan

After the return of Wazir Zorawar Singh from Ladakh, Raja Mourup Stanzin did well for sometime, later, he got indulged in luxurious activities. He got married to the princess of Pashkyum, and got constructed a beautiful palace at Murtse to accommodate her. Where, he did the arrangement for polo and other entertainments. Thereby he took much interest in his new queen and song and dance and paid less attention towards the administration of the country. Consequently, the power came in the hands of his ministers, like Kalon Tsewang Stobdan, Pangkhapa and Gyapacho Tsewang Shes and they misruled the country. In the meantime Col. Man Singh, who was the Subedar of Kashmir deputed by the Lahore Government, plotted against the Dogras in connivance with the prominent people of Purig. He deputed one of his employees Fateh Singh Jogi, along with some other persons to Kargil, and motivated the people of Purig to revolt against the Dogras. Kalon Rahim Khan easily became the prey of the Sikhs, he revolted against the Dogras with the hope that the Sikh promised to afford all sort of military assistance to him. He took Raja Mourup Stanzin and some of his ministers into confidence and asked them to request the Government of Lhasa for military assistance. He managed the assistance from

Skardo too. In short, he did the efforts to mobilize all the regions of Purig and Ladakh to revolt against the Dogras and get the assistance from Kashmir, Lhasa and Baltistan. In Purig the revolt took the practical shape, as Nidhan Singh Kardar of Drass and Kargil and some Dogra soldiers were assassinated at Karket. Beside the payment of tribute and taxes from Purig and Ladakh were ceased. In Ladakh the Dogra Thanedar appointed by the Wazir was humiliated. When Wazir Zorawar Singh came to know in Jammu about the new circumstances, he prepared himself for the third expedition in the summer of 1896 Bikrami according to the 1839 AD. There was a chaos and crisis in Paddar also, since the people of Chamba killed and imprisoned the Dogra soldiers and recaptured Paddar. Hence, Wazir marched towards Ladakh, along with 5,000 Dogra soldiers. As soon as he reached Kishtawar, he went to Paddar. He plundered the area and recaptured Chhatargarh and renamed it as Gulabgarh. He built a fort and deployed Dogra soldiers there. Later, he came back to Kishtawar and via Darun and Suru went to Ladakh.

Mohammad Shah the son of Raja Ahmad Shah of Skardo came to the Wazir, during his first expedition, probably he was in Zangskar and complained that his father declined him as successor and made Mohammad Ali Khan, the son of the second wife as crown prince and mentally tortured him. Since, as per the local tradition, it was the right of the elder son to succeed. Hence, he requested for military assistance. At that time Wazir was busy in Ladakh. So, he didn't want to indulge himself in other problems. Moreover he didn't want to miss the chance of capturing Baltistan. He assured Mohammad Shah, that you have come forward to help the Jammu Kingdom; hence, you will be provided full support. He made the arrangement of his accommodation at Suru. He stayed for one or two years in Suru and than he was sent to Ladakh, where he stayed with ease. But later when Raja Mourup Stanzin and his ministers were fed up with the Jammu Kingdom, they revolted against the Dogras, and wanted to make friendship with Ahmad Shah to grind their own axe. Instead of supporting Mohammad Shah they send a message to Ahmad Shah to depute his men to arrest the fugitive son, and have no objection in doing so. Ahmad Shah did the same he got arrested his fugitive son from Ladakh and imprisoned in Skardo, where he was tortured. When Wazir Zorawar Singh came to know about this event, he made the determination to teach a lesson to all these mischiefs. First of all he wrote a letter to Raja Ahmad Shah, revealing that your son came for the help of Jammu Government. You have interfered and invaded Ladakh through your men and had arrested him forcibly. If you fail to release and sent him back immediately to our camp, the Dogra soldiers will forcibly enter your capital and release him from your prison. But Raja Ahmad Shah didn't respond to it.

On arriving Suru, Wazir decided to precede Ladakh via Zangskar. He had to wait few days in Suru and Zangskar for a favourable climate. When the Ladakhies came to know that the Wazir has reached Zangskar with the intention to come to Leh. The plans of the mischievous failed. Leaving the idea of revolt aside, they began to think for self-defense. Out of fear, Raja Mourup Stanzin along with a group of people marched towards Zangskar and Spiti. He was of the opinion that if he could have a compromise with the Wazir, then he will attend the Wazir's camp and will express that he has come to receive him here otherwise if he found the situation unfavourable then he would fled to Spiti. Really, the situation was unfavourable, so instead of proceeding to Zangskar, he fled to Spiti. But because of his ill-luck, Wazir came to know this well in time he was followed by the Dogras and before crossing the border of Spiti he was overpowered. When he found no chance of fleeing, he made the last struggle before surrender and some people were killed from both sides. Finally, he was arrested at Taboo. Then he was locked up in Leh prison along with his companions. In the summer of 1897 Bikrami, according to 1840 AD. Wazir entered Ladakh for the third time and punished all those people who participated in the disturbance. Mourup Stanzin was dethroned and imprisoned in Leh fort, his property was ceased to pay the dues of tribute. Similarly, fines were imposed to Kalon Bazgo and Gyapacho, etc.

Now the time had come to annex Ladakh properly with the Jammu kingdom. Hence, he appointed Mian Magna as Thanedar and made him the administrator of the country. Onpo Rigzin, who is later known as Gobind Ram was appointed as Kalon for his assistance. Raja Tundup Namgyal was reinstated as nominal king, so as to keep continue the royal linage and the royal palaces and the seat of the Raja were handed over to him. As soon as he did the arrangements properly in Ladakh, he left for Kargil and Skardo. In the meantime the Rajas of Kargil did efforts to get the military assistance from Kashmir but neither did they receive help from Kashmir nor from Ladakh. So all Kargilies became silent and Kalon Rahim Khan fled to Skardo.

ANNEXION OF PURIG AND CONQUEST OF BALTISTAN

During the short period, the Ladakhies proved that they are not the men to rest in peace under the Jammu Government. Therefore, Zorawar hatched the plan to exploit the Ladakhies against the Baltis so as to keep Ladakh free from any form of revolt against the Dogra rulers. Therefore, Zorawar decided to do an expedition against Baltistan, pretending to come for the rescue of Mohammad Shah son of Raja Skardo. There is a contradictory statement about the number of soldiers, but it is considered that it was not more then seven or eight thousand, including the porters and warriors. The old Ladakhi General Kalon Pankhapa was appointed as the Commander, and the old Raja Tundup Namgyal was also deployed with him. In short wazir marched from Ladakh to Skardo including the Ladakhi soldiers, along with his own army. When they reached at Hanu, Wazir kept the Ladakhi Army under the Dogra commanders Mohiuddin Shah and Shahji, and deputed them via Hanula, Chhorbat and Khapulo. And he himself went to Garkono, along with the Dogra army. During those days the route from Leh to Skardo was via Garkono, Morol, and Kharmang. The present Olding route was not in existence at that time. At Garkono Wazir crossed the Indus River and reached at Pasri Khar Sot. Here he punished the people of Purig, who revolted against the Dogras. He annexed all the regions of Purig and appointed Dogra Thanedars at Kargil,

Daras and Suru. He also deployed a required number of soldiers with them. After making the administrative arrangements of Purig, Wazir mobilized army and porters from the region. Then Wazir crossed the mountains from Pasri-Khar and got down at Chey Chey-Thang and was ready to move towards Skardo. When the news of Wazir's invasion came to Skardo, Raja Ahmad Shah deputed his army at Morol and Chhorbat, to stop the way of the enemy. He deployed the soldiers from Keres and Khapulo at Chhorbat under the command of Yostrang Karim. The soldiers from the village of Rongdo to Kharmang were placed under the command of two brothers Botopa Wazir Ghulam Hassan and Wazir Ghulam Hussain and deployed at Morol, at the border of Baltistan to counter Wazir Zorawar Singh. It is difficult to reveal the correct number of the soldiers, but it is expected that it was about twenty thousand, including the warriors and the porters. The Balti army stationed themselves near Morol on a high plateau, before Wazir Zorawar reached at Chey Chey-Thang. The route of Chey Chey-Thang is just adjacent to this plateau after crossing the Indus on its right side, as its left side is closed because of the merger of Suru River. So, the Balti army stationed at such a place where no other passage is possible. This field is now known as "Thamo Khoni Thang", i.e. battle field. On the top of this field the Balti army of Skardo built Morchas for ambush, and they stopped the route which leads to the Wangko pass, which made the advancement of Zorawar impossible. Zorawar had to face two problems; first the river and secondly the enemy. Though it was the winter season but the whole river was not frozen, so as to cross the river on the surface of ice. Moreover, it was too difficult to construct a bridge under the threat of bullet from the enemy. Because of these problems Wazir had to stay at Chey Chey-Thang for two weeks, and had to face the shortage of ration and other provisions. It was awfully cold; hence, the army was discouraged. But because of the courageous and good strategy of Wazir, he was able to overcome all these problems. One night Wazir deputed Mehta Basti Ram along with some soldiers to look for a possible way to cross the river. But the water of the river was not frozen at any place. In the mean time the Dard of Village Garkono suggested that the part of the river which has not frozen can be made frozen to ice by adopting a local method and it would be possible to cross the river through the artificial ice. Therefore, in front of Nalah Chethang, just below the Wangko pass where Wazir Ghulam Hussain was stationed along with his army to stop the advancement of Wazir, the water was frozen from the both sides of the bank of river Indus and a very small portion of the river was open. They joined both the ends with some logs. It is said, that Raja Ali Sher Khan of Kartakshah made the correspondence secretly with the Wazir at Chey Chey-Thang. Though he had deputed his soldiers with the Balti army to counter Wazir at Thamo Khoni Thang and secretly he helped Wazir, so whoever may win the battle, he would not be in loss, and he also contributed in preparing the frozen artificial bridge. The time and the venue of the bridge was decided in collaboration between the people from Chey Chey-Thang and the people of Raja Ali Sher Khan from Morol. The pieces of ice which floats in the river during the winters got blocked and froze on the logs. The pieces of ice were joined together with one another and due to awfully cold of the winter; it became a sheet of ice, over the open space within some hours. Now it was possible to pass on over the frozen surface of the river. Wazir and his soldiers became very happy on this success. Before dawn, a group of Dogra soldiers under the command of Mehta Basti Ram passed through the newly created ice bridge and attacked the Balti soldiers of Wazir Ghulam Hussain. It is said, that the creation of the bridge and crossing the river was made with a good strategy that the Balti soldiers could not know about it, unless Mehta Basti Ram reached at Wangko pass. At that time the Balties were sleeping, when suddenly the Dogra soldiers appeared, and Wazir Ghulam Hussain himself was busy in ablution. He hurriedly arranged the army. It was a sudden attack by the Dogras and the bunkers became useless for the Balties. Though they fought hand to hand bravely and almost killed all the Dogra soldiers. Wazir was watching the scene from Chey Chey-Thang. He deputed reinforcement; Wazir Ghulam Hassan was killed in this battle. Because of his death and arrival of reinforcement, the Balties were discouraged and fled away and joined the soldiers of "Thamo Khon". Now the Dogras captured the Wangko pass, and they were free to cross the river without any hindrance. Wazir Zorawar Singh attacked the Balti soldiers of "Thamo Khon" along with all his soldiers. Since the Balties were on the top inside the "Morchas", they fired heavily on the Dogras, but Wazir Zorawar Singh deployed a group of Dogra soldiers on the top of the hill, through a narrow route. They destroyed the posts of the Balties and they were compelled to come out of their bunkers. They could not counter the Dogras in hand to hand fight. Finally, when many Balties got killed in the battle they fled away and the Dogras captured the battle field.

The exact number of casualty couldn't be ascertained but it is believed that almost one thousand Balties got killed in this battle including Commander Wazir Ghulam Hassan and many prominent Balti Officers. Wazir Ghulam Hussain and Wazir Sultan Beg were fleeing from the battlefield of Rongdo but before arriving at Morol they also got killed. The grave of Wazir Ghulam Hassan still exists at Thamo Khon and that of his brother Wazir Hussain at Morol. About Raja Ali Sher Khan, it is believed that his men who were on the side of Balti soldiers were secretly instructed by him not to fight with the Dogras but to keep themselves away from fighting. Therefore, they acted according to this instruction. As Zorawar Singh entered Morol beating the drums of his victory of Thamo Khon and chasing the fleeing army reached Hamzagund. This event happened around first of Phagun 1896 Bikrami. This battle was a deciding factor in the conquest of Baltistan. Though the Balties fought another war near Hamzagon but their retaliation was meek and ineffective the details of which follows as such.

Just after Morol the route passes through "Sanjak", which means soft sand dune, this dune is formed over a period of time, when the river gets stagnant at a plain on its course and takes the shape of a big lake, all the sands carried off by the river gets deposited here thus forming this dune. This dune is formed right from below Skardo, where the river got blocked because of the falling of a huge mountain, till Ladakh. The route again goes down to the bank of river. After this route passes through a tough terrain on which a footbridge is being built with wooden logs. This was destroyed by the Baltis. And they built their post in the Nullah right after this bridge and stayed there. The next day when Zorawar reached there he found that the route was closed due to the broken bridge. Visibly it was a huge bottleneck for him but after the victory of Thamo Khon the situation for him had changed and the inhabitants of Kharmang region were happily ready to serve the Wazir. People of Hamzagon suggested the Wazir to abandon the usual route and should crossover the hill from the area where the bridge is broken. Therefore, the Wazir along with his army marched on top of the hill and descended right there where Baltis had set up their bunkers. Because of the fact that the Wazir came from the top of the hill, the Baltis failed to counter him and ran away. Thereafter, he had to face no obstruction in the way, till he reached Skardo. During the first Ladakh expedition of Wazir Zorawar Singh, relation developed between him and Raja Ali Sher Khan, who has already been mentioned. After returning from Ladakh, he again became the ruler like that of the past, but due to the invasion of Raja Ahmad Shah to Kartakshah, he could not recover the humiliation and loss of property. To take the revenge, he never minded to sacrifice his own freedom. Probably, he wouldn't have done this, but there was no chance of compromise with Ahmad Shah. Nor the entire force of Baltistan had the strength to stop the invasion of Zorawar Singh. He made no mistake and took the advantage of the situation, as far as possible. Whereas, he deputed his soldiers along with Balti army under the command of Trangfa Abdul Ali to fight against Wazir Zorawar Singh, and was in the good book of Raja Ahmad Shah. On the other hand, he made secret correspondence with Wazir Zorawar Singh at Chey Chey-Thang and helped him secretly in the battle field and to cross the river, and was able to win the confidence of Wazir Zorawar Singh. I came to know in Skardo, that with the consultation of Wazir Zorawar Singh, the inhabitants of Kharmang were wearing a distinguish badge, and it had been decided that the Dogras would not harm the inhabitants with such batches. Therefore, neither these people attacked the Dogras nor the Dogras harassed them. Because of this strategy the soldiers of Kharmang came out of the battle field without any injury or loss. Besides, Raja Ali Sher Khan himself came at Hamza Gund to greet the Wazir and assured to extend all sort of cooperation to him. In recognition to his services the Wazir assured them that he would not interfere in the affairs of Kartaksha. This promise is almost still continuing. Raja Ali Sher Khan reached at Kharmang along with Wazir Zorawar Singh and performed properly the responsibilities of a host. And because if the intervention of Raja Ali Sher Khan, Raja Ahmad Khan Tolti along with Wazir Parkuta came to see Zorawar to express their loyalty. After four days of his departure from Kharmang, Wazir reached at Gol. The Ladakhi army who had proceeded from Hanu, via Chhorbat and Khapulo also reached at Gol and joined the Wazir's army. The travel via Hanula was also full of difficulties because of heavy snowfall and awful cold. But the Ladakhies are habitual of it. No other race of the world could show such courage. All the soldiers crossed the Hanula successfully. Though Raja Ahmad Shah had made full preparation to stop the army from crossing, his most confident person Yustrong Karim along with the soldiers of Keres, Khapolu and a few from Skardo were ready to fight. But the luck favoured Wazir Zorawar Singh and the nature helped him. Though Raja Mehdi Ali Khan of Khapulo had been imprisoned by Raja Ahmad Shah but the real heir of the throne Raja Doulat Ali Khan was at Nubra. When Wazir Zorawar Singh conquered Ladakh, the mode of administration changed. On the one hand he deputed his cousin brother Haider Khan to mobilize the people of Khapulo in his favour; on the other hand he did efforts to develop the relation with Wazir Zorawar Singh. When Wazir's army marched towards Hanu, in the mean time Doulat Ali Khan made the strategy and mobilized the people, through Haider Khan. When the Ladakhi army arrived near Poyon, Raja Doulat Ali Khan also marched from Nubra towards Poyon. Yustrong Karim stationed all the soldiers on a terrain between Kostang and Poyon, to counter the Wazir's army. When the Dogra army under the command of Mohiuddin Shah reached at Poyon, they stationed in the fort. In the mean time Raja Doulat Ali Khan left Siksa and met the Dogra officers at Poyon. His confident man Haider Khan deceived Yustrong Karim, by telling that I know about the topography of the area very well, I will go forward along with the half army and after crossing the river, I will reach Siksa via Poyon, where from crossing the river again, I will attack the Dogras at Poyon from the Siksa side and you attack them from Poyon side. Thus, it would be very difficult for the Wazir's army to counter the Baltis from both sides and they would be easily captured by us. Yustrong Karim could not understand this plot hatched by Haider Khan. He divided his army in two groups and Haider along with a huge army of Khapulo region arrived at Poyon fort. And after greeting Doulat Khan and Dogra officers he assured them to be loyal and faithful. This changed the whole situation and Doulat Ali Khan, who had been in house arrest for last 13 years, got a ray of hope to be a ruler again. When Yustrong Karim reached at Poyon, he got the message of Haider Khan, that we are loyal to Raja Doulat Ali Khan and he has accepted the authority of the Dogras, and we does not want to keep any relation with you. Yustrong Karim gunned down the messenger and after doing so, he returned back to Khapulo along with the soldiers of Skardo. The soldiers of Khapulo had been mobilized to counter the Wazir's army, but the joined with Raja Doulat Ali Khan and the Ladakhi army along with the army of Khapulo entered Khapulo. Since all the inhabitants of Khapulo showed their confidence in Doulat Ali Khan. Hence, Mehmood Shah alias Mehdi Ali Khan had to step down as ruler. And Raja Doulat Ali Khan captured the fort and once again became the ruler. Yustrong Karim marched from Poyon and positioned at Keres. The Ladakhi army took rest at Khapulo for some days and became the guest of Raja Doulat Ali Khan and moved forward. Raja Doulat Ali Khan performed his best services to the Dogras. Yustrong Karim positioned at Keres and fought with the Ladakhi army for two days but he came to know about the arrival of Wazir at Parkuta, he left the fort silently, crossed the river and accompanied the Ladakhi army. They crossed the river and attended before Wazir Zorawar Singh and assured him their full support and loyalty. In short Wazir Zorawar Singh entered Skardo without any interruption, along with Ladakhi and Dogra Joint army. All the rulers of the area where from his army passed were with him, and the Wazir of Doghonipa Bono Raja Mohammad Shah, who was at Ladakh during his arrest also accompanied him along with his supporters.

When the Wazir reached at Skardo, he found Raja Ahmad Shah fortified in the Kharpochhey fort. On the north of Skardo town, there is a high mountain, on the bank of Indus River. The mountain is formed in such a way, that nobody could climb the mountain from all sides. But on the east there is a small plateau, where the fort had been built. The wall of the fort had been built with big boulders. There were two passages to the fort, one in the east for communication and second towards north for domestic use and fetching water from the spring or river. A zigzag route on the rock leads to the fort for the common use and the entire passage was under the visible range of the fort. Except these there was no other route to reach the fort. The domestic route towards north leads to the spring and river was covered and could not be seen from outside. Beside it was not possible to reach at this route from the Skardo town or river. Above the fort on the top of the rock, is a small plateau. It has two routes to reach there. One is from inside the fort and another from the west, where the New Rangga village is situated. A tower had erected there to stop the route for enemy. This tower had been built at such a place wherefrom few people can create hindrance to proceed further, and there is no other route to climb the rock except it. Moreover the fort cannot be captured except from the said plateau. This fort was considered unbeatable in those days. Wazir surrounded the fort and it was very limited because both the routes of communication from east and west got blocked. Though the attack on the fort was continued but it was useless. Within fifteen days they were not able to capture the besieged; hence, efforts were made to act according to a new strategy, through Raja Ali Sher Khan. A Muslim officer Syed Mohiuddin Shah of Zorawar's army also joined Raja Ali Sher Khan in the plan. It is said that Raja Ali Sher Khan took the vow before Raja Ahmad Shah that nothing would happen with you. You come to the Wazir and greet him. Raja Ahmad Shah came out of the fort, to meet Wazir with confidence but was arrested. Thus, Wazir captured Skardo deceptively without any resistance. Wazir Zorawar Singh had the victory at the battle field of Thamo Khon, which made the conquest of Little Tibet, i.e. Baltistan very easy. Now the vassal kings of Kartakshah, Tolti, Khapolu, and Keres, etc., became obedience to the Wazir and were with him and the Baltis were fully discouraged after the conquest of Kharpochhey, i.e. Skardo. Therefore, Raja Haider Khan of Shigar and prominent personalities of Chhorbat also came to the Wazir to express their obedience and loyalty. But Raja Ali Khan of Rongdo and Raja Jabbar Khan of Astore did not come to the Wazir. However, before attending them Wazir thought it important to reduce the influence of deposed Raja Ahmad Shah and strengthen the government of his son Mohammad Shah. Therefore, Wazir Hussain Golwala and other courtiers of Raja Ahmad Shah were imprisoned and took all the movable properties of the deposed Raja as tribute and deposited in the government treasury, the total amount was approximately two lac rupees, consisting of cash and other valuable articles like, gold, silver and ornaments, etc. Thus after taking Ahmad Shah in confidence and consolidating his rule, he invaded Rongyul, i.e., Rongdo. Wazir deputed one thousand Dogra soldiers under the command of Mirza Rasool Beg and Mohammad Khan via Kachura, and the Balti soldiers under the command of Dogra officers and Raja of Kharmang via Baghardo Chhary. When, the Dogra soldiers reached at the fort of Rongdo, i.e. Mehendi, they found that Raja Ali Khan had fled away, leaving his fort and country. Hence, the fort was captured without any interruption. Later, they received fifteen thousand rupees as war penalty and reinstated him as ruler of Rongdo. In the mean time Kalon Rahim Khan who had fled from Pashkyum to Skardo. Later, when he came to know about Wazir's Skardo invasion, he left for Rongdo, wherefrom he was trying to proceed towards Gilgit, but he had been arrested and brought before the Wazir. This man had been the instigator of revolt in the Purig area. Wazir inquired him about his misdeeds in presence of the nobles of Ladakh and Baltistan, and finally he had been severely punished. Wazir ordered the executioner to cut off the limbs of the body and to dip the stump at once into the boiling oil, and then the executioner had also to cut off his nose, ears, and tongue and had been left in the field to die. Similarly, other persons of the Purig who were involved in the revolt were severely punished. Rahim Khan could not save his life and while crying, he died after three days. His family members went back to Kargil and the offspring's are still there.

After the conquest of Rongdo, Wazir deputed Mohiuddin Shah to invade Astore, along with five hundred Dogra soldiers and a good number of local soldiers. This army moved via Shakarthang. On knowing about the invasion Raja Jabbar Khan of Astore became fortified. Mohiuddin Shah besieged the fort and the battle continued for 20 days. There was no permanent arrangement of water. To bring water the external passage was blocked by the Dogras and Jabbar Khan was compelled to come out of the fort. Then he was arrested by Mohiuddin Shah. After the conquest of Astore, Mohiuddin Shah came to the Wazir along with Jabbar Khan. And Wazir kept Jabbar Khan as a prisoner for a short period because the Sikh ruler of Kashmir raised objection, that Astore is a territory of Sikh regime and Zorawar Singh has no right to interfere in their territories. Hence, Jabbar Khan was released and went from Skardo. Therefore, Zorawar Singh could not have a political gain from this invasion. However, after few years, the Sikh ruler invaded Gilgit and captured Astore too. Finally, Astore and Gilgit came under the Dogra Ruler of Jammu including Kashmir and the desire of Zorawar Singh was fulfilled.

In the beginning Zorawar Singh stayed in the Matam Sara of Kharidong and the soldiers in the camps. In the mean time he got constructed government quarters known as Ranbir Garh and a temporary fort on a top in the north of Khanqah Syed Mehmood. Later, he stayed there along with the Dogra army. Finally, he got built a very strong fort on the bank of Nallah Satpar, on the top of a hill. One portion of the fort had been completed under his supervision and deployed about one hundred Dogra soldiers there, under the command of Bhagwan Singh Kishtawari, who had been appointed as Thanedar and Bhupat and Mukhtar Khan as his Munshi. When, Wazir consolidated the administration of Baltistan, he left for Leh via Khapolu, in the summer of 1797 Bikrami according to 1840 AD, along with the Dogra and Ladakhi army, the deposed Raja Ahmad Shah, his Wazirs and nobles, and some people of Shigar, who were in the prison.

Since he decided to invade Lhasa, during his stay in Baltistan, therefore, he mobilized the soldiers of Baltistan and kept them under the command of the representative of their concern Rajas. At Khapolu Raja Ali Sher Khan also joined along with the soldiers of Kharmang and Tolti and deployed his brother Haider Khan and Ghulam Ali in the service of Wazir. The Raja Khapulo, Doulat Ali Khan agreed to proceed along with the Wazir. In the mean time the epidemic disease smallpox spread in Khapulo, because of that many soldiers had died. However, Raja Tundup Namgyal had seen many revolutions in his life; he had suffered more than his constitution could stand. Moreover, the long journey had been unbearable for him. When, the smallpox spread in the area, many Ladakhi soldiers were died. Among the nobles first of all Pangkhapa died with smallpox and then Raja Tundup Namgyal met with the same fate, and within a few days he died. His Steward Acho Gonbo was very faithful. Knowing the fact that smallpox is an epidemic disease, he, according to the local tradition, fastened the legs and arms jointly and put the body in a big pot, i.e. "Deeg" and put salt and other local medicines, as to protect the body from decomposing and stinking and closed the lead properly. Then, the corpse was carried to Stok palace, via Nubra, through his servants, where after performing the rituals and prayer, the body was cremated.

Wazir along with the whole army reached Ladakh, via Khapulo, Chhorbat, and Nubra. The first task, which he did in Leh, was the nomination of the successor of Late Raja Tundup Namgyal. Actually Chhogsphurul was the hire to the throne but he fled to Shimla via Spiti and died there. Before his departure to Spiti, the first Queen Skalzang Dolma gave birth to a son. His name was Jigsmet Chhosgi Singgay or in short Jigsmet Namgyal. He was putting up at Shay palace along with his mother. Though, the child was an infant, but he was the heir of the throne after Chhogsphurul and Wazir convened him at Leh along with his mother. He made the arrangement to perform the traditional rituals of succession at the royal palace of Leh. A court was arranged in a room of the palace called "Thagchhen Kongma". All the prominent persons and nobles of Ladakh and Baltistan participated in the function. Wazir got Jigsmet Namgyal ascended the throne with great pomp and show. Though, the dignity of the throne was only by name. Wazir put the turban on the head of Jigsmet Namgyal with his own hand and wore the gown and offered the shield and sword and said that your grand father has died in the service of the Jammu kingdom. I feel sorry for that and you are being made the vassal king in his place and placed on the throne. We would be responsible for your convenience and to look after you in future. Later, Raja Doulat Ali Khan of Khapulo, who had relation with the old regime, offered shield and sword. Similarly, the elites and nobles of Ladakh offered traditional "Khataks" and congratulated him. Now, Wazir began to prepare for his Tibet expedition, after performing the rituals. I got a copy of a note about the expedition of Baltistan, written by an eye-witness, which he has narrated in a very beautiful way, and some events have been revealed in detail, which I could not discard. Earlier, while explaining the events I did not included the notes with the reason, that it is bifurcated in parts, its beauty lost. He had written the notes in Hindi, which is translated as under.

I Ganga Ram Nakashi submit the application in the court of Shri Maharaja Gulab Singh Sahib, that there is no genius person like that of Wazir Zorawar Singh. I shall praise him till my death. He prayed at the temple of Satila Devi and promised, if he wins the battle, he would reconstruct it very strong. Since the Devi came in dream and gave blessings for his triumphant. However keep in mind the regards and respect of Maharaja Gulab Singh and Sochit Singh, and would be successful in every respect. At the movement Wazir promised that he would build a temple of the Devi in Baltistan. Since Wazir stationed at Chey Chey. He gheraoed the Baltis at Tental Watery. First he deputed the Maliks of Murwa under the command of Imam Malik. Zamindar Zafar Lone got prepared the posts. He had been an old and faithful servant of the Jammu Government. He has kept himself and his property for the service of the Jammu regime. Mukhtar and Mohammad Khan both are real brothers. Both went on the other side, along with the Maliks of Murwa. Both the brothers are very loyal. Maizban Khan and other soldiers were deployed with them along with the goods. It was very difficult because of heavy snow fall. They made the arrangement to cross the river. Rahim Khan was the leader of the Bhotis. He was not in a position to attack the Dogras, but because of fear he went across the river, otherwise he would loss his nose and ears. Mehta Basti Ram was convened by the Wazir, and ordered to cross the river and asked to see the possibilities to place the logs over the river for preparing Ice Bridge the people of Nagsen and Padar were deputed with him and ordered that the ice bridge should be get ready during the night. A man came to Wazir Zorawar Singh and said that it is difficult to place the logs and prepare the ice bridge here. Two men who knows to swim, should be deputed with me, so as to cross the river during the night therefore Wazir asked Kamanda resident of Jodhpur to cross the river with the help of cow skin bag and promised to pay 50 rupees as reward, if he succeds. Many other people were deployed with him, and requested him to be careful and keep in mind the dignity of the Dogras. With the folded hands, Mehta Basti Ram also requested to do efforts whole-heartedly. Mehta Basti Ram was able to cross the river through the logs. The first battle with the swords took place at Tatri. Mirza Rasool Beg is a brave and good administrator. He is the Jamadar in the army. He invaded the enemy just after crossing the river. He encouraged he soldiers to climb the hill and asked to be loyal to the regime, that you would be praised in both the world. Rana Jalim Singh of Arnoda and other soldiers are very brave. Samad Khan Jamadar of Pathan soldiers is an able person and his soldiers are also very brave.

All fought bravely with the enemy. Zorawar's servants Kalu Negi, Sokia Kumhar and Gopi shah, etc., followed them. These all people climbed the hill from the opposite side of the river. The Balti soldiers geraod them. When 3,000 Balti soldiers gathered there, our soldiers returned back. Later, they again invaded, and the Baltis had to face lot of human losses. Mian Mutssadi of Raina Rama fought with the sword bravely, and many Baltis got killed. Bhupat Mahan Singh of Kastigarh also killed many Balti soldiers. The cook of the Wazir Damodar is so stupid, that if we demand rice, he will give bread, but he too killed many Baltis like a soldier and enlightened the name of Brahmans. Ten to twenty porters were told to proceed on the other side. They fought with sword at Tatry. Two or three persons were killed in this battle. Dhana Sardar was shot in the belly and died. Bhaikam was his brother. The zamindar of Rajgarh Narban was killed. He was unmarried. Rahim Khan Jamadar was convened and deployed in the battle field. He along with Rana Bhagwan Singh of Badharwah fought bravely with sword and the enemies run away from the battle field. Rana Dilip Singh of Galhyanwala was a dull person but when he had the sword in the hand, use to fight bravely. Mian Mubarik Thanedar Sakta Kishtwar was a young man; he was a very good fighter. Azim Khan Jamadar of Moryan and his brother Saadullah Khan and their army were well prepared with weapon. They fought very bravely during the night along with another army. Mian Mubarik and the two brothers Mahan Singh and Manggal Singh fought courageously, which is praiseworthy. Phinu and Chadta, both were very good fighters. Hundred rupees have been conferred to them as reward. Wazir Laaba, who was along with the Dachhni soldiers against the soldiers of Skardo confiscated the weapons like guns and swords, etc. at village Katni. Kamon Kotwal and Mukhdam Bhago get the welfare news of our soldiers, only 10 killed and 9 injured. The loyal soldiers fought with sword bravely. Wazir Zorawar Singh observed the war on telescope, and found that each soldier has killed at least two enemies the man on telescope only knows, whether it is true or false. Now the Balti soldiers along with their commanders used to run away from the battle field. Many soldiers and Zamindars were got killed. Later, the Dogras attacked at the Morol village. Many soldiers of the enemy were got killed and they became very upset.

First of all, Raja Ali Sher Khan submitted and prayed that should not fight with us, as we are your subjects. Hence, he was conferred with rope of honor. The said Raja invited the Wazir to come at Hamza Gund. So as to have a rest there with ease, since it is the country of Jammu regime and should not worry for any danger. The Raja offered a sword and a gun as good will, and Wazir conferred rope of honor to Haider Khan, in whose village he stayed the night. Both the Rajas accompanied the Wazir. They were given "Kanggan and Kantha", i.e. ornament for the wrist and the pearl-necklace as reward and granted estates. From Hamza Gund the army proceeds for Kharmang. All the soldiers stationed in the village and Wazir stayed in the fort of Raja Ali Sher Khan. All the soldiers went to see the fort. It was lunar eclipse on that day, hence, parties were arranged. We marched from Kharmang and stayed at Mayurdo, the next day traveled on a hilly rout. There were two different routs for the foot soldiers and riders. It was a very dangerous rout that people, out of fear used to call "Ram Ram". From Mayurdo we reached at Parkuta and from Parkuta arrived at Gol and stayed there. Though we were ignorant of the routs of the region but Ali Sher Khan was there to guide us. Some soldiers were deployed to destroy the tower.

When Raja Ahmad Shah of Skardo came to know about the Dogras invasion, he became fortified along with his subjects and nobles. Gradually, the army reached at Skardo, and Ahmad Shah became fearful to see the Dogra army. The army stationed at Thurgo, and the tower which is between Thurgo and Skardo was ambushed. The guards at the tower fled away due to fear. Ahmad Shah also fled away. Both the armies on foot and riders attacked and burnt his house to ashes. The army reached at Skardo, set right the pickets and besieged the fort. Shot the missiles like Jamburay and Jazail, and fear was created in the mind of the people. The ambush ended after five days. Ahmad Shah was discouraged and came to the Wazir and surrendered. His elder son Mohammad Shah was made the ruler, and Wazir Bono was made his Wazir. The people used to call "Juju" (Instead of salam it is used in Ladakhi language). Ahmad Shah regretted but Mohammad Shah was conferred with rope of honor. Man proposes and God disposes. Mehta Basti Ram was deployed in the fort and brought out all the valuable things from inside the fort. It is because of the wills and blessings of God, that some are happy and some sad. All the belongings were got collected. The people of the fort were weeping. Mohiuddin Shah fled away, Wazir Abtara followed him. Though Mehta Basti Ram was an officer but was keeping no authority. The writer Ganga Ram Nakashi has written, that Wazir is an incarnation, an authority and super man. He reinstated the Government of Khapolu and Chhorbat to their concern Rajas, to rule as per their wishes. Ten thousand people along with the women and the children were gathered in the fort. The next day the men and the women were looted (raped) Wazir sahib also came there and Holi was played. The Baltis felt it very much, as hard like bullets. The Rahim Khan of pashkyum, who was Kalon and collector of the area was arrested by Mohammad Jan, and Wazir did the justice of Nosherwan with him. Wazir issued order, anyone who kills the cow and bull would be given life punishment. It was declared, that the subjects are safeguarded, they should not worry. My pen is helpless to admire the rule of Wazir sahib. Ganga Ram Nakashi has not made any exaggeration in writing the notes. Ahmad Shah showed some haughtiness, so Wazir Zorawar Singh got him arrested and handed over to the army, who got written an agreement, that he will pay 10,000 rupees, within a month, otherwise he would be got killed. The Ladakhi Raja died in the way because of smallpox. Later, Wazir sahib went to Shigar, along with 300, soldiers and stayed there for 5 days. Shigar is so beautiful; that one didn't like to return from that place. I can't resist myself by praising Shigar.

8

Wazir Zorawar Singh's Tibet Expedition, Conquest of Purang and Distruction of Dogra Army

As soon as Jigsmet Namgyal ascended the throne and the traditions were fulfilled, Wazir Zorawar Singh prepared for the expedition of Lhasa. At that time he was having more than three thousand Dogra soldiers, and to assist them, he mobilized 4-5 thousand local soldiers from Baltistan, Purig and Ladakh, besides a huge number of porters.

The Balti soldiers were under the command of their concerned rulers. The soldiers of Purig were also distributed under the command of prominent persons of their concern region. The name of the deposed Raja Mourup Stanzin was proposed to command the Ladakhi army who was in the prison at that time. But he didn't accept this honor, because of the religious attachment with Lhasa. Therefore, his younger brother, Nono Sonam, Ghulam Khan former Raja Chushot and Tsewang Stobdan former Kalon of Bazgo, who had been released from the prison, was made the commanders of Ladakhi army. All the local soldiers were distributed under the command of Dogra officers in different platoons. Later, the total army was distributed into two groups. The first had been put under the command of Mian Rai Singh and deputed via Rupsho and Anley and the second was under the command of Wazir himself, and marched via Changla and Tangtse. It happened on May 1841 AD. Both the army met just before Rudok and invaded Rudok, the Tibetan army was fortified which was not more than three hundred.

Mehta Basti Ram was deployed to conquer the fort, he invaded the fort and after a short battle the commander of the Tibetan army was killed and they were discouraged. On their request a compromise got settled between both the army and the battle was ended. The next day the "Zongspon" Rudok came to the Wazir along with his officers and Lamas and surrendered. Wazir captured the fort and the Tibetan army who were the inhabitants of the neighbouring villages was allowed to proceed to their home. Instead, he deployed his own army in the fort, and Alchi Lonpo Dawa Tundup was kept there to assist the Dogra officer.

There are two routes to proceed to Gar from Rudok One via Tashigang, along the Indus and the second via Lubra, directly to Gar. Wazir proceeded along with the army via Lubra whereas Mehta Basti Ram along with a small group of army went via Tashigang, to make the arrangements for surrender in case there were any inhabitants so as to ensure no interference of the enemy on the Ladakh route. Here a minor battle took place, and Mehta Basti Ram was able to overcome it easily. He got them surrendered and after getting the promise of loyalty from the Lamas and the public he proceeded towards Gar. At Gar the two armies met again. Here the people surrendered without any interference. There was scarcity of fuel in this area, there was no wood. Though, this place was colder than Ladakh, the people have not built houses, instead they live in tents, which are made of Yak wool and is warmer than a mud house. In Gar there was an ordinary house for the Tibetan officers, Wazir got it repaired and made it the store and kept some soldiers to guard it?

After departure from Gar, Wazir reached at Mansar without any interference and the people surrendered. Hereafter, at a distance the route follows via three streams. All these three streams flow along the Kailash and fall in river Sutluj. It is called "Tokpo Ralsum. The middle stream is called "Shar-Tokpo". Wazir stationed at the bank of this stream, but during the night the Tibetan army stationed at Purang suddenly ambushed Wazir's camp. There was a chaos and crisis among the Wazir's army, but he managed to overcome the situation and attacked the Tibetans. The battle continued for about three to four hours. Many soldiers got killed from both the parties. Mahan Singh's son also got killed in this battle. Finally, the Tibetan army was defeated. Wazir proceeded further, along with the Dogra army and reached "Tsomo-Mapham" called Mansarowar Lake. This is a sacred place for Hindus. Different historians have revealed differently about the length of this lake. Actually it is not so far. A man on foot can take a complete round of the lake within three days. The Kailash Mountain, which is just ahead of the lake, is not so long as considered in old books. A man can have a round of Kailash easily in a day. According to the old Shastar no Raja could have approached Kailash, except Raja Man Data till this time. But it was Wazir Zorawar Singh, who with the blessings of the Jammu kingdom captured Kailash Mansarovar and the surrounding areas and conquered Purang.

After the defeat at Tokpo-Ralsum the Tibetan army fled to Takla-Khar, and consolidated their position and prepared themselves to counter the enemy. When, Wazir marched from Mansarwar Lake, he reached Kartong fort on the Lhasa route, but found it empty. He captured the fort and deployed a group of Dogra army under the command of Wazir Atbara. He did the arrangement at Kartong and marched towards Takla-Khar, which is the capital of the Purang area. Here the Tibetan army fought bravely, but was ultimately defeated. Wazir conquered the fort and the Tibetants left the fort and fled away. The Tibetan General Darpon Shata also ran away towards Lhasa. Takla-Khar is one of the best places of Purang as far the climatic condition is concerned. Wazir made it his capital, and opposite to the Takla-Khar, on the left bank of River Karnali (Ghakra) near the route, built a grand fort on the top of a hill and deployed Mehta Basti Ram there along with the Dogra army. At that time the province of Naris Korsum comprising of Rudok, Kugay, and Purang and Spiti were under the control of Wazir, and to defend the areas, he deployed Ladakhi and

Dogra army at all the places. Mehta Basti Ram and Wazir Atara were at Purang. Rahim Khan Raja Tikchey along with his son in law Ghulam Khan was deployed at Spiti. Similarly, he deployed some soldiers at Tarthapuri. After this conquest the territories of Jammu kingdom got extended up to the boundaries of Nepal and Kumaon district of Allahabad province of British Government. The distance of Nepal's border and Kumaon district of Allahabad is about 15-20 miles from Takla-Khar. Since the border of Jammu touched with Nepal, after the conquest of Purang. Hence, the King of Nepal deputed his representative along with 120 soldiers, to the Wazir, expressing, that there had been peaceful relations between the two kingdoms in absentia, but suddenly it turned into neighbours. Hence, the two governments have to keep in mind the solidarity, unity and integrity of each other in future. But Wazir thought it unwise to develop relation with Nepal, unless he would have an agreement with the British Government in India. He hosted the representative of Nepal for few days and sent back by ensuring a better relation in future. In the meantime another event took place, that Cunningham Sahib requested the wazir to depute one of his officer at the border of the British Government, so as to develop the relations, friendship, unity and integrity between the two countries. Therefore, Wazir deputed Mehta Basti Ram and Kalu Jamadar to discuss. After the agreement of friendship was signed, Cunningham advised the Dogras, that the climate is unfavourable and cold. The enemy is waiting for such an opportunity. You are far away from the capital Ladakh and it is very difficult to arrange transportations and ration. If you are willing to conquer Tibet, it is better to wait for the spring to come.

Mehta Basti Ram returned and revealed it to Wazir, what Cunningham has suggested him. Wazir appreciated the suggestions. Alas! The mistake done by Mirza Haider Gorgan regarding the Tibet expedition was repeated by Wazir Zorawar Singh. He learned no lesson from it. He proceeded from Ladakh at such a time, that he arrived at Purang in winter. Neither was it a suitable time for invasion, nor to proceed further. History repeats itself; the result was very destructive, like that of Mirza Haider. Since Mirza had to return back from there during the winter, because of the bad relation with his own government, from where Lhasa was only eight days away. And because of declamation and unavailability of transportation and ration, his army got ruined on the way. However, he was able to save the lives of most of his army men. But the inhabitants of a warm country like the Dogras, could not face the extreme cold of Purang, against the Tibetan army, and almost all the Dogra soldiers including their General became the prey of the cold and high altitude and the Tibetans killed them. However the shortcoming of these brave invaders was fulfilled by Col. Young Husband in August 1904 AD, where he unfurled the British flag on the potala palace of Gyalwa Rinpochhey.

In short, keeping in view the unfavorable climatic condition Wazir stopped the advance and leaving Mehta Basti Ram in the Takla-Khar fort, he himself went to the pilgrimage of Gonpa Khoshaq. This Gonpa is considered a sacred place and is situated on the left bank of River Ghagra, just ahead of one halting place from the newly constructed fort of Wazir at Takla-Khar. Wazir halted there for few days and returned to Purang. Thereafter, Wazir deputed some soldiers at the Nepal border to observe the tower of the actual line of control. They came back with positive report and revealed that a big boulder had placed on the old border. On the one side of the boulder has written Sanskrit words and on the other side Tibetan. This indicates the old border and is in tact. When he was satisfied with the report, he began to consolidate his own army. Shortest of ration was there, it was not possible to transport it, except from Ladakh. But the distance was very long and the route was very difficult. So, this problem was under consideration.

Wazir thought that the winter season has started and has no intention to proceed further and there was no chance of attack from the enemy, and he thought it not necessary to stay in the battle field. Hence, he marched from Taghla-Kharto to Mansarowar Lake, with the intention to precede Leh. Wazir expanded the territories of Jammu regime from the sources of Indus and Sutluj to the upper reach of Ghagra valley and the border of Jammu touched with the Nepal. The sacred places like the Mansarowar Lake and Kailash Parbhat were also under his control. The Maryumla was the border between Lhasa and Jammu. It had been the border between Ladakh and Lhasa in the past too, during the reign of some able Ladakhi kings. Thereby, the source of River Brahamaputra was also under his control. In short Wazir extended the Kingdom of Jammu upto the famous place, wherefrom the following four popular rivers of India follows:

1. Singgay Khabab (Lion mouth) Indus.
2. Langchhen Khabab (Elephant mouth) Sutluj.
3. Mupja Khabab (Peacock beak) Ghagra.
4. Stachhok Khabab (Horse mouth) Brahamputra.

Since the luck of the victorious brave general had been reached at its climax, but there is down fall after every success. Now, he has to face the defeat. This courageous and brave person unfurled the victorious flag of Dogra's from Suru to Ladakh, Ladakh to Skardo and from Skardo to Purang. And with the same sprit he sacrificed himself on the flag of Government of Jammu. Though the European writers have special interest with the Asian conquerors, they had referred many crimes towards this brave man, but the Buddhists of great Tibet and Muslims of little Tibet still praise him. That Wazir neither harmed any innocent people, nor destroyed any religious structure during his invasion, for which he would be remembered for a long time in future.

When the Tibetan people in Lhasa came to know, about the interference of Wazir, they had been preparing for the counter attack. After performing the pilgrimage of Mansarowar Lake and Kailash, Wazir had preceded about two halting places, towards Ladakh, when he came to know about the arrival of the Tibetan Army, on 7th November 1841 AD, according to 22 Katak. He became so furious and emotional, that he never cared for his own security, and in order to stop the advance party, he deployed 300 soldiers under the command of Nono Sonam, to assist Atbara Thanedar at the Kartong fort. He sent back his family members to Ladakh escorted by some soldiers, and he himself was busy in arranging the army to encounter the Tibetans. When he got the news that the soldiers stationed at Kartong fort including the reinforcement headed by Nono Sonam were killed by the enemies. Nono Sonam and Jeeru Kotwal came to the Wazir with the news. Now Wazir deputed 600 strong soldiers under the command of Nono Sonam, Ghulam Khan, Mahan Singh, Bhupa Kotwal, and Mian Ssanggara, on 19th November 1841 AD, to stop the advance of the Tibetan army, and he himself followed them along with all the Dogra soldiers towards the battle field. Even his army could not meet the advance party, when he came to know that all the soldiers were got killed by the enemy, and the rest were arrested. Their commander Nono Sonam and Ghulam Khan were made prisoner. The number of Tibetan army was much larger, consisting of 10,000 soldiers, then that of Wazir. There was awfully cold in the region and it was at its climax. Transportation was not good. In spite of these hardships, Wazir considered them weak and jumped in the battle field like a lion. A fierce battle took place on 10th December 1841 AD at Toyu, situated between Kartong and Tagla-Khar. Gun battle started by both the parties and it continued for three days. Both the parties fought the battle bravely. Finally, on the third day the Wazir's army fought very bravely. It is said, that the Tibetan's was to face the defeat. Hence, on seeing this, Wazir himself jumped in the battle field to encourage his soldiers.

But luck not favoured him and the unvarnished time has come, a bullet of the enemy was struck on the right thigh of Wazir. He fell down in the battle field from his horse. On seeing this enemy ambushed him from all sides. But in this awkward position he never left his sword and attacked the enemy soldiers, whosever came in front of him. When the enemy observed that it is difficult to catch the injured lion alive, they deployed a person on the back side of Wazir to throw a spear on him, locally it is called "Dung". Its both ends are sharp like a spear, and a rope is fastened in the centre. It is being revolved over the head, with one end of the rope in the hand, and thrown on the target. The "Dung" struck on the back of Wazir and the sharp edge damaged his chest. Because of this injury, Wazir died in the battle field on 12th December 1841 AD, according to 27th Maghar 1898, Bikrami.

During Zorawar Singh's departure to Tibet expedition, he locked the window of the gate of Leh fort, and the word "Talaq" was inscribed on a sheet of iron connected with the lock. It is said, unless Tibet is conquered, the lock of the window should not be opened. The order is still followed, but the political condition has changed now and it seems to be very difficult to fulfill his desires. However, Wazir Zorawar Singh's memory still exists on the gate of the fort, and it will remain in tact in the future too. After the death of Wazir, the Dogra army discouraged, and the condition of the battle changed. The Dogras became helpless, and the soldiers run away every side. The Tibetans followed them and the maximum were got killed. It is said that the total army was about 6,000 including the porters, but hardly more than two thousand came back alive. Out of this about one thousand soldiers were imprisoned by the enemy and about one thousand five hundred soldiers arrived back at Leh. Among them the Dogra soldiers were not more than one hundred. Those Dogra officers who remained alive were got arrested. Wazir Zorawar Singh's army fought this battle in a very difficult and hardships position. The battle field was more than 15,000 feet high from the sea level, and the climatic condition was not good. It was awfully cold, even during the day the temperature remains minus, and during the night it is so cold, that only those who are habitual of such climatic condition can face the situation. They also kept the leather coats and fur dresses. But the Dogras were not having these types of clothes, and during the awfully cold they spent many nights in the open fields. Moreover the rain and heavy snowfall, made their journey unbearable. It is said that the toes and fingers of some soldiers were affected by frostbite, and almost the hands and feet of all the soldiers were got affected with cold. There are no wood in the area, so as to bask before a fire and save the life. Here people use a bush as a fuel. As long as it burns, it has the warmth, but after burning, nothing is left except the ashes. It was so cold, that some soldiers burnt the butt of their rifle, to save the life. Above all, there was shortage of ration and during the last few days they could have nothing to eat.

In spite of these hardships, the soldiers fought bravely with the enemy, till their last breath. On the last day of battle, half of the army was not able to use their arms properly.

They were discouraged, when their commander was killed and was left no option but to run away from the battle field. These are the causes for the destruction of the army. The Tibetans not followed the absconders; hence, most of the people came to Ladakh, along with the Ladakhies, and some arrived at Takla-Khar, with the sad news of destruction. The soldiers of the Takla fort thought it better to save their life, so all the soldiers along with Mehta Basti Ram went towards Almoda, via Changlao Chheyla. Though there was no danger on this route, but due to heavy snow fall and awfully cold half of the soldiers died in the way and hand and feet of rest of the soldiers became the prey of frostbite. In short among his army, the life of only those few people, who reached Almoda or were able to reach Ladakh fort, were saved. When the Dogra's in Leh came to know about the Tibetans invasion, the deputed reinforcement from Leh to help Zorawar, under the command of Pehalwan Singh Kamedan, Munshi Gorandata, and Subedar Teg Singh. Probably, the Wazir must have ordered them to do so. These soldiers were far away from the battle field, when they came to know about the battle of Toyu, and destruction of Dogra army. Hearing this sad news, they returned back to Ladakh and were busy in the consolidation of the fore. The conquests of Wazir Zorawar Singh have terrorized the mind of the Tibetan people. He was considered a very special man. It is said, that after his death his blood and flesh were distributed by the Tibetans among themselves, they took his head to Lhasa and built a "Chhorten" to keep it, which still exist. A piece of his body has been kept in Tashigang Gonpa. On the appointed days prayers are performed according to the Buddhist tradition, so that the spirit of the late Wazir may not enter in the body of a person to destroy Tibet once again. At the place, where Wazir died, the Tibetans had built a grand "Chhorten". About the cause of the erection of the "Chhorten" it is said, that in the process of reincarnation, the spirit of the General may not invade Tibet again. Therefore, because of the superstitious nature of the Tibetans, the memory of Wazir Zorawar Singh still exist in Purang, and refresh the memory of the great conqueror's Tibet invasion. The following Dogra Officers were made Prisoner of war at the battle of Toyu, by the Tibetans:

1. Mian Rai Singh 2nd in command.
2. Tsewang Stobdan Kalon Bazgo.
3. Nono Sonam brother of Kalon Bazgo.
4. Ghulam Khan Raja Chushot.
5. Mourup Stanzin.
6. Acho Gonbo.
7. Raja Ahmad Shah, deposed Raja Skardo.

Besides, all the prisoners were sent to Lhasa and the Tibetan army captured Naris Korsum, Gar, and Rudok during the winter season. The affect of the Wazir Zorawar Singh's defeat in the Tibet invasion was far lasting. Not only the conquered areas of Tibet were recaptured by the Tibetans, but the position of the previously conquered areas became shamble. To set the things on the right path two more expedition were sent to Ladakh and Baltistan. The details of the events are follows further.

9

Revolt of Ladakh, Purig and Baltistan

Tibets invasion on Ladakh. Revolt of Ladakh, Purig and Baltistan. Dogra's Ladakh invasion No. 4. Commanded by Dewan Hari Chand and Wazir Ratnu. Defeat of Tibetans Army and compromise with Government of Tibet.

The Tibetan Army thought, that none of the Dogra soldiers could save their life in the battle field of Toyu and the Ladakhies are not their enemy. They never followed the fugitives, and spent rest of the winter with ease in the surroundings of Naris Korsum, Gar, and Rudok. Beside consolidated their rule in these regions. Those soldiers, who were deployed by Wazir Zorawar Singh in the fort of Gar and Rudok, were captured by the Tibetans, after the battle of Toyu. Most of them were killed and the fugitives, who were able to save their life, arrived in Leh fort in a deplorable condition. About one hundred soldiers, who came from the Purang side, including the soldiers of these border forts, were able to reach Leh. Because of the destruction of the Dogras, the Ladakhies and Balties wished to be independent again, but due to their laziness and natural disturbances to some extent, it helped the Dogra rulers. Though the number of the Dogra soldiers at the Leh fort was very small, however, without the assistance of the neighbouring states, the Ladakhies were not having the courage of revolt. Although, the whole winter season expired, in discussion to obtain the cooperation of Purig and Baltistan and to acquire military assistance from Tibet, and could not take any action before the summer starts. When the plot against the Dogras was finalized, the process of deployment of the soldiers started. Acho Gonbo who had been Lobchhak (Head of the annual trade mission) used to go Tibet and had a good relation with the prominent persons of Tibet. He approached the Tibetan General P.C. Shata and decided to eradicate the Dogra soldiers from Ladakh and restore the rule of Ladakhi Raja, again. In the beginning of the year of 1842 AD, according to 1898-99 Bikrimi, the said general proceeded towards Ladakh, along with the 3,000 Tibetan army from the surroundings of the Gar area. Onpo Tsewang Rafstan was deployed to Sham area (Lower Ladakh) to mobilize the army. The army from upper Ladakh was mobilized by Acho Gonbo himself and reached at Leh, along with the Tibetant Army. In the mean time the army from Sham also reached at Leh. The whole army entered in the Leh palace during the night. Jigsmet Namgyal the grandson of Tundup Namgyal, who had been appointed as nominal Raja by Wazir Zorawar Singh in place of his grandfather, was declared as independent Raja. The weapons stored in the Tingmogang and Leh palace were distributed among the soldiers. Those who could not get the weapons were given wooden spears. However, when the arrangement was made, the Government of Raja Jigsmet Namgyal was declared. There were two groups of Dogras in Leh. One was under the command of Maghna Thanedar at the Leh fort and the second was under the command of Kamedan Pehalwan Singh at Karzoo Bagh. It was not a safe place. When Kamedan observed that the soldiers are gathering at the Leh palace, and the situation is not normal, he left the Karzoo bagh and shifted to a place just adjacent to the Leh fort, which was stable of the Ladakhi Kingdom since there was shortage of accommodation inside the fort. He got repaired the structure as far as possible, and the required arrangement were made. The rebels also came in action; they with the collaboration of the Tibetan Army surrounded the cantonment, fort and stable. But they were not able to stop their internal communications. The irritation continued for a long time. Finally, the rebels decided to attack the fort and the cantonment, during the night. But to their ill-luck, they spent most of the time in discussion and arrangements and attacked at the dawn. The Dogra army countered from the cantonment and inside the fort. The battle continued till morning. In the morning, Kamedan Pehalwan Singh from the cantonment and Maghna Thanedar from the fort came out with the army and attacked the rebels with courageously. They fought hand to hand and many Ladakhies were killed. Finally, they were defeated and began to run away. The Dogras followed them up to the town. It is said that thousands of Ladakhi and Tibetan soldiers were killed in this battle. Not only the Ladakhies but the Tibetan Army was also discouraged after this defeat.

They could not mobilize themselves for a long time and even could not besiege the Dogras any longer.

Wazir Zorawar Singh had have built a temple in the Leh town. During this rebellion period, the Ladakhis and Tibetan Bhudhists were not contented with the military activities but interfered in the religious activities and destroyed the Hindu temple called "Devi mandir" at Leh. Beside the religious goods which were inside the temple were also destroyed carelessly. This made the Dogras very irritated who till now honored the Buddhist religious places:

Later, during the invasions they took the revenge and looted the valuable goods of Buddhist Gonpas. Though, at this occasion, they only looted the valuable goods but not damaged the statues and sacred religious monuments. The religious harmony of the Dogras is praise worthy. When, these events were happening in Ladakh. Purig was also facing the same situation. Since the revolt tookplace in all the Border States at a time with the mutual understand and conspiracy. The Kalon Mulbe arrested the Dogra soldiers of Mulbe fort and thrown them away in Nallah Wakha from the Darket bridge the Raja Sot also got killed the Dogra soldiers of Pasri-Khar along with the soldiers of Chhubar-Khar and Chokyat-Beroi. Similar activities were done in Suru-Kartsey. Raja Pashkyum also imprisoned the Dogra soldiers but took least interest in the revolt. That is why he was convened at the capital Leh and he was allowed to go back with the strict warning, but unfortunately he could not reach back Pashkyum. In spite of all these efforts of the rebellion, there was peace in Daras. Revolt was at its peak at Baltistan too. The events are revealed as follows:

When Raja Ahmad Shah was released from the prison of Wazir Zorawar Singh, he was again arrested by the Tibetans at the battle of Purang. Being like minded he became their friends and plotted to fight against the Dogras. He deputed his representative Yustrong Karim to Skardo to mobilize the Baltis through his confident Haider Khan Shigar, and Kazim Beg Skardo. So, all the three prominent persons did efforts to create ill-will and hatred against the Dogras and gradually, came in agreement with other dignitaries, like Ali Khan Raja Rongdo, Doulat Ali Khan Raja Khapolu, Khorram Khan Raja Keres, and other nobles of Baltistan. Later, they arrested the Dogra Thanedar of Skardo Baghwandas and his soldiers and they destroyed the fort and the storeroom. Haider Khan deputed these prisoners to Nihali, and full arrangement of their security was made there. Then Suleman Khan Raja Shigar was arrested and ruled over his kingdom. Since Mohammad Shah Raja Askardo did not participated in the revolt, hence, he was arrested and imprisoned at Khanqah Kawardo, and captured Kharpochhey fort and Haider Khan ruled over Skardo. Thus, he left no sign of the Dogras in Baltistan. Haider Khan arranged the reinforcement from Ngar, wherefrom Wazir Shuja reached Skardo along with 140 warriors and remained assistant of Haider Khan. Therefore, after the death of Wazir Zorawar Singh, his conquests areas were confiscated by the ex-rulers. In Phagan 1898 Bikrami when Maharaja Gulab Singh was proceeding to Peshawar via Kashmir to make the arrangements and receive General Palak, he got the sad news of Zorawar's assassination at Barah-Kot of Hazara region. Therefore, he immediately made the arrangement to depute 2nd expedition to Ladakh. At that time Dewan Hari Chand, who along with Painda Khan were busy, on the bank of River Indus at Palyan as a representative of Government of Khalsa was called back? He was deployed from that very place by appointing the Commander-in-Chief of Ladakh expedition.

Dewan marched from Hassan Abdal and reached at Haripur Jammu within a day and night by crossing the distance of 150 "kos", wherefrom he went to Jammu along with Raja Dhayan Singh. Later, he reached at Mirpur, after making the arrangements of ration and weapons. Where he stayed for 15 days and mobilized the soldiers. When he arranged the requirements, he left along with 6,000 soldiers via Uri and reached at Kashmir, where Sheikh Ghulam Mohiuddin, who was the Subedar of Kashmir, appointed by Government of Khalsa Lahore, did all sort of arrangements for them. This army has to stay for 15 days in Kashmir, where from he deployed 500 soldiers each day towards Ladakh. Wazir Ratnu was the 2nd in command of this expedition. He marched one day earlier of Dewan, the next day Dewan himself marched towards Ladakh and staying at various destinations reached at Daras. The entire route from Sonamarg to Daras was covered with snow, and because of its shine the soldiers has to face eye sore, but recovered very soon. He has to stay three days in Daras. Suchita Thanedar Daras reported in detail, the obstructions at various places, from Daras to Kargil. That the enemy has erected posts right from terrain of Kharul to Nallah Kargil and has stationed soldiers with weapons. And it was difficult to pass through the rout. But Dewan never cared for it and marched forward. At Kharul the forward army has to face the enemy and returned back to Chhani-Gund. Dewan deputed some soldiers via Chhani-Gund Nallah to climb the hill, so as to attack the enemy from the top of the hill. But all the hill was covered with snow, therefore the plan failed, and the army returned back. Finally, Dewan waited till the snow is melt and after one month he deputed 3,000 soldiers with a gun via Nallah Chhani-Gund to climb the top of the hill, under the command of Ram Singh Jamadar. Under the hill on the plateau of Tiktikmo were the positions of the enemy and Dewan himself along with Wazir Ratnu and rest of the soldiers marched from the main rout and reached Kharul, where the soldiers of the enemy were ready to counter the Dogras, under the command of Bahadur Khan Kargili. Dewan stayed at Kharul and was waiting for Ram Singh to reach on the top of the hill. When Ram Singh's army arrived on the top of the hill, then Dewan fired the gun heavily on the positions of the enemy. Now the positions of the enemy were under the fire of the Dogras from both the sides, hence, there was no alternative for them but to run away. After the Tiktikmo, the Kargilies positioned at Lankore village but the gun of the Dogras was on the top, therefore it was difficult for them to continue there, hence, they run away from there too. Now there was no alternative for the fugitive soldiers of Purig to break the bridge over River Suru, after they cross it. But unfortunately their own senior people blocked the passage of the bridge with stone and wood, so that they did not dare to runaway. Dogra soldiers were following these fugitives and the firing continued from the hill. In such a situation, it was difficult to open the passage of the bridge. Hence, the people jumped into the river, out of fear. In the meantime, the Dogra soldiers also reached at the bank of the River. Those who were on the bank were killed with hands, those, who were swimming in the river, were killed with bullets. And those who were not expert in swimming became the prey of the wave of the River. In short, among the huge army of Purig, only those soldiers could save their lives, which were able to swim on the other part of the river. Their number was very low. The triumphant Dogra army stayed the night at Kargil. Instead of Choki Chhubar-Khar, Dewan arranged to build a strong fort, opposite to it on the left bank of River Suru. One Dogra officer was deputed to Sot, so as to destroy "Pasri-Khar" with fire. Thereafter, he marched from Kargil and reached at Pashkyum. Raja Pashkyum Mohammad Ali Khan was at Leh, his fort was destroyed with fire, and those who were instigator of the revolt were severely punished. Later, they proceeded ahead of Pashkyum. Dewan marched towards Ladakh after making the political arrangements of the villages on the road side on the way he burnt out the Malduk-Khar palace of Mulbe. The valuable goods of the forts, which he burnt out, like planks and logs, were sent to Kargil to re-use in the newly built fort of Kargil. Those people, who were found responsible for the revolt, were handed over to the Thanedar Kargil, so as to put them in the prison.

When the army reached ahead of Bodh-Kharbu, met with Mohammad Ali Khan Raja Pashkyum, who was coming back from Ladakh, attacked the 6,000 Dogra army along with his 30 soldiers. The details are as follows: the place where the Henasku Bridge over Nalah Kanji is situated, on its right they positioned on a rock and attacked the Dogra army on the other side of the river. The Dogra army never imagined to face such a situation. Because of this sudden attack some Dogra soldiers were killed. The Dogra army prepared to attack them, but the army was beneath on the bank of the river, and the Raja's soldiers were on the hill positioned behind a rock, so it was very difficult to counter them, and they were in a fix, how to overcome them. That suddenly, one of the companion of the Raja who was a former Dogra soldier, shouted loudly, that the gun men are not more than thirty, attack them without any hesitation. After performing this service, he sacrificed himself for the sack of the country. Thus, the Dogra soldiers advanced further and got killed all of them. Though some more Dogra soldiers were killed, but among the Raja's soldiers only one person reached at Chiktan to tell the sad story to them. Then the people came form the village, they took away the dead body of the Raja and buried at Chiktan. Thus, the Dogra soldiers cleared the obstructions and proceeded further. Raja Mohammad Ali Khan was remembering the punishment, which was given to his brother Kalon Rahim Khan by Zorawar Singh at Skardo, and he never dared to do so and abstained himself by involving in such crises again. But it was the Raja of Ladakh who misled him from the right track, and took the promise from him that he will stop the Dogra army at Kargil. It is said, that he was in a fix, what to do and what not, but he was afraid, that the Ladakhi Raja will invade him, therefore in order to keep them away to do so; he broke down the planks of the Khalsi Bridge in to the river. That is why, when the Dogra army reached at this place they had to face the problems to cross the river. They got repaired the bridge in a day and crossed the river and reached Khalsey. There are two routes ahead of Khalsey. One upper route goes from Tingmogang via Liker and comes down at Bazgo, another lower route which goes from the river bank via Nurla and Saspol and reaches at

Bazgo. Ahead of Bazgo this rout leads from a narrow gorge, wherefrom it is impossible to pass, if the enemy creates obstructions. Hence, to do the arrangements and to capture the Tingmogang fort which was considered one of the strongest for of Ladakh, he divided the army in two groups. He deputed Wazir Ratnu from the river bank rout to Bazgo, and Dewan himself from the hilly route proceeded towards Tingmogang. Dewan destroyed the fort of Tingmogang and ahead of village Liker surrounded the Nallah Kesar, so that the army of Wazir Ratnu can climb the Nallah safely. Later, both the army reached at Bazgo. There was a strong fort at Bazgo called Rafstan Lartsey, the army destroyed it partially. Later, on they marched towards Leh, Ladakh.

Kamidan Pehalwan Singh taught a good lesson to the Ladakhi and Tibetan joint army. Hence, they could not unite them again. However, after this defeat they did the efforts to mobilize them again, but before they are able to do some practical activities, they heard the news of arrival of the Dewan's army in Ladakh. This made them discouraged, and the number of the Ladakhi army gradually decreased. When Dewan's army reached near Leh, the Tibetan army came out of the Leh palace and instead of fighting with the Dogras, they straightly went towards the border of Lhasa. Besides, Raja Jigsmet Namgyal, along with his mother, who ruled over the rebels about six weeks, left the palace and fled away towards Lhasa. Thus, the palace of Ladakh, which was the centre of the rebels, became empty completely.

When the Dewan reached at Ladakh along with his huge army, he unfurled the flag adjacent to the Leh fort, and praised the bravery of Kamidan Pehalwan Singh's army. He rested at Leh for few days. Later, he deputed a group of soldiers to Zangskar under the command of Mian Jawahar Singh to crash the rebels, and some soldiers were sent to Nubra under the command of Mian Naraina. Those porters, who came from Kashmir along with his army, were given the wages and rewards and sent back. And among the nobles of Ladakh, Onpo Rigzin, Tsewang Stobdan, and Acho Gonbo were honored and rewarded. In the meantime, the valuable goods like the Chhorten of silver and gold and furniture's from the Leh palace were removed. Moreover in response to the destruction of the temple, the valuable goods of the Gonpas were shifted to the fort, but he neither disregarded the sacred things, nor damaged the religious articles. Besides he did justice with the rebels.

In the meantime, the General of the Tibetan army Darpon Pishi Shata, who fled from Ladakh to Rudok, made the efforts to get the detail information about Ladakh, through Raja Jigsmet Namgyal. When he came to know, that a major portion of the Dogra army has proceeded to Zagskar and Nubra and the Kashmiri porters has gone back, he determined to invade the Dogras once again he deputed immediately one thousand Tibetan soldiers to invade the Dogras, under the command of his younger brother Chhagchhung and Kalon Raga Shah's brother Karan Shah. After crossing the pass of "Changla" the army arrived at Chemdey. Onpo Rigzin and Acho Gonbo informed the Dewan about the current developments. Hence, Dewan immediately deputed a platoon to counter them, under the command of Kamidan Sardol Singh and Lala Ramji Mal Munshi. A battle took place at lower Chemrey between the two armies. The enemy fought bravely but finally was defeated and fortified in the Chemrey Gonpa. When Dewan came to know about this situation, he kept a required number of soldiers at Leh to defend the capital. And he himself marched towards Chemrey along with rest of the soldiers to fight the Tibetants. On the first day he stayed at Chushot. The next day he reached at Chemrey and besieged the Gonpa. A canon was fixed on a top of a hill just opposite to the Gonpa. The cannon-ball reached inside the Gonpa. The Gonpa is situated on the top of a hill, but have to fetch the water from the canal or spring. Dewan surrounded the Gonpa from all sides and stopped their way and finally the enemy was compelled to surrender. Dewan deployed Bakhshi Nihal Singh inside the Gonpa to sign the agreement of forgiveness. He did the needful and gets them out of the Gonpa. Dewan sent Chhagchung and Karan Shah along with their companions to Leh Ladakh guarded by Wazir Ratnu, and he himself stayed few days at Chemrey to fulfil the political arrangements. After doing the needful, he appointed Sardol Singh Kamidan and Ramjimal Munshi as Incharge Officers at Chemrey and he himself went back to Leh Ladakh. It is not out of place to mention here that the Chemrey Gonpa is under the Hemis monestry and it is the greatest and famous Gonpa in Ladakh and the lamas are popular for their far sightedness and good strategy. When the Tibetan army arrived at Chemrey, the "Chhagzot" of Hemis arranged all sort of arrangements for them similarly when the Dogra soldiers of Dewan reached at Chemrey to counter them, the "Chhagzot" of Hemis Gonpa remained ready to serve them and he fulfilled the need of transportation and other requirements. Thereby, he maintained an equal balance between he two groups, and both the parties were happy with him. In response to the services rendered by the Steward of Gonpa Hemis, Dewan neither seized the valuable goods of Gonpa, nor did he damage the sacred monuments.

In the meantime, after nine days in the prison, an event happened, one night the prisoners attacked the guards, killed some with stones and some were injured and they run away from the prison in the midnight. When Dewan came to know about this event, he followed the fugitives and surrounded them few miles away from Leh, Ladakh. The Tibetan fugitives positioned on a slope of a hill and began to throw stones over the Dogra army. The Dogra soldiers fired from the foothill and killed about 100 Tibetans and about 400 were re-arrested. A group of these fugitives run away from another route but they were also arrested. They were sent to Kashmir escorted by 200 riders. Those fugitives, who were able to run away from Ladakh, told the sad story to Darpon Pishi Shata, Kalon Ragasha Commander-in-Chief and Kalon Zoorkhang. Thereafter, 6,000 Tibetan soldiers, along with cannon, which they seized from the Dogras in the battle of Toyu, marched towards Ladakh with the intention of attack. They reached at Tangtse and built a strong cantonment at Lung-Yogma.

This information was brought to the notice of Dewan, by Sardol Singh Kamidan and Ramjimal Munshi. He ordered

Sardol Singh, to take position on the hill under which the enemy has built their cantonment. He himself marched along with all the soldiers, except he left one hundred soldiers at the Leh fort to guard it, and within two days he met with the army of Sardol Singh. They stayed the night at Durbuk. Even the soldiers had not cleared the dust of their weapons, when the guards informed that the enemy wanted to ambush during the night. Hence, the soldiers never took rest and get ready throughout the night. The enemy came forward at night with the intention of ambush, but the Dogras were ready to welcome them. The enemy soldiers were seen clearly in the moonlight. the Dogras shot the cannon balls and fired guns over them. Beside, the swords did their own job. Finally, Tibetan officer Daspon Aggyam was injured, he turned his horse back. On seeing this Tibetan army run away, the Dogras followed them up to the cantonment. When they entered inside the cantonment, the Dogras besieged it. The battle continued for eight days, and the cantonment was so strong that the Dogras failed to capture it. Finally, they were disgusted and on the eight day they invaded the cantonment once again but in vain. The enemy was ready for the counter; they throw out fire balls over the Dogra soldiers from inside the cantonment. Because of the fire about 300 soldiers of Damjad Singh Kamida were got killed, and many more were injured. The loss of lives of the Tibetan army was very few; however one of their officers Chhagzot Mikmar was died because of gun firing, however they failed to capture the cantonment.

The Dogra soldiers were morally discouraged, because of this failure. However, Dewan did efforts to boost their morale tactfully. Four days passed but there seems to be no alternative to capture the Tibetan cantonment. Finally the luck favored them. The details are as follows:

A person namely Thangpa Joldan of village Nurla was among the Dogra soldiers. He had been officer in charge of the stable in the past, during the Ladakhi kingdom. The horses of the Raja have to graze there at Lung Yogma and whenever there is lack of grass in the field; the land is being irrigated through the water of the Nallah. He told the

Dewan, that if we bring the water from the Nallah and put in the field, the cantonment would be filled with water and it would compel the enemy to come out. Dewan examined the spot and the proposal was found genuine and easy to execute. He did the arrangement immediately and diverted the whole water of the Nallah in the field. Thus, the water of the Nallah follows continuously for three days and the cantonment was filled with water. The enemy did efforts to save themselves from this calamity but found no way to get rid from this misfortune. Their belongings and weapons, etc., drowned into the water and was surrounded by the Dogras from the outside. Neither had they a dry place to sit in, nor a passage to come out. It compelled them to surrender and requested the Dewan for forgiveness. Dewan showed generosity towards the enemy and deployed two Dogra officers Qazi Nadir Ali and Wazir Mutasaddi to console and comfort them. All the Tibetan officers came to the Wazir without weapon. Dewan was kind enough to deal with them. All the weapons and other goods of the enemy were confiscated, and gave a way to the soldiers to come out of the cantonment. Beside, the weapon, etc., which they got in the battle field of Purang from Wazir Zorawar Singh, were received back. And Jawala Brahman, who was in their prison, also came before Dewan. The rebellions like Mourup Stanzin, Acho Gonbo, and the deposed Raja of Skardo Ahmad Shah, who were accompanying the Tibetans, were arrested. The cantonment was totally destroyed. In short Dewan got a victory over the Tibetans.

Now, he got an opportunity to fulfill the desires of Wazir Zorawar Singh, but he never did efforts to get back the region conquered by late Wazir. Instead, due to tiredness Dewan returned to Leh by enjoying the great victory and left Wazir Ratnu behind so as to escort the Tibetan officers and other prisoners to Leh. When Dewan left for Leh, the mind of the Tibetan officers changed and they refused to precede Leh, along with Wazir. In this struggle Kalon Ragashah was got killed at Aamtat hill near Shachukul. Only Pishi Shata, Tsepchhot and Zurkhang arrived at Leh. When Maharaja

Gulab Singh came to know about the fresh invasion of the Tibetans, he deployed 4,000 soldiers from Kashmir for reinforcement of Dewan. After the victory over the Tibetans, he was not in need of any reinforcement. Dewan asked them to go back. The Government of Lhasa, through Garpon Jorgais prayed for compromise. Garpon came to Leh in the court of Dewan. The Government of Lhasa appointed Pishi Shata and Kalon Zurkhang to participate in the talks, which were in prison at Leh, and the Government of Jammu empowered Dewan Hari Chand commander in Chief for Ladakh expedition and Wazir Ratnu 2nd in command to make the compromise. They on behalf of the Government of Jammu and Lhasa signed the agreement. When they signed the agreement, Dewan proceeded to Jammu along with the two Tibetan representatives, their officers and prisoner of war and got accorded the agreement, and the Tibetans officers were conferred with rope of honor and returned to Lhasa. Raja Ahmad Shah along with his companions was presented in the court as prisoners. He was kept in prison for some years, at Gomut Darwaza. In the meantime, one of his sons Mohammad Ali Khan fled to India and died at Ludhiana. Later, he was shifted to Kishtawar and kept house arrest till his death. After his death, his offspring's were granted estates in Kashmir. They are settled at Taral.

Wazir Ratnu stayed few days in Ladakh; he handed over the administration of Ladakh to Maghna Thanedar and went back to Jammu. Where as Onpo Rigzin was appointed his Assistant. According to the agreement the borders of Ladakh remained the same, as was during the reign of Raja Tundup Namgyal. When first time Zorawar Singh conquered Ladakh and those regions which he conquered later, like Rudok, Ghar, Kugay, and Purang, etc., which are known as Kangri region remained with Tibet. Beside the relation of Tibet which was with the Rajas of Ladakh during the Namgyal dynasty keep continued by both the Governments of Lhasa and Jammu and the prisoners of wars were exchanged. In recognition to his services, the Government of Lhasa conferred the status of "Kalon" to Darpon Pishi Shata, and after some years, he was elevated to a higher post of the Government of Lhasa. As far as Kalon Zurkhang is concerned, it is said that he died earlier. Dewan took the following rebbilions along with himself to Jammu; they are: (1) Deposed king Mourup Stanzin, (2) His son Gurmet, (3) Eshay Tundup, (4) Tsering Tobgais Ladokh and (5) Acho Gonbo. Among them only two persons Gurmet and Eshay Tundup returned Ladakh after few years and the rest were died at Jammu. Similarly, Dewan also took with him to Jammu, some Rajas and Nobles of Kargil; among them Salam Khan Raja of Sot died at Jammu and the rest returned to their home. After few years Raja Jigsmet Namgyal, his mother and his companions, were sent back to Ladakh by the Tibetan officers, escorted by their soldiers. It is because of Dewan Hari Chand's generosity that he restored to him, all the estates of his grandfather situated at Stok. Whereas, Chhogsphurul's second son Phuntsog Stanshong Yurgyal had already got 50 per cent estate of village Matho, which continuously remained in his possession. Since than the two brothers Jigsmet and Phuntsog stayed separately at their own estates. Thus, their ancestors have still occupied the concern estates.

After the death of Jigsmet Namgyal his son Sonam Namgyal was made nominal Raja, and the total estate of Jigsmet Namgyal remained in his name. When it could not make both ends meet, the government sanctioned an honorarium in his favour. He was the nominal Raja of Ladakh till 1914 AD. After becoming his father a Lama in the Gonpa, his son Jigsmet Dadul Namgyal became the nominal Raja and got the estates at Stok. Now it is said that he is a Member of Assembly and some more property has been allotted in his name at Nubra. When Chhogsphurul's second son Shongh Yurgyal was died, his son Lahwang Namgyal became the fief-holder of Matho, and after his death his second son Nangwa Thayas Namgyal was looking after his estates. His elder brother Thustobs was a Lama at Gonpa Hemis. After this expedition there was continuous peace in Ladakh, and never required to send a fresh expedition to Ladakh. The country is progressing day by day because of good governance. Now the

Ladakhies has learned English and Urdu education and has got government jobs. Its foundation was laid by me, and I am proud of it.

In this connection the efforts of the priests of Moravian Mission Ladakh is praise-worthy.

10

Removal of Disturbances in Baltistan, Purig and Zangskar

DOGRA'S EXPEDITION NO. 5 COMMANDED BY WAZIR LAKHPAT KISHTAWARIA

Though, according to the sequence, this expedition should be narrated in the events of Baltistan, but the revolt of Baltistan is related with the revolt in Ladakh. Hence, in order to keep the events intact and to mention all the expeditions of the Dogra's at one place, I have narrated this expedition with the events of Ladakh, so that all the expeditions of Dogra's concerning this region could be seen at a same place. I have already explained earlier about the revolt of Baltistan. Where as Suleman Khan Raja Shighar and Mohammad Shah Raja Skardo were in the prison and Kacho Haider Khan was ruling over Skardo and Shighar. The Dogra officers and soldiers deployed at Skardo were in prison at village Nyali and surrounding areas, thus the Dogra's rule in Baltistan came to an end. Therefore, to remove the chaos and crises in the region and to punish the rebellions, Maharaja Gulab Singh deputed his confident Wazir Lakhpat Kashtawaria to Baltistan.

Wazir Lakhpat, along with 3,000 Dogra warriors marched from Kishtawar and reached at Suru, via Nallah Chilung, so as to check the rebellions, because the people of Suru also revolted. Therefore, he had to face the rebellions everywhere in the way but he crashed them and arrived at Kargil. Before he arrived at Kargil Dewan Hari Chand and Wazir Ratnu had left for Ladakh by defeating the rebellions of Sot at Tiktikmo. Wazir Lakhpat first did the internal arrangement of the region and then with the consultation of Raja Ali Sher Khan of Kartaksha gets prepared for the travel of Baltistan. Wazir crossed the Daras River at the Karket briedge, wherefrom he reached at Shingho Shighar. Here the rulers of Skardo had built a tower, where he had kept some soldiers to guard. They fought with Wazir's army, but their number was very few and all of them were got arrested. Hereafter, Wazir's army arrived at the ahead of Devsai deseart, wherefrom the army descended in the Nallah of Kafchun. Wazir did the travel with good strategy and quickly, that nobody came to know unless they reached at Kafchun village. When Kacho Haider Khan was informed about the arrival of this army at Kafchun, instead of fighting he fortified himself in the Kharpochhey fort. When Wazir Lakhpat arrived at Skardo, he surrounded the fort, the fort because of its location was naturally very strong, as has mentioned earlier, that it was considered unbeatable. The fight continued for few days, but Wazir was helpless to capture the fort. Therefore, he with the support of Raja Ali Sher Khan and Raja Mohammad Shah bribed Wazir Mohammad Ali Chheykhatpa, who was the officer in-charge of the main gate of the fort. He agreed that the gate would be open during the night. There was a tower on the hill, which is towards New-Rangga, wherefrom the upper route of the fort is being guarded. The soldiers deployed at the tower were also under the command of Wazir Mohammad Ali. He assured on behalf of the soldiers, that they would not disturb them. Therefore, according to the agreement Wazir deputed a group of soldiers at night on the top of the hill from the New-Rangga side, and he himself along with rest of the army attacked the main gate of the fort. Since the gate was open. The Dogra soldiers entered the fort and a fierce battle took place. The soldiers of the fort fled away because of horror. Some crossed the river by swimming and some run away from the land. Many people drowned in the river. In short, the people inside the fort have to face a great destruction. In the morning the Dogra's unfurled the flag of triumphant on this hill.

When Kacho Haider Khan observed, that luck is not favouring him, and it is useless to counter the Dogra's, therefore in order to save his life he along with his companion run away to Shighar, during the night. Where he did the arrangement and planned to precede Yarkend along with his companions, via Nallah Thaley and Saltro. But here also luck not favoured him, when Raja Doulat Ali Khan came to know about it well in time. He as a loyal subordinate of the Government of Jammu deployed his men and got him arrested along with eighty companions, and brought at Khapulo where from, they were placed before Wazir Lakhpat. The sincere effort of Doulat Ali Khan Raja Khapulo was highly appreciated by Wazir Lakhpat, and Haider Khan and his companions were imprisoned. Later, Wazir took him to Jammu, along with himself and he died there. Since Kharpochhey was the centre of the mischievous; hence, Wazir set fire to the fort and destroyed it. But he spared the beautiful mosque inside the fort, and rest of the buildings was destroyed and was kept in a deplorable condition, so as to keep it unfit for reuse. The mosque is still in a good condition. Later the fort was repaired and renovated and have built small rooms which is being used as arms store and is under the possession of the army. Though Wazir Zorawar Singh had laid the foundation of the new fort towards the right bank of Nallah Satpar on the top of a hill, and the construction was in progress but it was Wazir Lakhpat who during his stay at Skardo got completed the fort and Bhagwan Singh, who was released from the prison of Nayali was appointed Qilladar and deployed there along with 300 Dogra soldiers. He made the villagers of Skardo region responsible for the arrangement of rations. Every village had to pay annually, two to four mds of agricultural seeds, 22 mds barley, 1 md butter, 10 md salt, 2 mds grass, 4 mds wood, besides the traditional taxes. Except it nothing was imposed on the villagers of Skardo. In this connection the Raja of Skardo was made responsible to collection of the goods and had to handover it to the Qilladar. Mohammad Shah was made the ruler of Skardo and never interfered in his administration. Doulat Khan of Khapulo and Khorram Khan of Keres were reinstated Raja's as usual and their estates were restored. Raja Ali Sher Khan of Kartaksha improved the relations with the Dogra's because of his sincere services to them. He remained the "Jagirdar" of Kartaksha as usual and never interfered in his area and the Raja of Tolti Ahmad Khan was reinstated. After making these arrangements Wazir Lakhpat went to Shighar. Here the real heir of the estate Suleman Khan had died, hence his son Imam Quli Khan was made the Raja, and his estate and powers were restored to him. Moreover, some soldiers were kept there to guard the area. Wazir proceeded to Rongdo to check the crises, after making the arrangements at Shighar after crossing the forest of Bhishu, the army attacked Rongdo, and the battle was won easily. But the Wazir of Raja Mohammad Shah Doghonipa Bono was killed in the battle, who was a faithful servant of Raja Mohammad Shah and a guide to Wazir Lakhpat. Here Ali Khan was the Raja at that time and Wazir also restored his estate. But his son Hussain Khan was took with himself as a hostage. And some soldiers were kept to guard at Astaq fort. Jabbar Khan was the Raja of Astore at that time. He was also responsible for creating disturbance in the area. As soon as he made the arrangements of Rongdo, Wazir Lakhpat invaded Astore via Harpola.

Jabbar Khan fortified and Wazir besieged the fort. When it took a long time and they felt shortage of food inside the fort, then the Raja came out and surrendered. Wazir punished them and went back to Skardo. When Wazir reached back to Skardo, the construction of the fort was completed, and the army was stationed inside the fort comfortably. There was peace and prosperous everywhere in the country. Thereafter, Wazir went back to Jammu via Kishtawar, along with the prisoners of Baltistan. When Wazir reached at Purig, he took the Rajas of Purig with himself to Jammu as prisoners, they are Hussain Khan Raja Pashkyum, Salam Khan Raja Sot, Rahim Khan Raja Tikchey, Tsewang Namgyal Kalon Mulbe, Chhaghdor Namgyal Raja Tambis, and his brother Kunga Namgyal, Wazir Quddus Beg of Sot and some other personalities who were responsible for the disturbance and participated in the revolt. Beside, such people who participated practically in the revolt or assassinated the Dogras in Baltistan and Purig were given capital punishment. Their heads were put on display at prominent places so as to terrorize others. He deployed forces at the forts of Kargil. Daras, and Suru for the defense of Purig. This arrangement was continued till the recent past. Over a period of time this fort system started to subside. Like wise the arrangements of the forts of Shighar and Stagh in Baltistan have ended. Now the regular armies are stationed only at Skardo and Leh forts.

In short, the Baltistan expedition of Wazir Lakhpat had been highly successful in every respect. Whatever arrangements he made in Baltistan and Purig, exists like a foundation stone even now. As soon as Wazir Lakhpat did the arrangement of Purig, he turned towards Zangskar because these people had also revolted. And the Thanedar Jamdar Dheenu appointed by Wazir Zorawar Singh and the Dogra soldiers under him got killed. Thus, the Raja of Chemur ended the Dogra rule and deputed his crown prince Balchu to Ladakh to convey this good news. When Wazir Lakhpat reached Zanskar the public surrendered without showing any form of resistance, and even the Wazir didn't bother the populace, although he made Raja Chemur hostage and took him along to Jammu and confiscated all his property. Balchu was not present there at that time therefore he escaped being made a prisoner, later he died in Kashmir due to smallpox. This way the entire family was finished.

Wazir Lakhpat appointed Mehta Basti Ram as Thanedar of Zanskar and deployed few soldiers with him. He abandoned the fort built by Wazir Zorawar Singh and constructed a new fort which still exists. During this time he also imposed tax on the population. After setting the military and civil administration right he left for Jammu.

11

Ladakh's Trade, Crafts, Agricultural Production, Minerals and Wonderful Objects

Leh city of Ladakh is a trade centre to exchange the goods of Chines Turkistan, Tibet, plain and hilly areas of India. The goods imported from Chines Turkistan are: namda, silk, carpets, skin, lambs skin, pashmina, coarse cloth, hashish, badakhshani and Yarkendi horses, silver, limited number of golden dust, Chines utensils, woolen duret and many other things. The goods exported from here are: Indian and foreign pieces of cotton cloth, sugar, ghurh, tea, soft skin, ruby and other similar things. The goods imported from Lahsa are: Chines tea, lucky stone, musks, chines medicen, pashmina, wool, Chines utensils, Chines silk cloth, and other things like coper and bronze pots, lamb's skin, and salt, etc. and the goods like, dry fruits, apricot, barley, woolen blanket and the shawal of Baltistan are being exported from Ladakh. There is no art and craft in Ladakh, to have trade at a large scale with India and central Asia. The major portion of goods wich comes from central Asia and Tibet for trade purposes are being sent to Kashmir and India and some indigenous goods like pashmina, wool, lamb's skin, and yak tail, etc. are being sent to India. Similarly, all sorts of daily use items are being imported from India. However, the woolen clothes and the duret made of goat and Yak's wool are prepared for their personel use. There is no special sect or tribe for manufacture of these goods, whereas almost every household prepare it in their houses.

The agricultural season is very short in Ladakh. Since most of the region are located at 10,000 to 15,000 feet high from the sea level. Almost all the agricultural lands are one crope field but the land is fertile, and the crop gets ready within a small time. Though the wind blows, yet there is no rain. Therefore, without irrigation no crop is possible in the valleys. The major agricultural productions are barley and grain. "Grim" is a kind of barley which has no stra, and this is the major food of the Ladakhies. Beside, the Rabi crops are: peas, mustard, masoor and baqla. Whereas the Kharif crop are tranba, kangni, and chanba. Among the vegetables the turnip is very famous and it is produced in a large number. Moreover, some vegetables and onion, etc., are also produced. The foreigners grow cabbage, karam-sag, cauli-flower, turnip, "chaqander", and potatoes. I have grown chilly, bottlegaurd, maize and other Indian vegetables for experiment but the local people have no interest to grow these vegetables.

At the government level mustard has been cultivated successfully in Ladakh it was not introduced among the local people. As far as fruits are concerned, the people of Nubra and lower Indus valley (Sham) grows walnut, apricote, apple, and a limited number of mulberry and grapes, but there is no fruit in the areas of upper Ladakh. Among the common tress only the white-lead and willow trees are seen, but at the high altitude areas these two types of trees are not found. In Leh town, there are some apricote trees but bears no fruit. I have planted walnut and chinar, though it was green in summer but dryed up in winter. There is a wild tree in Nallah Wanla which is called locally "Padam" and ceader in English, it is found in large number in other Nallahs. It is also used in construction purposes in special cases. The Buddhists consider it very sacred and used during the rituals. There is no forest in this area. The white-lead and willow trees are being planted for the domestic and constructional purposes. The people cultivate some types of grass as fodder for the animals. The fule in Ladakh is very few, except Nubra, where some sorts of trees are grown in the

Nallahs and around the hills and the wood is used as a fule. Usually, the people cook their foods with horse and cow-dung and small plants of herbs. In spite of awufly cold and lack of fule, the people are not habitual to bask before a fire. Instead with the increase of cold they increase their dresses. Even the strength of cold is measured by one gawn or two gaon's cold and so on. Though there is no rain or snow in the valleys, yet snow falls on the top of the hills and mountains, because of that the streams and rivers follows throught the year and there are springs at some places. Its water is being carried tactfully for the irrigation purposes. Wherever there is water for irrigation there is inhabitants otherwise the land is dry. Though the water is very valuable here, yet mostly falls in the river without having benifitted. As far as minerals are concerned, in the past the gold was dug out from the bank of River Shayok and Indus, but now the diging work has left because of none avalibility of the minerals. However, the gold mines are still available at some places. In the beginning of the Dogra's period "Phuli", a kind of Soda and sulpher were imported from Nubra and Rupsho respectively. Now this system has discontinued because of the less demand in the Indian market. The iron mines are at Charasa Nubra and Fotoksar at lower Leh. In the past these were in use but now it has discontinued. Because now, the cheap and best quality of iron is being imported from India. The copper mine is at Lingshed, but it is not in use. The lead mine is also in Chrasa. The mine of green stone is found in Bogdang Nubra but not benifitted and the mine of "Nila Totia" is situated at Hanu Ladakh but it is not in use. The mine of Alum is also in Nubra without any use. Salt is procured from Rupsho and Tangtsey Lakes but the process has left on nature, and because of bitterness it is not able to use. However, the local people take it for human and animal use, and are a great source of income. If it is extracted tactfully, one can have a very pure salt. Since I started the work, but I left the region without completion of the process. The diet of the people is "Zan" which is prepared by barley. The preparation of "Zan" is very simple. First the pimple of barley is cleared and than roasted. Later it is grinded to make "Sattu" and finally the "Sattu" is being put in the water to cook and balls are made, this is called "Zan". The people eat the "Zan" with tea or Chhang. In Ladakh only the animals drink the water. Instead of water people use Chhang and those who didn't drink Chhang use tea. The people drink the tea at a large scale, which is salty. Butter is mixed in salt tea. The Kashmiri rice is available in Ladakh but only the rich people use it. The dresses both for men and women are woolen during summer and winter. Men wear a necktied gaun which reaches up to the ankle. Women wear a garment like a gown its foot touches the ankle. Both men and women wear a tide trouser beneath the gown. The nobles wear a printed shirt under the gown. The rich person wears a jacket like garment over the gown during the winter and some people use the skin jacket. Both men and women fastend a belt around the waist. The women put on a goat skin over the gown with its wool inside. Sometimes it is prepared with lamb's skin. Without it the female dress is considered incomplete. The women keep a basket on the back to get the things to and fro and the strap of the basket lies at the chest. Beside the woman kept the child in the basket too. The women put on a valuable-cobra shaped cap over the head called "Perak" decorated with gold, silver, and luckey stones. Its pointed side lies on the forehead and goes downwards up to the back. The local people called it "Perak". It is the popular ornament of the women here. It costs rupees hundred to few thousands. To protect the ears from cold a lamb's skin is placed over the ears attached with the "Perak". The hair "Chuti" of the women touches the ankle and the back as that of men. Both men and women wear woolen shoes during winter and summer with skin on the soles. Among the peculiarities of Ladakh is the hot springs. Some springs have the smell of sulpher. Since the springs of Rupsho are situated near the mines of sulpher. Some springs have no smell of sulpher, like that of hot spring of panamik. It is too hot. It is said that rice can be cooked here. I did exprement, but failed. Probably, I have not kept the rice for a long time inside the water. Some patients took bath there for different disease. The hot water is being taken to a reservoir through a canal and took bath in it. The local people have great faith of its effectiveness. I also got opportunities to have a bath in these springs and I took bath almost in all the hot springs of Ladakh and Baltistan but I never felt them as effective. One of the specialities of Ladakh is the asthama. The details of it have been mentioned in the Mirza Haider's expeditions. The people of the plain areas have to face this difficaulty in Leh city itself. Neither they could sleep well and nor could work. I never felt it at the height of 14,000 or 15,000 feet but whenever, I got an opportunity to travel at the height of 18,000 or 20,000 feet high from the sea level. I also felt the problem and was senseless. Later, I regained the sense, when I was brought 2,000 or 3,000 feet downwards, and the next day I was quite well. But the Ladakhies have no affect of the high altitude. As far as wild animals are concerned, there are deer on the small hills and the "Kail" on the high mountains. There are Zebra in large number at Rupsho and wild Yak is also found in some Nallahs. The rabbits are found in large number at many places. Among the birds patridge and pegions are found every where. The fowls are found at some places. There are large numbers of fish in the river but the Buddhists have no intrest of fishing, since they considered it a great sin.

12

The Dogra Rulers of Ladakh

(1) Magn Thanedar, (2) Mehta Basti Ram Thanedar, (3) Mehta Manggal Thanedar, (4) Wazir Shipsaran Thanedar, (5) Syed Akbar Ali Shah Wazir, (6) Mr Doru Wazir, (7) Mr. Johonson Wazir, (8) Pandit Radha Kishan Koul Wazir, (9) Khan Bahadur Sardar Mohammad Akbar Khan Wazir, (10) Choudry Khoshi Mohammad Mohtamim Bondabast Wazir.

MAGNA THANEDAR (1898-1902 AD)

During the Dogra's rule, he was the first ruler of Ladakh. He was appointed by Wazir Zorawar Singh. The old fort of Ladakh was got constructed under his supervision. In the heart of Leh town, he built a beautiful house, which still known as Magna Haveli. Now the veterinary hospital and Kotwali have been accommodated in it. He planted tress on Leh-Kashmir road below the agricultural land of Leh, which is known as Magna Bagh.

MEHTA BASTI RAM THANEDAR (1903-1916 AD)

The polyandry system of marriage was prevellent among the Buddhist of Ladakh. Consequently, a large number of women were unmarried. Some of the women enter the Gonpas as nun; they are called "Chomos". Some are wanderer and vagabond and have illegal children oftenly. They remain homeless. Mehta Basti Ram renamed them as "Ghulam Zadah" and prepared a list of such children. He sanctioned rations for them and made the arrangement for their education. He established a handi-craft centre, where durets, etc., were being prepared. An officer was the incharge of the center. This continued till the period of Mr. Johnson. During the reign of the Ladakhi Raja's it was a custom to keep sheep and goats owned by the government. There are some tribes in Tangtsey and Rupsho, who looks after the sheep and goats of others on contract basis, on two conditions; the first condition was that the man has to return equal number of animals at any rate which he received at the time of contract. Secondly, he has to give in detail, the correct quantity of the increase and decrease of the animals. In both the conditions he has to pay annually, one seer butter per goat, one seer pashmina, one seer wool per sheep to the owner. Mehta Basti Ram started to keep the sheep and goats of the government, which became a source of income. This system continued for a long time but now it has discontinued because of ill-administration. He got constructed a beautiful bunglow in the Leh town, called Basti Haveli, which still exist. The drawing room of the building has been converted in to ration store and the quarters are being used by the Tehsildar and other officers. The construction of the present Bazar of Leh had been started by him. On the one side of the Bazar was built the court and treasury building and the quarters for the employees. These buildings are still being used for the said purpose. Mehta Basti Ram was an able and good administrator. His sympathetic rule is still remembered by the people.

MEHTA MANGGAL THANEDAR (1917-1922 AD)

Mehta Manggal was an able administrater. He made the revenue settlement of whole Ladakh for the first time, and made the reforms in the tax system. The second great achivement of the officer is the demarcation of the border between Tibet and Ladakh. The fort built by Magna Thanedar was so small; he extended the area of the fort by constructing buildings attached to it, and got constructed the wall and ditch around the old and new fort and consolidated the fort. There are so many new colonies founded by him. However, the following are very famous:

1. Ranbirpur, 2. Rampur Chushot, 3. Partapur, and 4. Mangal Chak (Martselang).

He got constructed the khuls for the above-mentioned villages and settled the homless people there. Residential houses were constructed for them and they were provided with plough, ox and grain for seeds for farming, imposed tax on subsidized rates and for some time they were exempted from the tax. In short he provided all sort of support to them, so as to improve them in agriculture, which was need of the hour at that time. The constructions of sarai at the halting places on Leh-Kashmir, Tibet and Kullu route and in the Nubra region, which still exists, are the contributions of this great builder. He planted trees all over Ladakh and planted white lead trees on the route side, where there is possible of water. In Leh town just adjacent to the court building, he planted trees after leveling the land called "Gulab Mandi Bagh". It is because of his wisdom, that he introduced the "Race" system at the halting places for the convenience of the travelers. Since in a country like Ladakh where there is less population and the inhabitants are scattered, this system is highly appreciable. Prior to that there was no postal system and at the time of emergencies special messengers were deployed. He appointed postmen and made the postal system regular. As far as education is concerned, he established a Pathshala in Leh town for Sanskrit language and the students were paid scholarships, so as to motivate them. The "Ghulam Zadey" illegal children were also admitted in this Pathshala to seek education. He made the arrangement to export and sell the Ladakhi salt at Kashmir and improved the trade. The construction of Leh Bazar, which was started earlier, was completed by him. As far as I know, in the hilly towns of Himalyan regions, this Bazar is very beautiful in every respect. He introduced "Hakim" system of treatment for the convenience of the government employees. The medicins were supplied to the "Hakim" by the government. And he has to treat the employees free of cost. Mehta Manggal was very favourite ruler. All the Ladakhies still remember him with great respect.

WAZIR SHIBSARAN THANEDAR (1922-1923 AD)

He planted tress in a garden in Leh, which is called Wazir Bagh. Within the garden the Yarkendi sarai, Charas Godown, Church, and Morvian Mission Charity Hospital have been constructed and the trees has finished now.

SYED AKBAR ALI WAZIR LADAKH (1923-1926 AD)

During his period, the status of Thanedar has been redesignated as Wazir. The Wazir introduced the law of Jammu kingdom here and introduced the coin 'Jao" in Ladakh in the name of Maharaja Jammu. It is he, who introduced "Chadar" instead of perak among the Muslim women. He encouraged physical cleanliness and abulution and made the people habitual of washing hands and face. He did efforts to eradicate some social evils but failed. He established a garden in Leh.

MR. DORU WAZIR (1927-1928 AD)

He introduced the "Jarib" of Punjab and Jammu and Kashmir into Ladakh. He was very much interested in agricultural improvement. He granted concessions to the hireless persons and outsiders in respect of construction of houses, excemption of taxes, and exemption from government duties, etc., and settled in the new colonies. But he didn't got a sufficient time to improve this system. He made reforms in the local administration. He was a scholar. He wrote a very good book on the geography and geology of Jammu and Kashmir state, which is a first detail geography of this state and has scholarly discussed the political and historical aspects also. Bai Ganga Singh was his assistant, who established the "Behesht Bagh".

MR. JOHONSON WAZIR (1928-1939 AD)

He was in the service of Government of India in the tourism department and visited Ladakh. Later, he joined the service of the state. He built a very beautiful bunglow for himself in Gulab Mandi. This was the first European type of bunglow in Ladakh, which is still in use as a capital. He got constructed a canal from the Indus to irrigate the desert of Gopuk just adjacent to village Spituk, but the water could not raise in the canal and the plan was failed. Later, he constructed another canal just below it and settled the population there. With the help of the said canal, he planted trees in a vast area and constructed a buglow inside the garden, which still exists. Beside, he constructed a canal for the barren land of Ule-tokpo and inhabitate the people there. He inhabitate the people at other places and planted trees in the gardens. He got constructed a grand fort at Chushot, it not exists now, however a damaged old sarai is there. He got constructed a Sarai, just adjacent to the Bazar, called Balti Sarai for the people of Baltistan who used to come Ladakh for the trade of dry fruits and butter and get purchase wool, Pashmina, salt, and tea, etc. from here. He raised the store of grain because of his good strategy and did reforms in the administration. He made amendmants in the land settlement system of Mehta Manggal, and made reforms in the contract of goats and sheep and to receive the amount of profit from the government traders. This increased the revenue of the government. He was a man of merriments and loved sports, dance and music. In spite of this, his system of administration was very admirable. His court was open for everybody, as per the eastern system. Chhang and tea were used to serve in the court as per the local system and all sorts of conversation were made in the office beside settlements of the cases and disputes. All the cases were settled verbally. There was no system of maintaining files. Usually, the decision was recorded on the backside of the application, and handover to the applicant. People still remember this quick judgement and disposal of cases and admire the system.

RAI BAHADUR PANDIT RADHA KISHEN KOUL WAZIR (1939-1943 AD)

His great contribution was the land settlement of Ladakh. Though the people didn't accept the newly imposed revenue tax and complained against the system. Finally, some modification was made in the proposal of Mr. Johonson and the public was satisfied with it, as a result the land settlement was not come in force. He made reforms in the system of forced labour. During his rule, post-office was properly established in Ladakh. Beside, he improved the plantation system in the region.

KHAN BAHADUR SARDAR MOHAMMAD AKBAR KHAN WAZIR (1955-1957 AD)

Khan Bahadur Sardar Mohammad Akbar Khan ruled over Ladakh for three years. He made reforms in the pervious system of administration and found a great corruption in the treasury because of misappropriation of funds. He also found some corruption in the import system of "soda", etc. He made the inquiry and rectified it, and recovered the losses of the government, and punished the defaulters. He improved the trade system of Lhasa.

CHOUDRY KHOSHI MOHAMMAD MOHTAMIM BONDABAST AND WAZIR (1963-1966 AD)

After him some more Wazir came, but they had been not as popular as per their performance. Finally, Choudry Khoshi Mohammad Mohtamim Bondabast and Wazir, made the legal land settlement of Zangskar and Ladakh under the supervision of commissioner settlement Mr. Talbot and the complain of imposition of heavy tax was removed. He made reforms in the system of forced labour and the arrangement of halting places.

13

Source of Revenue Old and New

1. The period of Buddhist dynasty, 2. The administration of Wazir Zorawar Singh, 3. The basic observation of revenue by Magna Thanedar and Wazir Ratnu, 4. The modification of Mehta Basti Ram, 5. More modification of Mehta Manggal, 6. The improvements made by Mr Johonson, 7. Land Revenue of Pandit Radha Kishen, 8. Administration of Mr Kalark, and 9. The legal land revenue of Mr Talbot and Choudry Khoshi Mohammad.

THE PERIOD OF BUDDHIST KINGDOM

There was no land revenue during the Buddhist rule. However, the peasants were responsible to make the arrangements of the domestic requirements of the king, and the peasants were themselves responsible for the administration and defence of the country, which are briefed as follows:

GRAIN, the twenty-four villages of Nubra region were responsible to arrange the grain for six months and the villages of Lamayuru, Skurbu-chan, Tingmogang, Saspol, Bazgo, Shay and Thiksay were arranging the grain for the rest six months. Moreover, the cultivation of the king's land had to be made by forced labour through the peasants, and all the productions have to be deposit in the state godown.

MEAT, the areas of Rupsho, Tangtsey and some villages of Rong were responsible to supply the requirements of meat for whole the year.

BUTTER, Zangskar region was responsible for the supply of butter and a small quantity of butter were procured from Rupsho, Tangtsey and Rong.

WOOD FOR FULE, The village in the Nallah's like Chiling-Sumdo, Khardong, and Hunder-Dok, etc., were responsible to arrange 3,000 Mds of wood for the Raja for the purpose of fule.

WOOLEN CLOTH, to prepare the woolen clothes for the members of the royal family, three pao of wool used to collect from all the household of the country and prepare the cloth by the peasants through forced labour. Mostly this task had to be done by the weavers of Tangtsey.

SHEEP AND GOAT, there was a tradition to conduct the census of the goat and sheep and after every ten animals one has to handover to the Raja. These animals had to be kept under the supervision of the royal shepherds, and at the time of emergencies, meat, butter and wool were procured from them.

CASH, every household had to pay one "Jao" annually to the king. Beside, the villagers were responsible to repair and renovate the Mane and Chhortens, without any honorarium. Moreover those villages where big Gonpas are situated like Hemis, Chemrey, Thiksay, Pethub, Phiyang, Likir, Lamayuru, Karsh and Rangdum were granted the payable dues and the Stewards of the Gonpas were responsible to collect the dues. But the correct figure of the income is not known. Besides the above-mentioned income the Raja was having some miscellaneous incomes too, thay are as follows:

TEA, the royal trader "Lobchhak" used to go from Ladakh to Tibet for trade purposes after every three years. The "Lobchhak" had to be provided transportation from Ladakh to Lhasa and Lhasa to Ladakh free of cost. In return to the concession he was responsible to arrange the tea for the royal family for whole the year.

THE ROYAL TRADERS, nobody was allowed to precede Chanthang and Lhasa for trade except the royal traders. Mostly, the Arghon traders were authorized to go there. They had to pay rupees 3,000 as advance amount and had to receive double of the amount at the time of return.

TAX ON THE GOODS, the Yarkendi traders, who bring their goods to sell in Ladakh, had to pay tax, but the correct figure is not available. However, there had been increase and decrease in the total amount of income subject to the quantity of goods. The approximate income was in between rupees twelfth thousand and thirty thousand.

SERVICES DURING WAR, the weapons and ammunitions had to be stored in the royal arms store. During the external invasion or attack by the king every household had to provide one soldier each, along with his food and clothes but the arms had to be provided by the king.

ROYAL POSTS, after the Raja there was a Kalon or prime minister and there were many other Kalons or Lonpos under him as head of the provinces and the Namberdar of the villages were under him. They had not been paid any salary from the royal treasury. However, every officer had to receive the "Rasum" from his subordinate officer and the grass-root level officer had to receive it from the peasants.

THE ADMINISTRATION OF WAZIR ZORAWAR SINGH

Wazir Zorawar Singh never interfered in the administration of Raja, during his first invasion. However, he imposed rupees 9,000 to Raja Tundup Namgyal as annual tribute and restored the country to him. During the next invasion, when he deposed Raja Tundup Namgyal and appointed Mourup Stanzin as nominal king and doubled the amount of tribute to rupees 18,000 annually.

MAGNA THANEDAR AND WAZIR RATNU

After the third invasion the administration had been undertook in the hand of the Jammu rulers. Finally, Wazir Ratnu and Magna Thanedar imposed the land revenue tax. They made the census in the country and made the grading system and imposed the revenue tax on different grades as per the following rates:

1. The Nobles like that of Kalon and Lonpo, etc., had to pay the tax at the rate of rupees ₹ 14, ₹ 25 and ₹ 30 per household.
2. The peasants were also distributed in three categories: first "gama" that is middle. Second "Phetma", i.e. half. Third "Yan phetma", i.e. one-fourth and imposed tax at the rate of rupees ₹ 9, ₹ 3.8 and ₹ 10 respectively.
3. The regions of Skurbuchan and Nubra are very fertile and gives two crops, so he increased the tax at the rate of ₹ 3.4, ₹ 4.1 and ₹ 20 respectively.
4. In the areas of Rupsho and Tangtsey the agricultural productions are by name only. And the peasants are dependent on animals only. Hence, the tax was fixed as per the quantity of the animal, but the rate and correct figure is not known.
5. The taxes on grain, woods and butter have not been fixed. It is said that it had to be received at the level of the expences of the government employees, as per the past practice. This was in addition to the cash revenue.
6. During the rule of Buddhist kingdom, the goats and sheep which were under the care of the royal shepherds was considered owned by the government and had been kept continuously under their care. And had to be received them, whatever number required compensating the requirement of meet for the government employees. The shephereds had to keep in tact the exact number of the animals as it was earlier.
7. During the reign of Bhuddist kings' the royal traders had been receiving rupees 3,000 as advance and had to pay back the double of the amount. This system continued during the Dogra's period.
8. The toll tax on the goods of the Yarkendi traders remained the same as per the past practice.
9. The tradition of the Buddhist kingdom to make the census of the animals and to receive one animal after every ten goats or sheep was banned.

10. The concessions granted in the past by the Buddhist kingdom to the Gonpa's were continued in the new system, and the land was not included in the list and kept tax free.

THE AMENDMENT OF MEHTA BASTI RAM

During the period of Mehta Basti Ram, the goats and sheep owned by the government were under the care of the shepherds, who had to pay annually 1 seer butter per goat, 1 seer pashmina per he goat or she-goat, 1 seer wool per sheep. This was the old system and made no amendment.

THE AMENDMENT OF MEHTA MANGGAL

As per the proposal of the Magna Thanedar, the land revenue system continued the same for about 20 years. Later, Mehta Manggal made some amendment in it. He kept continue the grading system and rate of revenue tax started by Magna Thanedar and Wazir Ratnu and renamed it as "real". And those where the payment of revenue was ceased or included in the list during the previous inquiry or the land which was demarcated after the said inquiry, all were added. Moreover, the land revenue tax of the two crops villages were increased, and partially reforms were made in other revenue arrangements. The above-mentioned detail indicates that the early Dogra administrators followed the principles of Buddhist kingdom and gradually made reforms in the revenue systems which improved the income. Thus, the differences between the harsh and lenient viewe was removed. The efficiency and far-sighted policy of these officers are praiseworthy. The latter administrations and arrangements are principally based on this very system.

JOHONSON'S DEVELOPMENTS AND REVENUE IMPROVEMENTS

Mr. Johonson who, like Mehta Manggal was very popular, efficient and good strategic administrater. He made reforms in the revenue systems. The details are as follows:

1. The tax was imposed on Mansar village which is in between Naris Korsum and Lhasa like an island.

2. The "Charu" used to collect from Rupsho and Tangtse. Lamb skin is called "Charu", and by joining them jacket is prepared.
3. Salt tax was imposed on the areas of Rupsho, Hemis and Rong, who used to take the benefits of salt from Thugjay Lake.
4. Nitre and coal were imported from Nubra valley and "Hartal" from Lingshed village. He imposed "Rasum" tax on these articles.
5. Soda which is lacally called "Phuli" is being procured from Nubar was given on contract.
6. "Nagtsur" is a color; the mine of nagtsur was properly guarded.
7. He introduced the system of cleaning the borax.
8. Got reforms in the systems of the iron mining and imposed tax.
9. He fixed the rate of "Zare-murakab" on the horses of transportation and fixed "Zare-mehtarana" on the animals, who enter Ladakh from Kargil and Kashmir.
10. The traders of Tibet who used to bring wool and salt in Ladakh and in return got purchased the grain of Ladakh. He imposed import tax on the goods.
11. He increased the agricultural revenue.
12. Grain was distributed from the government stores to the peasants for seeds.
13. Rasum of cash instead of kind was fixed on the animals owned by the state.
14. The gift received by the government employees were deposited in the treasury.
15. Reforms were made in the service of forced labours utilized by the government employees for their personel use.
16. Instead of cash as interest on the advance amount paid to the state traders, he arranged to receive "pashmina".

17. Beside the revenue in kind, he passed on the order of purchase.

LAND SETTLEMENT OF PANDIT RADHA KISHEN KOUL

Pandit Radha Kishen Koul did the land settlement in 1940 AD, but there had been a common hatredness against this system and the peasants complained against it. Consequently, instead of the new system kept continue the old system with slight modification and increase in the revenue.

THE 'BACHH' SYSTEM OF MR KLARK

Mr. Klark introduced the new "Bachh" system with slight modification in 1958, but the complaint of the peasants about the harsh system of the "Bachh" continued. Later, Mr. Talbot with the assistance of Choudry Khoshi Mohammad properly did the land measurement and repelled the complaints and imposed tax on pasture lands.

14

Buddhist Customs and Traditions

1. Caste and tribe, 2. Heridity, 3. Marriage, 4. Secret marriage, 5. Divorce, 6. Polyndry and polygamy, 7. Adoption, 8. Testament, gift and charity, 9. Birth, and 10. Death.

1. Caste and Tribe. There is no distinction of tribe within the Buddhists. The low or high caste came into existence because of profession. However, except the Beda, and gara (the musicians and blacksmith) there is no distinction of high and low, and every persons drink and dine together. However, the men of different status don't utilize the used utensils of others. The caste which exists presently as per the professions are as follows:

1. Gyalpo, i.e. Raja.
2. Kalon; whose ancestors had been Prime Minister or Governor of the province.
3. Lonpo; whose ancestors were ministers.
4. Nangso; whose ancestors were the royal cashiers or store man.
5. Larjey; Hakim by profession.
6. Onpo; Astrologer.
7. Phalpa; general peasants/farmers.
8. Shingkhan; carpenter.
9. Sergar zergar (gold smith).
10. Gara, Iron smith.

11. Lamkhan, Shoe maker.
12. Mon; Musicians.
13. Beda; Musicians.

Actually, Beda is Mon. But those who converted to Islam are called "Beda". The rest of the twelfth castes mentioned above are Buddhists. Many Muslims from Kashmir and Baltistan are settled in Ladakh. The Kashmiris are settled in Leh town, whereas the Baltis are settled in two big villages, Shay and Chushot. The Kashmiris are Sunni Muslims whereas the Baltis are Shia Muslims. A third tribe is in existence in Ladakh, because of the inter marriage of the Kashmiris and Yarkendis with the Ladakhi women; those are called "Argons". There is no difference of caste and creed between the Muslims. As far as customs and traditions are concerned, they follow the Islamic Shariya. Those minor differences are not necessary to mention here, hence, I am narrating the Buddhist customs and traditions only.

2. Heridity. Among the Buddhist the elder son has the right of inheritance. If there is no male issue, then the elder daughter would be the successor, conditionally, that she is not married to a man out of the family. If she is married then the second eldest daughter would be the successor. If all the daughters might have gone outside the faimly as "Pagma" (marriage). Then none have the right to claim the inheritance. Instead a second grade relative can claim it, unless one among the daughters return to the parental house by divorce. Though there are instances in Ladakh that a married girl had been the owner of her husband's property as well as the successor of her own father. But this is an extraordinary case, it can't be acceptable generally. If the real successors raise the objections than it can be null and void. A childless person generally adopts a son or daughter among his nearest relatives. If there is none among his nearest relatives then, with the consultation of the relatives and "Phaspun", he adopts one among the "Phaspuns" or outsiders. In that case the adoptee would have the full rights like a real successor. (Phaspun is the outsiders who under a contract support to arrange all sorts of functions whenever required among them.) According to the tradition, the system of succession is as under. As far as the adoptions of the far relatives are concerned, it is an extra-ordinary case, generally it is not acceptable. In the said case, the relatives should not have any objection.

1. Elder son, 2. Elder daughter, 3. Brother (the elder among the brothers), 4. Elder daughter, 5. Uncle, 6. Mother, 7. Widow, 8. The widowed daughter-in-law, and 9. Phaspun.

The son, brother, or uncle and daughter and sister might have gone in another house as son-in-law or daughter-in-law or have become Lama or Chomo have no right of succession, unless and until after divorce they come back in the parental house, with the consent of the relatives and successors. The offsprings of those abodoned from inheritance would become successors after widow no. 8 mentioned above, conditionally if he or she resides in the house of the inheriter. After them the "Phaspun" would be the successor. The widows of the successor would get the succession conditionally, that she would reside in the house of the successor. Moreover, there is option to get a husband as "Makpa" and it did not affect their inheritance. Otherwise if she marries out of the faimly, then she would loss the right of inheritance. In case if she marries living in the family and gets a man as "Makpa" their offsprings have the right of inheritance. Phaspun is called to those relatives, who support the person during the functions of sorrow and happiness. Usually, they are the far relatives but sometimes the outsiders are also included among the Phaspuns. Traditionally, every household is affiliated with some other households in the name of Phaspun, but it happens seldomly that in search of inheritance one might have reached up to the Phaspun. If one has to face the situation off and on, then traditionally, all the members of the Phaspun get together and decide to make a boy or girl among themselves as inheriter of the childless person. If it is not possible then amalgamate the property of the poorest person among the "Phaspuns" with the childless one. However, the propery of the childless person is never devided among the phaspuns. If a person possesses more than one wife then their offsprings would be the successors as per the seniority. If a person gets married his daughter in the family considering her his successor, later his own wife gave birth to a son. In that case the son has no right of inheritance; however he can have the maintenance. If a woman dies childless, then his husband would be the successor and he has the right to remarry. If they failed to produce an issue, then in the absence of the husband his widow would be the successor, but after her death, the property woud be transferred to the members of the forefathers. In the absence of a legal child, the illegal one would be the heir. In case of conversion, no one has igonored or abandoned from inheritance. There are so many instances in Ladakh that after the conversion, the offsprings remained the heir of their ancesters. But now the efforts are being made that after the conversion one has no right to claim the inheritance, but it is not in practice till now.

3. Marriage. Those persons whose paternal or maternal heredity meets with one another, within seven generations are not allowed to marry. The nobles marry after five generations, but the members of the royal families never bothered even for five generations, while the ordinary people have the regards for this tradition beyond seven generations. Marraige is not celebrated within the "Phaspuns". However, there is no ban to marry their relatives who are not among the Phaspuns. One can't marry with the widow of his deceased son. There are two system of marriage; one, the woman has to go to the house of the husband as bride, it is called "Pagma". In this case, the woman has no right to claim the inheritance of her parents. She is compelled to be loyal to her husband. The second system is that the man goes to the house of his wife as bridegroom called "Makpa". Such man has no right to claim the property of his father and he is also compelled to be loyal to his wife. Usually, it is being done by those men who are abandoned the inheritance of his parents customarily. If later he is entitled to inherit because of the removal of the barriers, even though he is not considered as heir. Such husband gets the divorce from his wife. In short, the relation of the husband "Makpa" is equallent to the wife "Pagma".

As far as the custom of marriage is concerned, the parents of the boy propose the name of the girl. First they consult the astrologer. If he approves according to his methods of astronomy, then they secretly approach the parents of the girl and gets their approval. Finally, the father of the boy along with his relatives go to the house of the girl and offer "Chhang" and Khatak, and prayed to give the consent. If the parants of the girl accepts the "Chhang" it indicates that they had informally accepted the proposal. But they never express the willingness for the first time. This practice is repeated again and again. It is called "Tichhang" or the custom of "Request". When the father of the girl catagoricaly approves the proposal and usually the father has to say, I am happy with this proposal but I have to consult my relatives and accordingly you will be replied. Then date is being fixed for the "Holchhang" and all the relatives of the girl are convened to attend a function. Hence, the father of the boy and his relatives along with the demanded goods proceed to the house of the girl and offer the Chhang and "Khatak" to the relatives of the girl. Those edible raw matrials which has brought by the father of the boy is being prepared in the house of the girl by and served to the guests of both sides. At this festival the father of the boy offers Khatak to every relatives of the girl and prayed. After thorough discussion they give the consent and the agreement is considered final. Later, the date of "Chhang" is fixed on that day and all the far and nearest relatives of the girl, the Phaspun and the neighbours are invited for the function. The father of the son (bridegroom) along with some of his nearest relatives and "Phaspuns" take all the goods for feast at the house of the girl (bride). Everybody is entertained there and piece of white cloth is being put on the head of the bride, which is called "Goras", i.e. head-cloth. After fulfilling this custom, it is considered that all the systems have been completed. At this occasion the father of the bridegroom offer some ornaments, cash, lucky stone, or some dresses to the bride as presents. In return the father of the bride gives a "Tabak" big plate and some other things as present. Later, the relation cannot be terminated. If it terminates by the bridegroom, then he has no right to claim the expenses, on the other hand if the bride does so, she has to pay all the expenses.

Later, "Rinto" is fixed. The literary meaning of "Rinto" is cost. Whatever the father of the girl gives her in kind, he fix the price of the goods and says that such an amount be paid as Rinto. The bridegroom's father is bind to pay the fixed amount to the bride's father before the date of marriage. Moreover, the bride's father prepared a list of the required goods and handover to the bridegroom's father. Which have to bring on the day of marriage to host the guests? The list includes usally, Chhang, bread, meat, butter, tea, rice and appricote, etc., to serve the guest. These articles have to deposit in the house of the bride before the day of marriage. Thereafter, the customs of "tabchhang" is celebrated at both the places. The relatives and neighbours gathered and one say I will arrange the "Chhang" another took the responsibility of butter tea. One arranges the lunch and another dinner. One offers the grain and another give the cash. In short the whole expences of the marriage is being distributed among the relatives, friends, and neighbours, and none has to take the burden. Later, with the consultation of both the parties the date of marriage is fixed, which is called "Pakston". Regarding the number of the "Baratis" and the dancers, the permission has to seek from the bride's father. On the day of marriage the "Baratis" consisting of the friends and relatives along with the dancers arrive at the house of the bride in the evening. But the bridegroom is not included among the baratis. They have to stay at the house of the bridegroom till midnight. In the meantime dinner is served and the dances continued. The Lama performs the religious rituals. As soon as, the dinner is over, the bride is being prepared to depart. She has to put on beautiful and expensive dresses. She put on a round cap over the "Perak" where the "Gores" is kept. All the goods are being collected which has to be given to the bride as dowry. At the movement the Lama performs the ritual of "Yangkhuk" before the bride. Its main aim is to retain the blessings in the house of the father. The bride's father handover a document to his daughter in which the detail list of the goods given as dowry is recorded.

Besides, it is mentioned that the girl has married with the so and so boy. These boy and girl would be the inheriter of the properties at the bridegroom's house. The girl would have the same rights at the bridegroom's house whatever the boy possesses. The "Nerpon" (leader of the bartis) and the relatives confirm the document on behalf of the bridegroom's father and aggress to fulfill the terms and conditions. In the meantime, the "Nyatitpa" comes forward and request the bride to have departed. She took the permissions from her parents, relatives, friends and all of them offer "Khatak" to her and take the leave of all of them with happily. A woman is deputed from the house of her father, along with the bride is called "Pakrok", i.e. helper.

When the bride arrives at the house of the bridegroom, she is received by a Lama at the gate. He performs some religious rituals in front of the bride. The bride has to stay at the gate till the rituals are over. At the end of the rituals the Lama broke an earthen vessel; so that the eveil spirit may not enter in the house, along with the bride or the dowries. Then the bride enters the house and goes in to the "Chansa", i.e. kitchen-cum-drawing room. Here the sitting arrangements for the couple are made, by making the sign of two "Sawastika" (Yundung) on carpet with grain. Both the bride and bridegroom sit together over the signs of sawastika. The relatives and baratis also sits there as per the capacity. A meal is served to the couple. They took a morsel with their own hands. Later, the festivals ends, it is called "Pakston". The next day a function is organized at the house of the bridegroom. The guests drink and dance and the couple have to participate in the dance. A Chhorten shaped feast called "Danggair" is prepared by the "Sattu" (barley powder) for that purpose 4 to 30 maunds of "sattu" is utilized according to one's status or capacity. The vessels of "Chhang" (wine) are being kept around the "chhorten" shaped feast. The bride and bridegroom sit near it. All the guests gathered there and they are served with "Chhang". All of them congratulate the couple and offer "Khatak" and present gifts in cash and kind. Finally, they distribute the barley feast among all the participants. It is also called "Pakston".

The next day a special feast is organized in honour of those people who have presented gifts. It is called "Nendon".

Besides, those people who made all arrangements for the marriage and the relatives are called on the other day. It is called "Don Chhung" or small feast. If the houses of the bride and groom are located in the same locality or near then the newly-wedded couple visit the house of the bride along with some relatives to pay regards to the parents and comes back on the same day. The relatives of the bride did not participate in the feast "Pakston" arranged by the bridegroom but her parents and relatives participate in the "Nendon". The next very day the "Nendon" feast is arranged at the house of the bride, where the newly-wedded couple the parents and the relatives are invited. The next day "Donchhung" is arranged at the house of the bridegroom. Similarly, Donchhung feast is arranged at the house of the bride. The bride and bridegroom and their relative's participats in all these functions. After the "Donchhung" the marriage rituals comes to an end. The "Pakrok" stays with the bride at least 15 days to one month and goes back to her house. The relatives of the bride and bridegroom invite them turn by turn to their house for feast and offer them some cash and Khatak and depart. Pakrok also gets some cash. This system continued for a long time. It is binding for every relatives to invite them once. Those people who are not able to arrange the feast or who are not expecting a huge amont as gifts, etc., they don't arrange this function and be content on the ordinary feast, whatever, they might have arranged for the guests at the time of depart.

If the boy and girl are minor, then neither they are consulted regarding the marriage nor seek their consent. But if youths are wedded, then both boy and girl are consulted. If the parents have expired, then a nearest relative has to fulfil this responsibility. The widow and widower marry as per their own wills. Except "Gores" no other rituals are performed. Some people marry in the old age because of some compulsion; in such cases even the custom of "Gores" is not performed. The woman directly enters in the house of her husband. This type of marriage is not formal, but it is not considered sin. The important custom in marriage is the "Gores", without it the marriage is not considered a complete. Those women who have not performed this ritual, they are not considered as formal wife in the society, and they can separate themselves, without any payment, whenever they like.

4. Secret Marriage. The rituals of marriage mentioned above are the formal system, but usually the people not act upon on this system. Mostly, the people perform the "Secret marriage" which is also called "Chori ki shadi". Its custom is that the "Tichhang" is served as per the above-mentioned system, and after obtaining the consent of the girl's father, one of the nearest relative of the girl is approached and requested to handover the girl to the father of the bridegroom and his relatives from his house. On the appointed night the father of the bridegroom and some of his relatives proceed to the house of the bride's relative along with the goods for feast and entertain there. This man brings the girl at his house with the consent of girl's mother or with connivance, and never cared for the consent or refusal of the girl. A peice of white cloth or a "Khatak" is placed on her head as "Gores". The man brings the girl from the house of her father to his own house and handover to the bridegroom's father and his relatives. The baratis along with the girl reached at the house of the bridegroom. Here a Lama performs the religious rituals; thereafter the couple has to sit side by side in the "Chansa" (kitchen-cum-drawing room). Gores are also placed on the head of the boy and a dish is placed before them and the marriage concludes.

The next day the father of the bridegroom along with some relatives proceeds to the house of the girl with "Chhang" and appologise for the act. Some people refuse to take the Chhang and abuse and accuse the father of the boy, stating that he performed the marriage without our permission. Then the similar action is repeated again and again, till the parents of the girl accepts the "Chhang" and appoligised. Later, the parents of the girl called the bride and bridegroom to their house for feast and the marriage is considered completed. On the night when the secret marriage took place and the girl is brought to the house of the bridegroom, right from the next morning the relatives of the boy began to arrive at the house of the boy with "Chhang" to congratulate the newly-wedded couple. This process continous for months together. When the feast is over at the house of the girl then the relatives of both the sides invite them for feast and offer some cash and "Khatak". And depart, as is done in the case of the "Pakston".

There is another system of this marriage. The adult boy and girl confirm the marriage at their own. If there is no expectation of willingness from the girl's parents, then they are not informed. And the custom of "Tichhang" is not performed. But with the coloboration of a relative of the girl, arrange to bring her at the house of the bridegroom. The rest of the customes are being performed as mentioned above, and the consent of the girl's parents is also sought. Some times they give the consent at a late stage. But unless they get the consent, have to go again and again with Chhang.

Finally, the parents of the girl have to give the consent without any delay, as they are helpless now. This type of marriage usually occurs, because the father of the boy is not in a position to arrange the expenses of the marriage party, and if delayed, there is the fear of cancellation of the engagement. Or the father of the girl is not willing to arrange the marriage party but father of the boy is in hurry. In such cases all the cusomes of the marriage as mentioned above are being performed but the celebration of the marriage have to perform later by both the parties.

5. Divorce. If the treatment of the "Pakma" wife is not congenial with his husband, the husband has the full right to divorce her. He has to pay rupees twelve or thirteen in cash and a cow, and has to return the dowry brought by the wife. If the wife intends to separte, she can't compel the husband for divorce, unless she prove his un-faithfulness. If it is proved, then the husband is compelled to divorce. In such cases the wife has to pay rupees twenty five or thirty in cash and a horse as compensation to the husband. However, the wife has the right to get back the dowries she has brought.

In case of "Makpa" the wife can divorce her husband, after the payment of rupees twelve or thirteen in cash and a cow. If they are in matrimonial relation for a long time and there are children between them, then the wife has to prove the ill-treatment or immorality. On the cotarary, if the "Makpa" husband intends to divorce, he has to pay rupees twenty-five or thirty in cash and a horse to his wife. But if they are in marriage contract for a long time and there are offsprings between them, then he has to prove the ill-treatment and misbehavior, etc. If the "Makpa" has brought some goods with him in this house, he has the right to take them back. After the divorce, when they compromise themselves, they can reunite as wife and husband without performing any rituals or custom, and there would be no hindrance to unite as couple again. Later, if they intend to separate, there is no need of formal divorce. Hence, after divorce if adultation starts again with mitual consent it will consider like that of formal marriage and the divorce will be automatically cancelled. In case of the separation of husband and wife, there is no custom for payment of allownces for maintenance. But after the marriage, if the husband proves impotence, then the marriage will consider null and void and no compensation will be paid to any party.

6. Polyndry and Polygamy. The man has the right to keep several wives in presence of the first wife. But there is no tradition to keep more than three wives at a time. And usually people don't keep more than one wife, but in special cases, when there is no issue from the first wife, or she is physically disabled or due to illness she is not fit to perform the domestic activities. There is no restriction, if anybody keeps more than one wife without the above-mentioned reasons, provided he will arrange good maintenance to all. The "Makpa" husband has the right to keep sexual relations with all the sisters of his wife and he will be considered a joint husband to all these sisters. The brothers of the husband would have the rights to keep sexual relation with the wife of their brother and she would be considered a joint wife of all these brothers. Usually not more than three brothers share a wife. If the quantity is more than that, then the younger brothers will marry a woman, who is called "Chan-chung" or younger wife, but her offsprings have no right of inheritance. Either they have to marry outside the family or to become a Lama. Similar, norms have to be opt for the offsprings of the "Chan-chen". However, if the Chan Chhen is issueless then the children of the Chan-Chung would be the heir. Except the brothers no other person can share with one wife. Some people under special circumstances have legalized the "Phortsaks" additional husband other than the brothers. But this system is the rarest of the rare in Ladakh now. Usually, this practice is in force in such cases, that initially a man is kept as a servant in a house but he develops illegal relation with his wife and the husband knowingly did the connivance and keep silient. These types of instances are there in Ladakh. Moreover, some people have kept the "Phortsaks" additional husband knowingly in the house and it is considered illegal and vicious.

7. Adoption. Only those people make the adoption, which are childless. No body can adopt in presence of a son or daughter. There is no difference of a boy or girl in case of adoption. The tradition is that among the husband and wife who is the real owner of the property choose a boy or girl among his or her nearest relatives to make the adopted son or daughter. Similarly, the second party chooses a boy or girl as per need among the nearest relatives to marry with the adopted person of the house owner. Thereby the husband and wife both the party have equal participation in case of adoption. No special custom or tradition is followed in case of adoption. Only the person is brought in the house after finalizing the terms and conditions with his parents. If the adopted person refuse to follow the direction of the adopter or show negligence to serve them or misbehave the adopter, in such cases the adopter has the right to expel him, and no compensation is paid to the adoptee. If and when the adoptee doesn't intend to continue the adoption, then he can also terminate the adoption at his own. In such cases, the adopter too has no right to claim compensation. An adoptee has the full right and duties in the house of the adopter like that of a real successor. The widows have to make the adoption with the consultation of their nearest relatives and "Phaspuns" otherwise it is considered illegal.

In the case of adoption usually those offsprings are spared who have no right of inheritance in their parental house. One man cannot be the successor of two houses. If the adoptee becomes the successor of his own parent for any reason, he has to forgo it, and the next person in the relatives would be considered as successor. If one fails to get an adoptee among the nearest relatives then he can choose one among the other relatives. If he fails to get here too then he has to choose one among the "Phaspuns". If he is helpless to get a suitable person among the relatives and "Phaspuns" then he can choose one among the strangers, but he has to get the consent of his relatives in such cases. If and when the adopter gets his own issue after the adoption is made then the adoption will remain continue and the adoptee will be considered as his real successor and the issue of the adopter, who has born after the deal of adoption will be considered as younger brother or sister.

8. Testament, Gift and Charity. Almost all the three, mentioned above are not in force in Ladakh. There is no custom of will, and the practice of gift is also very few. And the custom of charity is very low. In special cases the charity is being made in favour of the "Gonpas". The rule is that no one has the authority to distribute his parental property, nor one can give his parental property in gift or charity by ignoring the real successors, however, one can offer his own property to his daughter or one of his son or the Gonpa. One can offer one or two canal of land out of his inherited property to the Gonpa, provided he gets the approval of his nearest relatives, but he can't offer land in a large quantity. One who is issueless he also cannot offer his inherited property to the Gonpa unless he gets the approval of his nearest relatives. There are very rare instances that one might have offered all his ancesteral property to the Gonpa with the consent of his relatives.

9. Birth. When the child is born, a pot full of grain is placed on a small table in front of the baby, and an arrow is kept inside it. A Khatak is placed over the table. All the relatives and neighbours come to congratulate the newly born baby. Usually, they bring meals duly prepared with Khatak and distribute among the family members and Khatak is placed on the table. This process continues for about a month. In the end of the month a day is fixed for celebration on the appointed day the family members prepare some meal, tea and "Chhang". All the relatives and neighbours get cooked food from their houses at the venu and all the guests are entertained with tea and chhang. The food brought by them are also distributes among them. The function ends after drink and dine. Till the appointed day the relatives and neighbours never eats the cooked food from that house except the "Phaspuns". However, this ban is lifted after the function. Except the function no other celebration is performed.

The rich people celebrate another function after six months or a year on the first issue, where the relatives and neighbours are invited, and grand feast is prepared, people use to drink and dance. They also present gifts. The poor people do not celebrate this function. After one year or two goes to the Kushok and he proposes the name, but some people propose the name by themselves. No celebration is made at the time of name keeping. There is no system of giving bath to the newly born baby or the mother among the common people in Ladakh. But it is said that the nobles and elite people give bath to the baby with the saffron water. After the bath the Bodhi letter "Aa" is written on a silver spoon and the child is made to suck it. Later, the child is feeded with milk. When a child is born in a royal family no one abstain in taking the cooked food from the palace.

10. Death. When a man dies in a house, first the "Lobon" of the Gonpa is convened of whome he or she is the disciple or follower. The Lobon recite some verses from the religious book. Later, the "Phaspuns" put off the clothes from the body and join the knees with the neck and tie a rope around it. Later, wraped in a cloth, kept the body in a corner of the prayer room. Here, the Lamas recite the verses from the religious books, and find out the date from the astrologer, that which day is appropriate for cremation. He fixes the date and arrangement is made to take the body out for crematiom. The rich people kept the body for two weeks together at home and the poor people don't keep more than four or five days. How long the death body remains in the house, the Lamas perform the Puja called "Chhoga" continuously. They have to offer the meals. However, the relatives take the responsibility to serve the meals to the Lamas turn by turn for one day. Those who could not arrange the meal, pay in cash. Thus, the expenses is shared by the relatives. At this occasion at least five to fifty Lamas are convened to perform the ceremonial prayer. On the day of cremation, all the relatives and neighbours gathered. The Lamas goes ahead by reciting religious verses. The Phaspuns took the dead body from inside the house to the out door of the house. From the outer door of the house the body has to carry by the successor of the house whether the person is a male or female. Later, the relatives put it in a palanquin and took upto the cremation ground. The palanquin system is restricted up to Leh town only. In villages the successor carries the body up to the cremation ground. There are different cremation grounds for different habitates of Leh. Here every household has their own separate cemetery. It is like a "Tanur" oven. This is built above the ground level. Here in the "Spurkhang" cowdung and wood are kept on the ground and then the corpse is kept over the wood. The Phaspun set on the fire. Then all the people return. The relatives have to perform three rounds around the oven-shaped cemetery called "Spurkhang", and prostrate before the Lamas and returns. The Lamas stay there and perform some rituals. It is called "Chenseq", which means the prayer of the fire goddess. In the meantime the Lama puts several times the butter, oil and other things in the "Spurkhang" over the flame of the dead body. Its main purpose is to burn the copse easily and stop the foul smell. After performing this rituals they kept there two Lamas only, the rest of the Lamas return. The two Lamas and Phaspuns stay near the Spurkhang, and put wood in it as per the requirement. When the bons of the corpse separate, a bone is drawn out of the Spurkhang and kept on a plate filled with grain. A piece of cloth is placed over the bone and a man among the "Phaspun" carry the plate. The two Lamas go ahead of the man playing the music on the "Gyaling" surnai and the man with the plate follow the Lamas. When they reach at the house of the breaved family, the plate is being kept there and the Lamas depart. When the dead body burns to ashes the Phaspuns also returns from the cremation ground.

The nobles and middle man are having their separate "Spurkhang" but the poor fellows are not having a permanent one to burn the corpse. They kept the dead body over few big boulders and burns. The members of the royal families are having separate Spurkhang for every individual.

All the dresses of the deceased person of good qualities and one share of the ornaments on his body at the time of death and other articles like pot. Tables, bedding items, carpet and horse, etc., as per once capacity, offers to the Lamas. After four days the Phaspuns withdraw the ashes from the oven. If the river is at a near distance then throw it in the river otherwise sepread it over the hill. The noble families carry the ashes on the horse back, put valuabe cloth over it and take towards the river. The Lamas goes ahead by playing music on "Gyaling". After perfoming this rituals the Lamas once again gather at the house of the deceased person and recite the verses from the religious book. After few days the piece of bone brought from the oven is grinded to powder. Mix it with dust and make mortar and mould to small "Chhortens" and statues of god and goddess. There are big "Chhortens" in the habitates to keep these things for the common people but the nobles have their own separate chortens for that purpose and kept the memory of the deceased person there. After one month a religious ritual is performed. No body except the Phaspun and the Lamas take the cooked food of the deceased house till this ritual is performed, and the ban is lifted. After one year another prayer is performed by the Lamas by reciting the religious cermons. The rich people perform this ritual for many years. Even some rich people keep continue this annual prayer for their ancestors throught their life. There is no system of cremation of the corpse upto three years. The body of the death child is kept in a earthen pot and burries on the hillside, and the body of very small children are put in a earthen pot and kept between the wall of their own house and plustered.

No religious rituals are performed in such cases. There is no custom of giving bath to the dead body.

During Losar on the night of the 9th day of the 10th month different type of dishes are kept on the "Spurkhang" of the deceased person. The system is that the people according to their capacity get prepared tea, bread, and rice, etc. and kept on the Spurkhang in the name of their deceased persons and returns. At this occasion the beggars comes and sit in the cremation ground and takes the benefit. The deciples of the Matho Gonpa, i.e. saskyapa get built new "Spurkhang" for every deceased person and after the cremation of the cropse they dismantle it. Usually, the dead bodies of the Lamas are also cremated. But it is said about some great Lamas that their cropse are dried by putting salt on it, and then it is being kept under a Chorten. Or the corpse is kept on the gound inside the Gonpa and a big statue is get prepared. The special organs of some Lamas are kept inside a statue. It is said that the heart of Lama Tsultim Nima, the founder of the Gonpa Ridzong has kept in a statue. The statue has placed carefully in a glazed almirah.

15

The Buddhist Functions and Festivals of the Gonpas

1. The Buddhist functions, 2. The sect of the Lamas, 3. The annual festivals of the Gonpas, 4. The designations of the Gonpas, 5. The right, duties and inheritance of the Lamas, 6. Bhodhi calendar, and 7. The renumeration of Ladakh and the border districts.

Losar the New Year. Losar is the great festival of Ladakh. In the past it was the tradition to celebrate the function on the eve of the New Year. But Gyalpo Jamyang Namgyal celebrated it two months earlier, on the first day of the eleventh month, because of political reasons. Since then the same date is fixed for the Lasar festival. The tradition is that the Losar Rituals start from the 25th day of the 10th month. It is practiced since long time. About more than hundred horse riders among the nobles and the common people gathered at the main gate of the palace, at noon in good dresses. In the evening the Raja comes out of the palace. All the horse riders follow the king. There are "Chhortens" and mane wall at a distance of one and half miles from the palace on Leh-Lhasa road. According to Buddhist faith, to have a round of the religious places is considered a virtuous deed. The horses processions of the king goes from the upper side of these buildings, and have a round of the Raja Deldan Namgyal's Mane wall, and comes back from the lower side. Thus, the Raja arrives in the Leh Bazar along with the procession after performing a round of the religious monuments. The Leh Bazar is very wide, and its length is also good. The Raja stays at a place in the Bazar, where as the horse riders run their horses from one end to the other in the Bazar in pairs of two each. When the show of the running of horses comes to an end, the Raja comes back to the palace, and the horse riders follow the king upto the singgay palace and returns. On the night of this day people light the earthen lamps at their houses and makes marry.

The process of horse race continous till the 30th day. On the night of 30th day the nobles and elites are invited at the palace for feast. When the feast is over, one of Raja's man comes out of the palace with a flame (torch) in his hand, and the people also comes out of their houses with flames in their hands and all gather in the Bazar. They come out of the Bazar calling the sologan "Hasha-le-hasha" and throw the flames in a field. This tradition looks like a Holy festival in India. The next day, on the 1st day of 11th month people celebrates the Losar at their houses. They congratulate their friends and relatives, on the arrival of the New Year. The nobles and elite people go to the palace to congratulate and express their good wishes to the king. The king along with the members of the royal family sits in the court according to their status. The room is furnished with the Ladakhi type of furniture along the wall. The nobles after expressing their good wishes to the king sit on the carpets as per their status. They are served with tea and drinks. The "Jung-Tsong" of Lhasa, who is considered the representative of the Dalai Lama, also gets the opportunity to meet the king at this occasion. He offers the presents to the king, which he has brought from Lhasa. The day ends in a very happy mood. On the next day on 2nd and 3rd dates, the horse race starts. The entire horse rider's gets together at the main gate of the palace. When the king comes out of the palace, the riders follow him upto the bazaar. Where the Raja sits in the room of his personel house, its balcony opens towards the Bazar. Later, the musicians beat the drums and surnai and the race starts. A representative of the Raja called "Lardak" starts the race; whose dress is very special and beautiful. All the riders have the race in the pairs of two, from one end to other end of the Bazar. After completing the first race the next race starts. Similarly, when they complete eight races, the king comes out of the house and from the main Bazar returns to the place. All the riders also follow him up to the palace and come back. Same custom is repeated on the next day, but instead of eight nine races are performed on that day. The custom ends, when the king returns to the palace.

Dosmochhey. According to the faiths of the Ladakhi Buddhist, whenever a person face some problems, they prepare certain things as per the instructions of the Astrologers, so as to get rid from such misfortune and evil sprits, which is called "Dos". The religious books are being recited by the Lamas before the "Dos" and it is considered that the spirit of the "La" goddess has entered the "Dos". This process is considered a sign to get rid from all such misfortunes. Later, the "Dos" is droped out. Similarly, to save the whole country of Ladakh from such misfortunes in the future days, a "Dos" is prepared which is called "Dosmochhey", i.e. the great "Dos". The tradition is that on 25th day of the 12th month, the Lamas of Thiksay, Hemis, Chemray, and Pethup gonpa, headed by a Kushok of one of the Gonpa and the next year the Lamas of Mangtho Gonpa headed by their Kushok gathered at the king's palace. The numbers of the Lamas are more than one hundred. The Astrologers also joine them and get prepared the "Dos" as per their guidance. The Lamas also get prepared other articles. The religious books are recited there till 29th day of the 12th month. In the evening of 28th day, the great "Dos" is taken out from the palace, in small groups and kept standing like a tree in a row, in a vast field just opposite to the Muslim grave yard and recite the verses from the religious books.

The Lamas are busy in this work from 25th day of the month and the Raja has to have a round of the "Mane wall" daily. The system is the same as mentioned above. The only difference is that the numbers of the horse riders are about one hundred and seventy-five. The Raja comes out on the horse back daily, till the 28th day and after a round of the Bazar goes back to the palace. On 28th the Dosmochhey festivals starts from morning in the Gonpa Soma, which is just adjacent to the palace. In the festival the Lamas wear masks and particular dresses and perform a religions dance which is called "Serkaim" in Ladakhi and devil dance in English. People both men and women use to come from far off places to watch the dance.

The king along with the members of the royal family watches this dance from the balcony of his palace. The other nobles and dignateries also got make the sitting arrangements for themselves. In short, till noon there remains the hustle and bustle in and around the Gonpa soma. At the end of the festival the king comes out of the palace for his usual round. In the afternoon of the 29th day, the Lamas carry out the articles prepared by them in a procession from the main Bazar, at the place where they had already kept the Dosmochhey trees. This procession comes out in different groups in different traditions. When all the goods are arrived in the field, then the Raja comes here riding on a horse in a procession. After performing the religious rituals by the Lamas the tree is broken into pieces. The spectators collect the pieces of the wood and carry it to their homes to keep in the store of grain as a token of honour for blessings. The other goods which have prepared by the Lamas are burnt to ashesh. When the rituals are over the Raja along with the procession comes in the Bazar and the horse riders have a horse race from the beginning to the end of the Bazar in a pair of two each and they escort the Raja upto the palace and comes back. On 30th day the Lamas returns to their respective Gonpas. The Raja also goes to the Gonpa of the Shay palace and fills the big lamp with butter which burns throught the year in front of the statue of Lord Buddha, which has prepared by bronze and is gold coated. Nothing is added in the said lamp during the whole year. After performing this ritual, he returns to the Leh palace on that very day. During his return to Leh all those processions which have referred above gathered at the Mane wall of King Deldan Namgyal and wait for the arrival of the king. The length of the Mane wall is about eight hundred and fifty steps. All the horse riders have a race here and the king march towardrs the town. The procession accompany him and escort the king upto the palace and returns.

On the 1st, 2nd, and 3rd day of the first month, the horse races are organized in the Bazar. The details are the same as already mentioned earlier in the Losar rituals. The difference is that on the first day the race held for seven times, the next day for eight times and on the third day it helds for nine times, with these the Dosmochhey rituals ends.

Recitation of Kangyur and Stangyur. Kangyur is a book of 108 volumes, which is considered a very sacred religious book by the Buddhists of Lhasa and Ladakh. The Stangyur is a religious book of 202 volumes, which is a detail commentary of the Kangyur. The Ladakhi Buddhist considers it a virtuous deed to recite both the sacred religious books. It is beyond the power of every Tom, Dick, and Harray. During the rule of the Namgyal kings, it was done under the royal patronage. It is said that during the beginning of the Dogra rules it was done on the expenses of the government. The tradition is that on 5th, 15th, or 25th of 2nd month of the Buddhist year, about 230 Lamas of different Gonpas of Ladakh gathered at Leh headed by their concern Kushoks. Previously, they use to recite the religious books in a government bunglow. Since there is shortage of accommodation for government itself, now they gathered in a vaste room called "Chhandazig-Karpo" and recites the books which end in five days. In the meantime some religious goods are being prepared in Gonpa Soma, which is called "Storma". 9th, 19th or 29th day of the Buddhist month the concern Kushok of the village Gonpa leads to carry the Storma, etc., from Gonpa Soma and takes at a ground outside the town. The Storma is being burnt to ashes and a horn full of blood fastened with a rope is hung between two poles. A statue called "Ghram Singh" is being kept on the slope of the hill. The soldier from the Zorawar fort uses to come here along with the gun and fires a salute of five guns. Later, the soldiers first fire the hanging horn and then the statue of Gharam Singh. When the bullet strucks on the point then the things are buried in the ground and returns back. The next day the Lamas also returns to their concern Gonpas. The Ladakhi Buddhist does believe that this worship is a virtuous deed for whole the country.

The Sect of the Lamas. There are slight differences among the Lamas in Lhasa, as far as the secondary principles are concerned. Due to this different sects came in to existence, which is known from the name of their Gonpas. The Ladakhi Gonpas are associated with the different Gonpas of Lhasa. Thus, the big Gonpas of Ladakh belongs to the following idealogical sects.

1. Dukpa; it is the old idealogy. The Lamas use to wear red cap and red dresses. The Gonpas of this idealogy are in Hemis and Chemray.
2. Galdan; it is the moderates. Its Lamas use to wear red dresses and yellow cap. The Lama's of this idealogy are at Pethub, Thiksay, Liker, Diskit and Ridzong, etc.
3. Dikong; it is also an old idealogy. Its Lama's use to wear red cap. The Gonpas of this idealogy are situated at Lamayuru and Phiyang.
4. Saskya; It is a sect of an old idealogy. Its Lamas too wears red cap. Saskyas is having only one Gonpa at Matho.
5. Sningma; it is an old idealogy. This sect is having only one Gonpa at Taktak, Sakti.
6. Lodok in Bhutan; its idealogy is similar to Dukpa. It is having one Gonpa in Stakna.

The Annual Festivals of the Gonpas. The annual festivals are being held in these Gonpas on different dates. About the festivals, it is said that it have been organized to have an inside feelings of the God and Goddess in the mind of the common people. The religious names and the date of the festivals are as under:

1. Hemis Tses Chhu—10th and 11th day of the 5th month.
2. Chhemrey Wangchhok—28th and 29th day of the ninth month.

3. Pethub Gustor—28th and 29th days of the 11th month.
4. Thiksay Gustor—28th and 29th days of the 12th month.
5. Liker Dosmochhey—28th and 29th days of the 12th month.
6. Diskit Dosmochhey—28th and 29th days of the 12th month.
7. Gaon Tsesdup—28th and 29th days of the 1st month.
8. Lamayuru Kapgyat—8th and 9th days of the 11th month.
9. Matho nagrang—13th, 14th, and 15th days of the 1st month.
10. Daktak Wangchog—28th and 29th days of the ninth month.
11. Shay Shubla—9th and 10th days of the 7th month.

During these festivals in the Gonpas the systems are almost same, except Matho Nagrang and Shay Shubla, about them will be narrated separately. The details of the festivals are as follows: After the main gate of the Gonpas, there is a big hall called "Chhamra". On the two or three sides of the main hall, there are verandahs. In a vast balcony sits the Head Lama and other senior Lama's as per their status. The seats of the Lamas are three feet to six feet high from the floor. It is prepared as per their religious status. In the other side of the verandah, the Lamas sit in a row and play music on Dhol. Trumpet Surnai and Damru, etc., on the instruction of the Head Lama. The Lamas comes out of the Gonpa turn by turn in group, wearing bright silk dresses and masks and have a dance in the compound on musical tune. They took the steps jointly and in a disciplined manner. When the dance of a group ends, the second group appears wearing new and beautiful dresses and different masks. This process continuous till the end of the festival. The Buddhist considers it a religious prayer but the foreigners call it the "Devil dance". People use to come from the far off places to watch this festival. Almost all the festivals are so crowdy that the local administration of the Gonpas has to make the arrangement of their own police, who maintain the discipline humorously and never use the sticks. Among the Ladakhi spectators, the number of female are more than the male members. Since the women are more prone to religion than that of men. There are separate sitting arrangements for the nobles, furnished with carpets, etc., and the Gonpa makes the arrangement for their stay inside the Gonpas own buildings. The common people stay outside and spent the night under the trees.

HEMIS TSES-CHU

The Hemis Tses-chu is very popular among other festivals of the Gonpas. It is famous among the tourist, the reason is that the other festivals celebrate in the winter and the tourists don't get the opportunity to watch them. Besides, the Hemis Gonpa is the richest Gonpa of Ladakh and the strength of the Lamas are much more than other Gonpas. The goods and other instruments of the Gonpa are very valuable and best. These are the old antiquities of about one hundred and fifty years back, when the son of Raja Saskyong Namgyal, called Gyalshas Mipham Tsewang Thinles, who was one of the Head Lama of Hemis Gonpa, get purchased these articles from Lhasa, which are still in a good condition.

MATHO NAGRANG

The above-mentioned systems are also happen in Matho Gonpa and the appearance of "Lah" Oracle is worth seeing. The details are as follows: those two Lamas of this Gonpa are being selected for the said purpose, who worships in isolation for about two to three months. It is considered that due to cleanliness of the soul the Lah (Goddess) enters in them. This practice has to repeat every year. The Lah appears in them at about 3 P.M. or 4 P.M. for which they have to do the arrangement earlier. When the Lah appear in them, they enthusiastically comes out of the Gonpa, in a special dress holding sword in one hand and spear in another hand. For a while they dance in the main hall on the tune of music, and then go on the roof of the balconies of the Gonpa and runs on the ridge of the walls. They jump from one roof to another.

They walk among the pilgrims and the pople inquires from the Lahs about their desires and future plans. They reply accordingly and usually it is having two meanings and sometimes it comes true. The Lahs also send sword and spear, etc. to the nobles as a token and according to the tradition it has to return the next very day wrapped in silk cloths. On 13th and the 14th day of the month, their eyes are open and their body ahead of the waist is nacked. On 15th their eyes are hidden with thick black cloths, which hang upto the chin. They are totally nacked except a cloth tied to hide the sex organs. The whole body is coloured with black and the face of the Goddess with three eyes, is prepared with color on the belly and back. They carry the prayer instruments in the hand like "Damru" and "Tilu" and comes out of the Gonpa and go from one room to another. Go up on the stairs and comes down. Whoever ask question, they answer. The hill where this Gonpa is situated, there is a house of the Gonpa at a little distance downwards. They use to go inside the house from the hilly route and while returning they had a round of the "Mane" and "Chhortens". All the piligrims and spectators enjoy their appearance and they go back to the Gonpa. Here they go from one place to another and runs on the ridge of the Gonpas wall. They go in the room of the officers and nobles and talk to them in their special styel. When they came to me (the author). I observed their face very closely and I am of the opinion that their face is totally covered. However, they face no difficulties to find out the way. Since the way inside the Gonpa is very narrow, uneven and un level but they runs fearlessly. They jumps from one roof to another and I observed that they never did a mistake in doing so. The local Buddhist are of the opinion, that they see every where through the eyes prepared on their belly and back.

When their task is over, a Lama of the Gonpa keep his hand over the heart of the Lahs and the power of the Lah disappear from them. They are senseless for the time being. On the day when they are nacked and their body has coloured with black. Hence, to get them back in sense they are put in hot water and colour is being washed by rubbing piece of cloth on their dodies. When they take the bath the Lah disappears from them and they again come in sense. At that time they caugh heavily and sometimes they vomit. For a while they seem to be restless but regain their power immediately.

Later on, the 8th day of the 2nd month the "Lah" again appears in them. They come out of the Gonpa riding on the horse back and proceeds in the "Nallah" abot five miles, where there are two "Latos" (the sacred place of the Goddess) they got repaire the Latos and replace the old branches of cyphere tree with new one. When the process is over they put their head inside the Lato and the Lah disappears from their body. Later, they return to the Gonpa. The spectators also gathered at this occasion to have a view of the Lahs.

THE SHUBLA OF SHAY VILLAGE

There is a Gonpa at Shay near the old palace of the king. In one part of the Gonpa has kept the statue of "Dorjay Chhenmo" who is considered the Lah of Lotsava Rinchen Zangpo. The pious man is considered to be the founder of Buddhism in Ladakh. In another two rooms there is the statue of Lord Buddha, one made of clay and another with bronze with gold coated. All such statues as I observed in Zangskar and Ladakh are almost of the same size, and are 6 to 7 "Gona" bigger than the human stature.

On 9th and 10th days of the 7th Bodhi month, there is the appearance of the "Lah". The detail follows: Among the common people a man is selected for this purpose. Before that he has to live in isolation for about two months. On the appointed day, he comes out from the isolated room and sits before the "Deshaq Gyatpa" (Eight Chhortens). Here few Lamas' recite some verses from the religion book and perform the rituals and the man comes under the influence of the appearance of Lah. At that time water comes out from his nose and the eyes. First he has a round of the Chhortens in sitting position, when he feels the appearance of Lah then he stands up. He has put on very beautiful silk cloths which the king of Ladakh has got prepared for the said purpose. First he goes in the palace, where the nobles are gathered. People ask different question as per their desire and he replies all immediately. Then he comes out of the palace, and replies the questions of the common people. Later, he goes on the roof of the Gonpa and runs on the ridge of the walls. He is offered boiling tea and he takes the tea without any difficulty. It is said that once a queen was in doubt that Lah has not appeared in the man and he is only doing hypocritical imposture. She desired to taste the person with hot tea. She thought, if he drinks the hot tea without any problem then I will trust his miracle. This system is still continued. The process repeats on the next day also. In the meantime the Lah have a race riding on a horse. Goes to the nobles and elites, talk to them and common people. The ritual ends in the evening. At this occasion people have a dance and other show and funs. A large number of spectator gather there to watch them. The people have much regards and respect of this Lah then that of Matho and the representative of all the Gonpas participate in this festival and ask different questions. These arrangements have been made by Lama Rigzin Tsewang Nurboo, who came to Ladakh during the reign of King Phuntsog Namgyal to mediate and compromise the infighting among the members of the royal families.

THOSE GONPAS WHO ARE NOT CONVINCED WITH THE RITUALS

The Ridzong Gonpa is one of the new Gonpa in Ladakh. The Lamas of this Gonpa is very disciplinarian and participates regularly in prayers. They never take wine and meat and took a simple meal for two times only. They are not convinced with the customs and rituals which are exist in other Gonpas of Ladakh. Neither they participate in the festival of Lahs, etc., nor do they organize any function. Similarly, no function is organized in Stakna Gonpa. This Gonpa too is not convinced with the rituals and no annual festival is organized in Takthak Gonpa.

THE DESIGNATION OF THE GONPAS

The Chairman of a Gonpa is a Head Lama. Who is usually a founder of the Gonpa or a reincarnation of a senior religious Head. He is known as Kushok in Ladakh. Kushok is the final authority in the social and religious affairs of the Gonpa. Except Ridzong, where the power rest with the senior most Lama of the Gonpa. The following "Kushok" are in Ladakh and Zangskar, and the Gonpas which falls against the name of each Kushok are under his jurisdiction:

1. Kushok Stagtsang Raspa: Gonpa Hemis, Chhemrey, Anley, and small Gonpas, almost in every village.
2. Kushok Bakula: Gonpa Pethub, Samkar, Stok, and small Gonpas in many villages.
3. Kushok Naris Tulku: Gonpa Liker, Lingshed, Rangdum, Karsha, Phugtal, and Stongdey. Besides, there are many small Gonpas in Ladakh and Zangskar.
4. Kushok Tokdan: Gonpa Gawn (Phiyang) Lama Yuru, Shachukul, Chhushul, Shang, Bodh-Kharboo, and some small Gonpas.
5. Kushok Chamba Stanba Chhosphel: Gonpa Thiksay, Diskit, and some small Gonpas.
6. Kushok Tsultim Legshed Stanzin and Shash Kushok Lobzang Tsultim Chhosphel Gonpa Ridzong and Samstangling.
7. Kushok Gonpa Matho: Matho, Kitmang and Spiti.

As far as the succession of the Kushok are concerned, it is done by the great Lamas of Lhasa, like Gyalwa Rinpochhe (Dalai Lama) and Panchhen Rinpochhee (Tashi Lama) the tradition is that finalization of the succession, a conference of four to five hundred senior Lamas are covened. They gather and recite the sacred religious books for few days and keep themselves busy in prayer. Later, the name of the different children to whom they believe to be the reincarnation of the deceased Lama are written on paper and put in the separate small ball of atta. These balls are collected in a gold cup. The Chinese representative stationed in Lhasa comes here and tookout one of the ball. Whoever name comes out, he is considered as successor. This tradition is called "Serpum". A huge amount has to spend to perform this tradition. No one has the authority to perform "Serpum" except the above mentioned two great Lamas.

As far as the reincarnation of the Kushok in Ladakh are concerned, the tradition is that after about one year of the death of the Kushok, the prominent Lamas of the Gonpa depute a representative to Lhasa to meet the Head Lama under whose jurisdiction the Gonpa is. The person inquiries from the Head Lama that where our Kushok has took the rebirth. The Lama find out astrologically the distance, direction, and some times the name of the region of the newly born baby. Some people also inquire from the Lah of the said Gonpa and some never consult with the Lah. If the Lah confirms the decision of the Lama, it is considered very auspicious; otherwise they agreed the decision of the Lama. The man returns to Ladakh after getting all this infomation. And he goes in search of the Kushok in the direction and the region where the rebirth of the deceased Kushok have been told in Lhasa. According to the Buddhist idealogy, it is necessary to every spirit to take re-birth within seven days of the death. Hence, they search such children, who have born within seven days of the death of deceased Kushok. Some of the events also help to find out the Kushok. Suppose, after the birth of the child the parents have got more happiness, or the child must have performed some miracles or the Lamas of the Gonpa must have learn something about a child in dream. Or the child recognizes one of the servants of the deceased Kushok or his belongings. But such happens rarest of the rare. However, they considered about a child of being the incarnation of the deceased Kushok, they present some of the belongings and animals before the child. If he recognizes some of the articles, then it is considered that he is the reincarnation of the deceased Kushok. Later, to confirm it, the daily use items of the deceased Kushok like cup, rosary and other prayer articles mixed with same other articles are presented before the child and he is asked to lift his own belongings. If he chooses wrong articles then he is rejected. But the search continued, and the same method is applied here also. If he recognize mixed articles some his own and some of others, then the case is submitted to the Head Lama of Lhasa, who has informed earlier about his birth. In shot correct or partly correct in both the cases, the Head Lama of Lhasa is consulted. If the child has recognized the things correctly, then the case is clear. The Head Lama of Lhasa certifies it. Otherwise if it is partly correct, then the names of such children are submitted to the Head Lama of Lhasa. Here as per the knowledge of astrology he finds out the name of one of the boy and selects, it is considered final and unchallengeble.

Now the Lamas of the said Gonpa bring the child in the Gonpa and make the arrangement of his nourishment and knowledge. When he becomes a clever boy and has completed the basic religious education then he is deputed to Lhasa to seek higher education in the concern Gonpa to which his Gonpa is affiliated. When he returns from Lhasa after the completion of religious education then the affairs of the Gonpa is handed over to him.

Those Kushok who are considerd the reincarnation of the founder of the Gonpa, like Hemis and Ridzong, they inherit the position, and can't be isolated from the post during their life time. The rest of the Kushok have been appointed by the concern Head Lama of their headquarter at Lhasa.

There are some Kushoks about whom it is considered that they are the reincarnation of some great religious personalities, have got the consent of being the Head Lama of the concern Gonpa from their Headquarter at Lhasa. Therefore, they too can't be separated from their religious post. The Kushok of Thiksay and Liker are of such type. It is also said about Kushok Bakula that he has got this position for lifetime. The Kushok of Gaon and Matho are being appointed for the appointed time. The present Kushok of Matho is not a reincarnated one. As far as the Gonpas of Pethub and Thiksay are concerned, the old tradition was to appoint one of the princes of the Namgyal dynasty as the Head Lama of these Gonpas. Since for a long time no prince of Namgyal Dynesty has become a Lama, hence other people have been appointed as Head Lamas. May be the old tradition will be restored, whenever the real successor is available. Except the Gonpas of "Gelukspa" the rest of the head of the Gonpas, when they are shifted back to Lhasa sends a great share of their income to their Headquarte at Lhasa. The Kushok of Hemis and Gaon send their representatives with valuable gifts to Lhasa after every three years along with the "Lobchhak" trade mission. They also get the gifts, etc., from Lhasa. In short through these Gonpas the administrative and religious influence of Government of Lhasa is still prevelent in the mind and heart of the people of Ladakh.

The officers of the Gonpa are further divided in two parts under the supereme command of the Kushok. One for the performance of religious activities and second for running the day-to-day administration. The religious officers are as follows:

1. Lobon. Because of seniority a Lama can achieve this post and he is considered the 2nd in command after the Kushok. He is responsible to perform the religious affairs in the Gonpa, under the Kushok.
2. Uzat. While performing prayer, he is holding the status of a prayer leader.
3. Uchhung. He is the Deputy of the Uzat.
4. Chhamspon. When the Lamas perform the mask dance during annual festival. He is responsible for direction and supervision of the "Chhams". He is also having an Assistant in some Gonpas.
5. Chhosthrimspa. He is like the police officer of the Gonpa. His duties are to maintain strict discipline in the Gonpa and to have a strict vigilance on the behaviour of the Lamas. This assignment is shifted annually.
6. Chhot-Shumpa. Chhotpa means the statues of grain powder and the preparater of other articles. These articles are being used during the religious functions and day-to-day prayer.
7. Chhotpon. He is responsible for preparation of the status of "atta and sattu".
8. Dunair. He is the store-keeper of the religious articles of the Gonpa which are not in daily use.

9. Konair. He is responsible for the lightening of the Gonpa, and has to guard the articles of the Gonpa, which are in daily use.

The above-referred post from Nos. 1 to 8 are being appointed by the order of the Head-Lama (Kushok) and the appointment to the posts from Nos. 2 to 8 are being made by the Kushok on the recommendation of the Lobon. The post No. 9 Konair is appointed by the "Chhagzot" himself.

The following are the administrative posts of the Gonpa:

1. Chhagzot. He holds the full power in general administration of the Gonpa under the Kushok. He maintains the income and expenditure of the Gonpa, and runs the business. The Gonpa is responsible to pay the debt if any; through him. However, he can't separate the property of the Gonpa. Such powers rest with the Kushok only. He does so with the consultation of the senior Lamas.
2. Nairchhen. He is the assistant of the Chhagzot. He is the storekeeper. He has to perform the agricultural duties, and to collect the land tax from the peasants. Actually, he is an officer and Chhagzot is his superior. In small Gonpas this duty is performrd by the Chhagzot himself.
3. Nairchhung. He is the assistant of the Nairchhen.
4. Nairpa. He is the attendant of the Chhagzot. He does the agricultural and other day-to-day arrangements by the order of the Chhagzot.

The appointment of Chhagzot is made by the Kushok and the Nairchhen and Nairchhung is also appointed by the Kushok on the recommendation of the Chhagzot. These all officers are among the Lamas. Lobon and Chhagzot are considered equallent post. A Lama who is having lot of religious knowledge is promoted as Lobon and one who is having administrative skills is appointed as Chhagzot. Konair is the basic post which a Lama can obtain. There are no such posts in small Gonpas.

THE RIGHT, DUTIES AND SUCCESSION OF LAMAS IN VARIOUS GONPAS

It was the tradition in the past, when a person enters in a Gonpa as a Lama, he has to perish his own personality. He can't make his own property. Whatever he aquires, it was considered as property of Gonpa. In return the Gonpa was responsible to provide all his expenses. Later, the system became defective, because of the negligence of both sides. The Gonpas paid less attention to fulfill their requirements and on the other hand the Lamas started to build their own property.

In Ladakh, Ridzong is the only Gonpa who's Lamas can't make personel properties, and the Gonpa is responsible to full fill their needs there is a limitation of the requirements, accordingly the needful of every Lama is done on the appointed time. Beside, whatever the Lama gets had to deposit in the Gonpa. Wine and meat is strictly prohibited in the Gonpa, and one has to be observance of continence. My friend Shash Kushok of Ridzond Gonpa Tsultim Chhosphel committed a mistake. He married with a lady of Nubra, after informing the Lamas, but they expelled him out of the Gonpa, in spite of being an influential, pious, and a scholar person. Which created frustration. Since such instances are being heard about some of the Lamas of Lhasa also, but in spite of that, they continued on the religious post. Therefore, I became a mediator and did efforts to remove the confusion and frustration. I did the compromise between the Shash Kuskok and the Lamas and finally they took back Shash Kushok in the Gonpa, and they provided his wife maintenance allowance and a house at a distance of few miles from the Gonpa. Thus, the administration of the Gonpa began to run in a fair manner. When, I visited Ladakh again in 1830 AD. I found that Shash Kushok had passed away and his widow was living in a house of the Gonpa and she was receiving the maintenance from the Gonpa.

Similarly, another Kushok of this Gonpa also done a mistake, he was expelled from the Gonpa on the charge of his bad character. Since he was not so influential person; hence his expulsion could not harm or influence the administration of the Gonpa. Here is another example of a Kushok of Thiksay. It is heard that he was expelled from the Gonpa by the Lamas and took the administration of the Gonpa in their hands. The rest of the Lamas of the Gonpas of Ladakh keep their own private property. Every Gonpa provide them the maintenance according to the scale. As far as the succession at Gonpa Ridzong is concern, the inheritance is only limited to books and dresses, which is produced in the assembly of the Lamas for verification and later on, is deposited in the treasury of the Gonpa. And if there are some books it is distributed among the Lamas. Usually, it is not deposited to the Library of the Gonps, but there is no objection in doing so.

The Lamas of Liker Gonpa can possess personel wealth or property and at their death it is inherited by the decilpes. The expenditure for his last rites is deducted from his wealth. Out of the leftover the diciples can take their share as per their will and the rest is distributed among the "Khamsan-Lamas". Khamsan means a group of Lamas. There are presently four "Khamsans" in Gonpa Liker. Neither the Gonpa gets the belongings, nor does his real successors. The Kushok of Gaon Gonpa use to send present in cash and kind to the Head of Degungpa in Lhasa through his representative, along with the trade mission. The Lamas of this Gonpa gets one time meal from the Gonpa and one has to arrange the rest by his own. The dresses have to prepare from their houses. Whenever there is a religious function, then they get all the meal from the Gonpa.

The Lamas have the right to possess personel property. The Lamas kept separately their own horse, goat, sheep, grain, and cash. Make the business. The belongings of a Lama go to his paternal relatives and they are responsible for his cremation and last rites, conditionally that the last rites has to be performed by the Lamas of the Gonpa to which he was affiliated. The books, dresses and religious goods shall go to the Gonpa. If there is a Lama among his parental relatives then he will be considered more righfull successor than others. He will also be responsible to pay the debt of the deceased. Whenever a Kushok get transferred from here, he took the personel belongings and properties with him. If he dies, then his belongings do not go to his paternal relatives but it will go to the reincarnated child. The property is being kept safely in the Gonpa till the child gets maturity. The Lamas have no restriction of wine and meat, but it is necessary to restrain from taking wife. In Pethub Gonpa Lamas can possess their own property. After the death of a Lama, his inheriter is responsible to perform his last rites. He does the rituals of the last rites through the Lamas of the Gonpa to which the deceased belongs. In such case, the Lamas gets their due share, the rest of the property goes to the paternal inheritors. The test of the Lamas of Hemis, Matho, Stagna, Ridzong, Tak-Thak, helds in their own Gonpas, it is not necessary for them to go Lhasa for this purpose. If they get success in the religious test then they are made "Gelong", now he has been included in the group of Lamas. If one fails to become a Gelong, then he has to serve the Lamas and has to do the agricultural works too or becomes a "Nairpa". It is very necessary for a "Gelong" to restrain from a wife. Those who are not "Gelong" are called "Bandey". They can marry. Gelong has no restriction of wine and meat. In Hemis Gonpa one has to pay rupees one thousand five hundred to become a Gelong, otherwise he is not made a "Gelong". Those Lamas who remains in the Gonpa will get 12th "Khal" grain annually from the Gonpa for their food. The rest have to manage by the Lamas themselves. Those Lamas who are appointed in sub-Gonpas, they are not given the grain. When there is a religious function in the Gonpa, the Lamas are provided three times meal, by the Gonpa.

The Lamas can acquire their own property. After his death when there is a disciple among his ancesteral relatives then the property goes to him otherwise it goes to the parental relatives. If the disciple is a stranger he has no right to occupy the property. First the expenditure of the last rites is deducted from his wealth and the leftover is goes to the seccessors. It is the condition that the last rites have to perform by the Lamas of the Gonpa to which the deceased belongs. The disciple gets the books but the dresses and utensils goes to the Lamas who perform the last rites. If there are a large number of utensils and dresses, etc., then one part is given to the Gonpa. The successer is also responsible to pay the debt if any. The Kushok of this Gopa is not transferrable. When a Kushok is died, the last rites are performed out of his own wealth. The rest of the wealth is brought in the assembly of the Lamas, puts stamps of the Gonpa and kept in a store. Later, it is handed over to the reincarnated Kushok when he becomes matured enough neither his successers from the parental side, nor the Gonpa gets the wealth.

The Lamas of Pethub, Thiksay, Liker, and Gaon Gonpas have to qualify the test of "Gelong" from Lhasa, otherwise they will not becom a "Gelong". They have to pay nothing to their concern Gonpas in this regard.

TIBETAN CALANDAR

In Tibet the year and months are calculated as per the lunar system. Probably, it has been derived from India. The said system is in force in Ladakh also. There are 12th months of 29th and 30th days. The months have no name, only it is being counted. Among the 36 months, thirty months are of 29 days, and six months of 30 days. Whenever there is the difference of 30 days in this system as comparison to solar system, in such cases an additional month is added. This usually happens after 30 or 32 months. Thereby the calculation which is based on lunar system, equalize with the solar system within three years. There are two types of calculation of the years; one is of twelfth years and another of sixty years. The small calculation is called "Loskor", i.e. the period of twelfth years. The names of the years are as follows:

> 1. Rat, 2. Ox, 3. Tiger, 4. Rabbit, 5. Dragon 6. Snake, 7. Horse, 8. Sheep, 9. Monkey, 10. Sparrow, 11. Dog, and 12. Pigs.

As far as the long calculation are concerned, there are five signs of wood, Fire, Earth, Iron, and Water. Which are called "Khams". The "Khams" which have been mentioned above added twice on the above cited years. It ends at the 10th year and restarted from 11th year. Thus, it complets 60 years, which is called "Rabjung". A Rabjung consists of five "Loskor" and six "Khams". Which are as follows:

1. Wood-rat 58	2. Wood-ox 59	3. Fire-tiger 60
4. Fire-rabit 1	5. earth-dragon 2	6. Earth-snake 3
7. iron-horse 4	8. Iron-sheep 5	9. Water monkey 6
10. water-sparrow 7	11. wood-dog 8	12. wood-pig 9
13. fire-rat 10	14. fire- ox 11	15. Earth-tiger 12
16. earth-rabit 13	17. Iron-dragon 14	18. Iron-snake 15
19, water-horse 17	20. Water-sheep 17	21. Wood-monkey 18
22. wood-sparrow 19	23. fire-dog 20	24. Fire-pig 21
25. earth-rat 22	26. earth- ox 23	27. iron-tiger 24
28. iron-rabit 25	29. Water-Dragon 26	30. Water-snake 27
31. wood-horse 28	32. Wood-sheep 29	33. Fire-monkey 30
34. fire-sparrow 31	35. Earth-dog 32	36. Earth-pig 33
37. iron-rat 34	38. Iron-ox 35	39. Water-tiger 36
40. water-rabit 37	41. Wood-dragon 38	42. Wood-snake 39
43. fire-horse 40	44. Fire-sheep 41	45. earth-monkey 42
46. earth-sparrow 42	47. Iron-dog 44	48. iron-pig 45
49. water-rat 46	50. Water-ox 47	51. wood-tiger 48
52. wood-rabit 49	53. Fire-dragon50	54. Fire-snake 51
55. earth-horse 52	56. Earth-sheep 53	57. Iron-monkey 54
58. iron- sparrow 55	59. Water-dog 56	60. Water-pig 57

Here, it is to be noted, that "Rabjung" starts from the 4th year, i.e. fire-rabit instead of the 1st year and the 4th year is considered the 1st year of "Rabjung". It is because of the fact that earlier "Loskor" was in practice in this country. Later, when calander was prepared then "Rabjung" was made in practice. At that it was the 4th year. However, its use is very rare, because usually the period ends with the count of the date and month. If we enquire with a scholar, he refers the case through "Loskor". I have never seen the use of "Rabjung" anywhere. The "Rabjung" is like this, if we compare it with the "Bikrimi" and Christian era.

Beginning of rabjung	Christian era	Bikrami
1. Ist	1027 AD	1084
2. 2nd	1087 AD	1144
3. 3rd	1147 AD	1204
4. 4rth	1207 AD	1264
5. 5th	1267 AD	1324
6. 6th	1327 AD	1384

7.	7th	1387 AD	1444
8.	8th	1447 AD	1904
9.	9th	1507 AD	1564
10.	10th	1567 AD	1624
11.	11th	1627 AD	1684
12.	12th	1687 AD	1744
13.	13th	1747 AD	1804
14.	14th	1807 AD	1864
15.	15th	1867 AD	1024
16.	16th	1927 AD	1984

Accordingly, the 1 January 1913 AD, according to 19 poh, 1969 Bikrimi is equallent to 25th day of 11th month, 46 year of 15th Rabjung. Which is recorded as follows, 25/11/46/15. Similarly, 1st Baisakh 1970 Bikrimi will be Bodhi date 7/3/47/15, i.e. 7th day, 3rd month, 47 year of 15th Rabjung. In this book the Bodhi year and "Rabjung" as per Bikrami and Christian era have been calculated according to the above given chart.

The name of the days of the week in Ladakhi is as under:

Sunday	Zanima	Monday	Zadawa
Tuesday	Zamikjmar	Wegnesday	Zalakhpa
Thursday	Zaphurbu	Friday	Zapasang
Saturday	Zaspenba		

I am highly grateful to the following authers, whose books have been benifited, me to accomplish this part of history.

1.	Gulab Nama Farsi by	Dewan kirpa Ram
2.	Mukammal Tarikhe Kasmir	Mohammad Din Foq
3.	Guldasta Kashmir	Hargopal Khasta
4.	Jammu & Kashmir jn English	Doru
5.	The making of a forienter	Col. Duerent
6.	The three empire meet	Knight.
7.	Chitral	Sir Georg Robertson
8.	Tarikhe Chitral	Azizuddin

Hashmatullh Khan Muslim Univesity, Aligarh
14th December, 1936 AD.

Census of Tehsil Ladakh

Year	Male	Female	Total
1837AD Summary	11106	9515	20631
1891AD Summary	14350	13934	28274
1901 AD Formal	15905	15715	31620

Region-wise systematic censue 1911 AD

Name of the region	Male	Female	Total
1. Nubra	2059	2108	4167
2. Tantse	833	845	1678
3. Rupsho	822	729	1551
4. Rong	842	844	1686
5. Hemis	676	570	1246
6. Indis Valley	8927	8950	17977
7. Lamayuru	843	864	1707
8. Grand total	16144	15980	32122

Recent systematic census of Tehsil Leh Ladakh

Year	Male	Female	Total
1921 AD	16616	16436	33052
1931 AD	17332	17091	34423

Sect wise statement of Forienter District for 1911 AD

Wazarat	Tehsil	Muslim	Bhuddist	Hindu	Christian	Others	Total
Ladakh	Leh	3505	28495	55	63	45	32182
Ladakh	Kargil	39985	7545	157	—	41	47727
Ladakh	Skardo	106570	—	165	—	16	106795
Tpotal		150060	36200	407	63	61	186645
Gilgit	Gilgit	14805	—	794	19	57	15675
Gilgit	Astor	8270	—	22	2	—	8294
Total		23075	—	816	21	57	43969
Political A.Gilgit		56341	—	77	—	17	54435
Grand Total =		225476	36200	1300	84	135	265046

1921 AD

Tehsil	Muslims	Buddhist	Hindu	Christian	Others	Total
Leh	3356	29412	54	70	—	33593
Mansar	—	160	—	—	—	160
Kargil	39790	4572	95	—	22	47479
Skardo	102518	57	120	—	50	102745
Total	145664	37201	269	70	72	283476
Gilgit	27894	—	711	15	86	28706
PA Gilgit	60749	—	220	1	21	60991
Total	234207	37201	1300	86	179	272973

1931 AD						
Leh	4073	30137	95	115	3	34418
Kargil	40123	8011	77	7	20	34481
Skardo	107192	64	147	—	74	107477
Total	152328	38212	29	122	90	192138
Gilgit	30741	—	1035	38	88	31902
PA Gilgit	64199	—	336	11	8	64544
Total	248328	38212	1580	171	193	288584